New Roles for Leaders

D1274208

New Roles for Leaders

A Step-by-Step Guide to Competitive Advantage

Tom Hornsby   Larry Warkoczeski

HILLSBORO PRESS

Franklin, Tennessee

Copyright 2000 by VisionWorks, LLC

All rights reserved. Written permission must be secured from the publisher to use or reproduce any part of this book, except for brief quotations in critical reviews or articles.

Printed in the United States of America

04   03   02   01   00   1   2   3   4   5

Library of Congress Catalog Card Number: 00-101334

ISBN: 1-57736-184-9

Cover design by Gary Bozeman

Published by
HILLSBORO PRESS
an imprint of
PROVIDENCE HOUSE PUBLISHERS
238 Seaboard Lane • Franklin, Tennessee 37067
800-321-5692
www.providencehouse.com

Come to the edge
We can't, we are afraid

Come to the edge
We can't, we will fall

And they came to the edge

And he pushed them

And they flew

—Appollinaire

CONTENTS

FOREWORD

IT IS NO secret that effective leadership is essential to business success. It *is* a secret that to attain business success, a balanced focus upon people, issues, and technical advances is critical.

In a competitive environment, an effective quality management system is essential in managing change. However, few people understand that effective quality management systems only work when leaders understand and embrace proper leadership roles.

Leaders must understand and carry out three key functions: leading, coaching, and managing. Tom Hornsby and Larry Warkoczeski's book *New Roles for Leaders* superbly blends these three functions, integrating leadership, coaching, and quality management. If you implement these tools in your workplace, the result will be a more involved, higher performing workforce.

This is a breakthrough book that I highly recommend to all levels of leaders to help them grow and succeed.

William R. Garwood
President (retired), Europe, Middle East, and Africa Region
Eastman Chemical Company
Winner of first Ishikawa Medal for Quality

ACKNOWLEDGMENTS

PEOPLE WRITE BOOKS for many reasons. I simply wanted to write a book to help make a positive difference in the professional and personal lives of employed people. My thirty years as a leader and consultant have led me to draw some conclusions about leadership in today's fast paced, changing world. This book is a synergistic product of many people to whom I am deeply grateful. In particular, I offer my thanks to:

—Lynnis, Melanie, and Mark, my immediate family. Their encouragement, ideas, editorial assistance, and life experiences which they shared so freely has a tremendous positive influence on me.

—Larry, my coauthor. His "stick-to-it" attitude kept our vision alive. The ability to value differences is our strength.

—Vicki and Craig, Larry's wife and son. Their willingness to share Larry and provide their personal support helped us keep focused.

—My parents, William and Rosa Jackson. I regret not completing the book before their death. They would have been proud.

—My numerous coworkers, David Gordon, Mark Hecht, and the Team Managers at Eastman Chemical Company. They shared their lives in ways that helped me grow.

—Many unnamed people worldwide who demonstrated their knowledge and skills in being a leader. Their contributions, many times unknowingly, provided a catalyst for convincing me the project was a worthwhile journey.

—Tom

This book is a symphony of my experiences and knowledge. To that end, I owe major gratitude to many people:

—The creation of this book has required many sacrifices on the part of my wife, Vicki, and son, Craig. Vicki has graciously provided many suggestions to improve the content and format of this book. Without her technical contribution, we could not have completed this effort. Craig has generously given love, humor, and inquiry and in so doing has helped me grow as a leader and father.

—Deep gratitude goes to my father and mother, Harold and Beverly, for teaching me values to live by, a strong work ethic, and a deep belief in continual learning. My sisters, Carol and Sue, have always been there when I needed them the most, inquiring how the book was coming.

—My coauthor, Tom, has helped me grow. He has helped me fine-tune my view of work and people providing me with more tools and skills. His wife, Lynnis, has also been critical to the success of this project driving us to complete this work and share the message with others.

—With over twenty-two years of formal education and three advanced degrees, I am a product of many minds working diligently to nurture my ability to think and create; I am deeply indebted to them. A heartfelt thanks also to Dee Gorham, Becky Ramsey, and E. Lee Feller because they helped me to understand and appreciate life. Thanks to Leigh Hornsby for her patience and editorial efforts.

Finally, my appreciation to those people I have worked with over the past twenty years as I practiced being something called a leader-coach-manager.

—Larry

New Roles
for Leaders

INTRODUCTION

THE STATUS QUO is no longer acceptable. You hear it in corporate America every day: "Why isn't our organization more successful? Why haven't our added efforts in empowerment, quality improvement, reengineering, and team building created greater profits?"

Leaders are also fed up with the status quo asking: "How can my work be more meaningful to me personally and professionally? What is my role now that employees are empowered and performing some of the tasks I used to perform?"

After decades of resistance, corporate management has embraced employee input and collective thought, leaving behind the traditional organization. Employees have taken on new roles and new responsibilities. Like the traditional organization, traditional leader roles are disappearing, leaving a barren cavern. The fatal flaw in today's leadership approach is a failure to learn and embrace new leader roles. Instead, leaders are using the latest skill-of-the-month or fad, such as empowerment, learning organization, or coaching, while exhausting the traditional leader roles. Leaders are essentially building new skills on top of traditional leader roles. The results are disappointing for organizations and leaders alike. Organizations are not continuously achieving greater than industry average success, despite all of the added efforts and expectations. Leader frustration and stress levels remain high because the old leader roles don't work, new leader roles are ill-defined, and personal meaning from work is fleeting.

Corporate America is like a contractor tearing down an old home and leaving the original, crumbling foundation to support a new, expensive, and

3

larger home. After a while, the walls crack and heave as the foundation further deteriorates. The old foundation is like the traditional leader roles, which are the functions leaders provide. The new frame of the house is like the new skills used by leaders that enhance their ability to perform certain tasks. The old leader roles are not in alignment with the new skills, and vice versa. At best, old roles and new skills create a wobbling house, perched on the edge of failure. These roles and skills don't support the changing organization.

Ask yourself, would you spend your hard-earned money to build a new home upon an old foundation? Are you willing to spend thousands of dollars to educate leaders when new leader roles and associated competencies have not been defined or learned?

New leader roles are the solution to the "wobbling house" of management. This book is the first of its kind to provide a proven and comprehensive program, which guides readers through the transition from traditional roles to new leader roles. New leader roles generate an excitement in the workplace that extends to the personal lives of employees. This excitement translates to increased productivity, long term financial success, and refreshing personal satisfaction at work and at home.

Stress and lackluster business results do not have to be the necessary by-product of corporate America. Both corporate America and leaders need the proper foundation for success. The keys are to recognize and implement new leader roles and align the appropriate competencies. However, the starting point is to recognize why organizations and leaders are changing and what roles are required to succeed in the future business environment. With that understanding, new leader roles can become the new foundation for business success.

FROM HANDCRAFT TO HEADCRAFT INDUSTRY — WHY ORGANIZATIONS AND LEADERS ARE CHANGING

Casey Stengel could have been talking about the management revolution when he said, "the future ain't what it used to be." Some leaders and employees feel like they are riding a merry-go-round that is reaching a maddening pace because so much has happened in the last ten to fifteen years. By 1997, the nation's top five hundred industrial corporations collectively shrank their work forces by more than 1.3 million jobs. Basically, leaders and employees are learning to do more with less.

The American Management Association states that mid-level leaders make up 5 to 8 percent of all jobs; however, they have accounted for 19 percent of all layoffs since 1989. As a result, the span of responsibility for senior leaders and remaining mid-level leaders is increasing. Leaders must learn how to help individuals and teams to be more self-directed.

By 1800, information was doubling approximately every one hundred years. By 1930, it was doubling every thirty years. Today, information is doubling every two to three years and the amount of information is well over one thousand times the amount of information available in 1800. Traditional management practices cannot succeed because the staggering amount of information and span of responsibility won't allow leaders to keep up with the information overload. Leaders need help to tap the intellectual capacity of all employees.

At one point, it was easy to tell employees to "leave their heads at the gate" when less than 20 percent of the population had more than a high school education. Now, more than 45 percent of the population twenty-five years and older has a college education, while 80 percent of all Ph.D.s ever born are alive today. With an increase in education, there is an increase in those who want to learn more on the job. It's no longer enough for leaders and employees to simply have a job. They want a job that has meaning and provides self-fulfillment. Children of parents who worked during the Great Depression have grown to expect more than just a paycheck. It's astonishing to see the growing percentages of leaders and employees that want to leave organizations and start second careers because they feel they've lost meaning in their work. Organizations must provide work opportunities that are meaningful to leaders and employees.

Some companies continue to focus on old paradigms—the way we were. According to the National Center of Education and the Economy's 1990 study, "America's Choice: High Skills or Low Wages," 95 percent of U.S. corporations still organize work in the same way as at the turn of the century. This may have worked well with a work force that had little or no formal education and organizations that were more dependent on physical labor, but as we stated earlier, competition is fierce—not just in the marketplace, but among companies in search of technologically advanced employees. Work opportunities must be reorganized.

In-command used to mean in-control. For more than a century, leaders were most effective where they used the command and control management style, looking over the shoulder of employees and telling them how to do their work. However, technological advances changed everything. The competitive environment accelerated, leaving command and control leaders behind because they were unable to cope with the speed and demands of the marketplace. As competition increased, so did the consumer's desire for quality supplies. Technological advances provided better goods and services, which outstripped leaders' abilities to grow.

As a result, a vast number of leaders today are in-command but out-of-control. The more leaders struggle to command and control employees, the more organizations are out of control, and vice versa. A new environment requires new leader roles.

YOU NO LONGER NEED TO LEAVE YOUR HEAD AT THE GATE— THE RISE OF NEW ROLES FOR LEADERS

At the start of the century, jobs were designed to be simple, narrow, specific, and repetitive. In addition, organization structures were designed with a recognizable hierarchy. Now, leaders are beginning to realize that employees are capable of more than hard labor. Because employees in quality oriented organizations are no longer "leaving their heads at the gate," they're encouraged to work in team-based structures to increase the opportunity for synergy.

As if culture shock were not enough, some leaders have further developed the team concept to reflect the growth of team members. The leader's role in the advanced stage of team management requires more concentration on managing relationships with other areas of the organization, while remaining a visible part of the team. Employees at this stage are given some of the responsibilities once held by a leader, such as office space management, vacation requests, and business travel requests. Some leaders and teams have advanced even farther reaching a point referred to as shared leadership. Employees are given even greater responsibilities—such as budget development—while the leader focuses on projects and relationships crossing team boundaries.

Despite the success of teams, some leaders have found that teams did not fit their culture or work process. Empowerment is used to fill the void. It's also a management tool used to increase team and individual productivity.

As leaders empower employees and/or teams, mid-level leaders, in particular, often become suspect because they are often perceived as shuffling paper or passing on decisions made by others. As a result, the number of mid-level leaders has decreased because less time is required for directing and overseeing employees. The number of employees reporting to leaders has steadily increased as a result.

As shown below in the Team Maturity Continuum, the levels of capability, ownership, authority, and purpose for leaders and employees are changing from one end of the continuum (traditional) to the other end of the continuum (shared leadership). Some organizations are progressing from one model to the next along the continuum, but many organizations are attempting to jump over points in the continuum. With the change in the structure of work, the leader's role must be redefined. However, efforts have focused on individual and team roles leaving leaders with old roles and new challenges. As a result, leaders are unprepared to solve today's problems.

Team Maturity Continuum

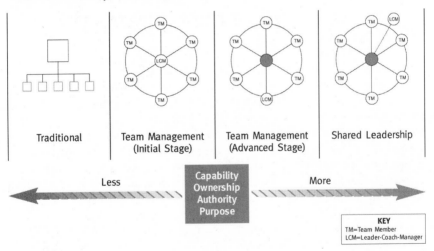

FADS AND FUZZWORDS—THE FINAL CHAPTER BEFORE NEW ROLES FOR LEADERS

Caught in the transition using old roles to address modern issues, too often leaders use fads and fuzzwords to fill the void. Fads and fuzz are truly four letter words. Fads are the programs-of-the-month, which we have all experienced. Fads are used to try and create enthusiasm because employee morale tends to dip during the organization transition to increased team and individual responsibilities. Fuzzwords are those words, like empowerment and quality management, which are frequently thrown around in conversations by leaders. Because the new roles for leaders are not defined or understood at this point, fads and fuzzwords create confusion and frustration for both employees and leaders instead of enthusiasm and alignment as originally expected. Leaders lack enthusiasm because they do not have a clear or thorough understanding how fads and fuzzwords relate to their roles. If leaders lack a clear view, employees certainly don't exude enthusiasm because they have less of a clue how fads and fuzzwords relate to their jobs.

The good news related to fads and fuzzwords is they are the last chapter in the transition. New roles for leaders replace the fuzziness. Fads will no longer be necessary because these new roles provide the desired outcomes and excitement for leaders and employees. Fuzzwords evaporate because both leader and employee roles are more clearly defined and related to the organization's journey toward its vision.

LEARN ELEVEN NEW ROLES FOR LEADERS

The dinner began without fanfare. Everyone sat down to enjoy a meal celebrating the passage of a milestone. A class of department leaders from a manufacturing firm had completed the foundational course in their journey to master the new leader roles. The room was buzzing as leaders exchanged quips, jokes, and war stories. At the end of the meal and before the close of the evening, the leaders made a presentation of a wall plaque to the session facilitator recognizing the group's accomplishments. The most poignant moment was the reading of the cryptic notes written on the back of the plaque by those leaders who had worked diligently over the past months to change their paradigms. The most telling notes read:

> Thanks for helping me change the way I think about life and my job. . . .
> The time you have spent with us over these past two years has helped each
> of us become more effective both at work and in our personal lives. Our
> company will survive these difficulties, and I will always remember the
> important role you have played in this turnaround and in our future
> success. . . . Thanks for helping us make our company a better place to
> work. . . . Thank you for all that you have done for our company and myself.
> I will always remember our talks. What you have shared with me will help
> me throughout my life. Wishing you my best.

As if they were the scribbled notes on a cave wall left by discoverers of a new land, these leaders committed their minds, hearts, and souls to a journey. Like these leaders, all leaders are on a long journey with many peaks and valleys. The journey has a virtual destination created by goals and strategic planning; however, there is no end to this organization's travels or the leader's trail. Leaders and employees must continue moving forward and sometimes changing course. Leaders and employees must always strive to increase knowledge, skills, and contributions.

In this journey, everyone's role must change, including a leader's role because the organization is leaving behind the old traditional organization. Like any successful journey, the transition requires a commitment. This book focuses on the starting point of that journey—new roles for leaders.

THE NEW ROLES FOR LEADERS

New roles for leaders are the most vital component of an organization's transition because they are the foundation or building blocks upon which the new organization will be built. Without new roles for leaders, quality improvement, employee empowerment, teams, and empowerment will be inconsequential. Leader roles are critical because leaders are the important linchpin between an organization's mission, vision, and values and employees. Leaders are the ones who will instill fervor and support the transition or allow new skills and techniques to decay. This section opened with the statement that new leader roles are like the foundation of a building. Leader roles are the base that supports the entire structure. With an appropriate foundation, the structure will be strong and enduring. However, a weak foundation will create ever widening cracks in the structure, heaving walls, and an unstable future.

The old foundation cannot be used to create a new, larger, and more dynamic structure. An old foundation cannot support the weight and stress of this new structure long term. Recognizing the importance of the foundation, new leader roles are the starting point for a transitioning organization. Unfortunately, many organizations are learning this point the hard way. These organizations have created new structures, teams, and new skills before changing their foundation—new leader roles. New leader roles must be built to align with the future, desired structure. There should be at least eleven new leader roles.

However, two roles, Create a New Mindset and Adopt the Leader-Coach-Manager Paradigm, must be firmly engrained prior to development of the other nine roles. These two roles are the foundation. An organization can effectively establish the other nine leader roles without these two key foundational roles but will fail in the leader roles transition because Create a New Mindset and Adopt the Leader-Coach-Manager Paradigm must support and permeate each of the nine roles. They tie together the other nine roles because of the basic philosophy and focus included in these two roles.

Leader's House

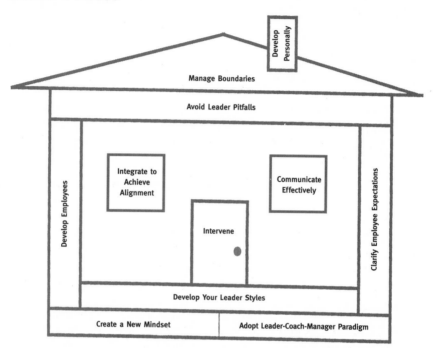

One way for leaders to understand how new leader roles are integrated is to use a picture. We have used the analogy of a house as shown above in the Leader's House diagram.

The foundation consists of **Create a New Mindset** and **Adopt the Leader-Coach-Manager Paradigm**. With the foundation appropriately laid for the Leader's House, the other nine roles can form the superstructure. The step to the house is the use of appropriate **Styles** by leaders when working with employees. Leaders must **Intervene** through positive and development approaches. Once within the house, the outer walls hold the house together as shown by **Develop Employees** and **Clarify Employee Expectations**. As with any house, it is important to have sufficient light. Light is needed to see and understand the vision and mission of an organization. Light streams into the house through the windows of **Integrate To Achieve Alignment** and **Communicate Effectively**. Without an over-arching beam, a house will cave in from the pressure of the outer walls. **Avoid Leader Pitfalls** is the support beam that keeps the house from caving in. Just as a roof protects a building from the elements, leaders provide protection through **Manage Boundaries.** Last, but not least, the chimney represents the intrinsic burning force that each leader must have for a successful journey—**Develop Personally**. Together the eleven roles form the new Leader's House.

LEADERS TAKING OWNERSHIP OF THE TRANSITION

All persons participating in the organization's transition must be willing to change their roles, expecting change from others and eventually the entire organization. More importantly, both leaders and employees must take "ownership" of the transition.

The word "ownership" underscores the point that transitions are successful where employees and leaders treat the organization as if they owned it. This also places leaders in a more comfortable transitional position because they do not feel that the responsibility for change falls only on their shoulders.

Before leaders and employees commit to change, they must first know and understand the roadmap—where they are, where they've been, and where they're going (in that order). Views vary when reading a roadmap. Attempting to locate an organization's present position can be complex because of the pace of change. In other words, it's usually more difficult to assess current reality than to develop a vision. Most employees can more easily agree on a desired future state than on what is actually taking place.

Current reality can be assessed by both formal and informal means. Informally, leaders can gain input from their supervisors, employees, and others to assess where they are relative to their desired role change. This can be done subtly or overtly through questions. The leader should hold employee meetings where part of the agenda is designed to elicit feedback on the transition process. Leaders need to be direct with their questions, such as—how are we doing on our transition to a more empowered environment? how well are we making the transition to new leader roles? what do we need to do to reach our vision of an empowered environment and new leader roles? and what might leaders do to help us in our journey to a more empowered environment?

A more formal means of assessing the transition is to use a focused, written survey where employees and leaders are asked to provide their perceptions about the current status of the transition. Questions in the survey should relate to the new leader roles recognized by the organization. All employees need to complete the survey. Survey results should be reported to all employees and by each area. The data should be benchmarked against data available from other organizations, if possible. It is best to perform surveys at least biannually because it provides sufficient time for employees to show substantial progress. Where possible, a survey should be conducted prior to the transition to provide a baseline for future comparison with survey results.

When the current reality is identified, the vision must be developed through participation by leaders and employees and clearly outlined and communicated to all. Once the vision is agreed upon, the gap between current reality and vision should be easy to identify. Finally, a transition plan can be developed to move leader(s) and employees from current reality toward the vision. The transition plan shows how an organization will narrow the gap. It is best to have a transition plan for the organization and each leader. A leader's personal transition plan should be included in a development plan which is covered in greater detail in part 2.

The transition plan would normally include such things as development required, leader and employee tasks to implement the transition, and monitors for the change process. Transitions require a change in beliefs, behaviors, and methods of operation, all of which should be underscored in the transition plan.

New roles for leaders are essential to support and develop employees and transition the organization in this journey. However, leaders must realize that the roles of a leader are not neatly wrapped in separate and distinct packages. The eleven roles are interdependent. As outlined in the Leader's House diagram above, one role affects all others. For convenience and clarity, each role will be explored separately.

There are two important points to understand when reviewing these roles. First, each role is important and not discussed in any priority, except for the two key foundational roles, Create a New Mindset and Adopt the Leader-Coach-Manager Paradigm. Second, roles will differ from one organization to another. The importance assigned to specific roles is affected by each organization's corporate culture, key operational areas for its industry, organizational philosophy (mission, vision, values, and strategic plan) and developmental needs of its leaders and employees.

ROLLING ALONG—NEW LEADER ROLES FOR ORGANIZATIONS

Because of the dynamic environment all organizations are experiencing, organizations are adapting to survive and thrive, streamlining the leader and employee ranks, utilizing teams and empowerment to quicken the pace, and embracing continuous quality improvement for enhanced efficiency and effectiveness. The roles of employees are also changing because of employee abilities to add value in a competitive world. Last but not least, we are witnessing the most revolutionary adaptation of leader roles to align with the organization and employees since the advent of the first Industrial Revolution. How we think of leaders and what we expect of leaders are reflected in the new roles for leaders. For leaders of the twenty-first century, these new roles will create new challenges but will offer greater meaning and rewards than the traditional roles.

This book is the product of practical role applications by practitioners who have used these new leader roles in organizations of different size, industry, and nationality. From the start, the book has been designed with outcomes as its focus. It is about the difficult and challenging roles of leaders.

The book is divided into three parts. The first part of the book defines and applies the eleven new roles for leaders. The second part of the book takes one more step forward and deals with the transition from command and control management to new roles for leaders, identifying how to select and develop leaders for these new roles. Leaders are advised to read part 1 which covers the eleven roles prior to part 2. This will provide greater context and appreciation for the processes outlined in part 2. Each section is designed with CEOs and other leaders in mind including real life stories of how these roles are applied. Part 3 offers practical exercises intended to fine-tune the newly found roles of a leader. One caveat for all readers, the eleven new roles for leaders provided in this book are based on the needs of many different organizations in diverse industries. Your organization may require greater emphasis upon certain roles or consideration of other leader roles to complement the major roles outlined in this book.

Being a leader of an organization, division, or department is about adding value to an organization and to a leader's own life. Enjoy the journey shared within these pages. It is about challenge, soul, quality improvement, superior business results, personal rewards, and connecting to a better way—a better foundation.

PART 1

New Leader Roles

CREATE A NEW MINDSET

Where Your Stress Takes a Rest

A MANUFACTURER OF defense weapons faced a bleak future. Productivity was decreasing, union problems were skyrocketing, government contracts were declining, and waste was rampant. A new CEO was hired to turn the company around or sell it. The new CEO met with leaders of the departments to discuss how to deal with the company's problems. Dressed in casual clothes similar to non-management employees, he carefully outlined the problems facing the company. He then talked about the organization's mission, vision, and values. He related these guiding documents to their specific problems. Unlike past leaders, the new CEO asked how these documents could provide direction for the company and how these grave problems might be addressed. Silence answered the CEO until one leader slowly stood. The leader said that a good solution was to ask for input from employees. This was revolutionary thinking because employees had always been managed closely. After a few snide whispers among the group, the CEO praised the courage shown and ideas shared by the leader. The CEO stated that unless someone had a better idea, he would personally meet with small groups of employees to share the challenge and gain input. The CEO also asked for improvement ideas from each leader. As a result of the employee input, the company abolished a number of human resource rules, changed the manufacturing processes, and revised a stringent dress code. Productivity climbed, the waste ratio became one of the lowest in the industry, and employee-leader relationships improved.

This true story illustrates the powerful impact of thinking differently, believing in the capability of people, and proactively pursuing business solutions. The story's positive results would not have occurred if leaders in that organization had used their old traditional management philosophy (i.e., only leaders think and employees do).

 SO, WHAT'S THE POINT?
If leaders always do what they always did, leaders will always get what they always got. Status quo is the enemy. Growth requires change.

ACHIEVING A NEW MINDSET

New leader roles are not business as usual. New leader roles are fundamentally different from past management behavior, traditional beliefs about employees and work, and leaders' commitment to continuous improvement. Thoughts, beliefs, and ownership are essential parts of the leader's job. It is a mindset, a new way of thinking about things.

This new mindset requires that leaders be "learning" leaders at all times and continuously challenge their beliefs ("Think"), have a basic foundation of beliefs ("Believe"), and, finally, be strongly committed to the new leader roles and transition ("Own"). The Think-Believe-Own mindset is a foundational role, because it forms the new management way of thinking and new beliefs about employees.

Think: Creating New Paradigms

How can leaders be sure they see things as they really are? In fact, leaders can't be sure. All act in accordance with their own individual perceptions of reality, or what is popularly referred to as a "paradigm." Whether or not these perceptions accurately reflect reality is not the point. The important issue is that the perceptions are real. These perceptions provide the basis for action. The word "paradigm" is generally defined as a point of view or, to use the vernacular, a paradigm indicates where one is coming from. Thus, a paradigm shift means a change in point of view. A paradigm shift occurs when a leader changes from the command and control paradigm to new roles for leaders paradigm. This type of major shift usually occurs over long periods of time, although small shifts can occur within very short time frames.

A good example of a small, quick paradigm shift happened to us several years ago. We had an important meeting with a company. Tim, a young leader responsible for the company's new service area, was to be present at the meeting to provide much needed support. Tim showed up at the meeting but said very little. Needless to say, we weren't too pleased with his lack of support. We viewed Tim as being unresponsive and uncommitted to the project. After the meeting, we confronted Tim. He explained that, immediately prior to the meeting, he and his wife were informed that she had a rare brain cancer and wasn't expected to live beyond five or six weeks. All at once, Tim's behavior at the meeting was perfectly logical. We had experienced a paradigm shift with respect to our impression of Tim. Our perception of his lack of support and unresponsiveness to our needs totally changed in light of this new information.

Leaders are prejudiced by information stored in their minds. This information can be very helpful or it can become their worst enemy. In order to be a continuously changing, learning organization, leaders and employees need to treat everything as a working hypothesis. Nothing should be accepted as an absolute. Everything is open to continual improvement. The willingness to shift paradigms—our points of view—is vital.

Sarah was appointed as the president of a regional health insurance company, which was part of a national company. The regional company had experienced stagnant sales for several years prior to Sarah's arrival. Sarah addressed the sales problem by reviewing all phases of the sales department. She found that the problem required a change in the sales commission program for internal sales staff and insurance brokers. Sarah spent countless hours preparing for a meeting with her supervisor, the CEO of the national company. She had data to support her assessment of the problem and alternative solutions. She even prepared a proposal that her CEO could use with the chairman of the board. Sarah carefully outlined the elements to change in their sales department and how to accomplish this change in a traditional environment. When Sarah presented the idea to her CEO, he said that it was radical and did not fit the tradition of the company. Sarah's perception of the sales philosophy was that it was only a hypothesis. Her CEO's perception of the sales philosophy was that it was a written-in-stone reality, never to be changed. The company has continued to suffer from lackluster sales because of traditional thinking. Sarah realized she could not be effective for the company if its leaders would not stretch their thinking. As a result, she accepted a job offer from a competitor. Today, Sarah is successfully implementing her dynamic ideas because she is surrounded by leaders who appreciate the value of challenging old paradigms.

Why do we have paradigms? What creates them? The best way to understand the answers to these questions is to review how the mind works. The following diagram, Decision Process, illustrates how people, in general, make decisions. A leader receives information, referred to as input. The input is received in the conscious level of awareness.

Automatically, the mind searches the subconscious or storage area for relevant information, which directly impacts the raw input. This transformed information is transferred back to the conscious level where a final decision takes place. The final decision is referred to as the output.

A new CEO announced to Bob and other leaders that new leader roles would soon be used, instead of the traditional management approach of command and control. In addition, all leaders would receive extensive training and prepare individual development plans. Finally, the incentive pay system would be changed to reward leaders who had effectively made the transition.

The new information or input entered the conscious level of Bob's mind. Bob's mind recalled relevant information stored in the subconscious. Bob's subconscious recalled that his managing skill always worked well in the past, and employees tried to take advantage of the company when a past CEO tried to utilize self-directed teams. However, Bob also remembered that the past CEO did not provide education for employees to make the transition and the pay system was not changed to reflect the new direction. At the conscious level, Bob made the decision that the CEO's directive might work because the CEO was taking a different approach. Therefore, Bob decided to proactively participate in the transition program.

Decision Process

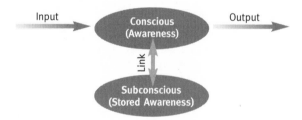

The mind is obviously more complex than is shown in the diagram outlined above. It does, however, highlight the fact that the subconscious can prejudice (pre-judge) decisions and actions. In essence, the way each leader and employee thinks can be one of the biggest hindrances to a transitioning organization. This is why a paradigm shift can be so difficult to achieve. However, if leaders don't change the way they think, it is almost impossible to solve the major issues confronting organizations today.

To take the example one step further, leaders sometimes permit unrelated factors to prejudice their opinions of employees. Leaders allow themselves to be influenced inappropriately by previous experiences. For example, children have been told by their parents to distrust people who have a soft handshake. Similar statements and subconscious beliefs could be held about eye contact, hairstyle, clothing, or virtually anything. Some leaders use these factors to make judgments about important issues such as trust, sincerity, respect, and integrity. These judgments create significant and unnecessary conflict between a leader and employees. Other leaders may use other factors to make judgments about the capabilities of people. For example, leaders might assume that an aggressive and controlling employee has the ingredients for success but, in empowered environments, these attributes are often ingredients for failure.

The "think" component of the Create a New Mindset role means a leader must make a commitment to, and develop skills in, three areas: (1) change organization paradigms by questioning or rethinking existing policies, systems, and goals; (2) shift employee paradigms by their reconsideration of assumptions made in the past about the leader/employee relationship; and (3) continually assess reality and identify the journey required to reach the organization's vision.

SO, WHAT'S THE POINT?
The way a leader thinks and then behaves will directly impact whether or not an organization will achieve its vision. Organizations can learn, imitate, or vegetate. The leader must think in an uncontaminated, unprejudiced way to provide the foundation for a transitioning organization.

Believe—Building Foundations

Beliefs are powerful. Beliefs can prejudice or "pre-judge" your thinking. Whatever leaders have stored in their subconscious will automatically surface in their consciousness to affect decision making. Some beliefs are good and should be kept. Other beliefs can be harmful because they tie leaders and employees to a tradition, which may no longer be applicable in today's changing environment.

"Think" was covered in this role prior to "believe" because it is critical that leaders think through their mental storage banks (beliefs). Leaders must consistently evaluate their own personal beliefs in order to maximize the impact of the decision-making process.

WHAT ARE BASIC BELIEFS?

Beliefs are firmly held convictions, which either determine or heavily influence our actions. In the workplace, leader's beliefs about employees directly impact the leader's actions toward the employees. The leader's actions or behaviors positively or negatively impact employees' behaviors.

The bottom line is that leaders must try to increase the discretionary effort of employees. Discretionary effort, shown in the following diagram, is the difference between what employees must do to meet minimum job requirements and what they could do if they wanted to. It is the difference between minimum and maximum mental and physical effort. This difference represents real bottom-line dollars to the organization.

Discretionary Effort

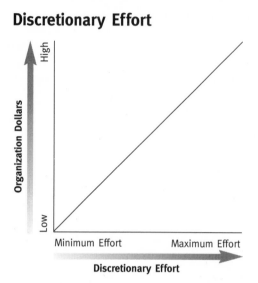

Leaders hold many beliefs and values. However, there are nine basic beliefs/values which leaders must have in order to be effective and maximize employee discretionary effort:

1. Satisfy stakeholders
2. People are the potential
3. Value is diversity
4. Power is delegation
5. Manage the journey
6. Dare to care
7. Face the consequences
8. Loyalty is challenge up, support down
9. Leaders needback the feedback

Let's take a closer look at these nine basic beliefs.

1. Satisfy Stakeholders—The S.P.I.C.E. of an Organization's Life

Stakeholders include suppliers, the public, investors, customers, and employees (S.P.I.C.E.) and, quite likely, are the "spice" of an organization's life.

Jobs will not exist unless stakeholders' needs are anticipated, met or exceeded.

Most organizations have mission statements which in essence explain the reason or purpose the organization exists. Many organizations are now pursuing statements of vision, values, and principles which are focused on meeting stakeholders' needs. Collectively, the mission, vision, values, and principles are philosophy statements. Philosophy statements provide a comprehensive explanation about why the organization exists and how it operates and meets the needs of stakeholders.

Vision is a desired future position or state. It identifies where the organization would like to be in five years or some other specified time period. Values reflect what beliefs are important to the organization. For example, leaders may believe that jobs exist only because the business is successful in meeting customer needs. As a result, customer satisfaction is one of the values that leaders and employees are expected to respect and use. Principles are actions or behaviors based on beliefs and values. A customer satisfaction survey may be used as an active measure of the company's principles. Utilization of the survey results to initiate improvement projects is an example of putting principles in action. All in all, stakeholder satisfaction is a foundational belief for the organization starting with the creation and implementation of its philosophy statements.

In addition to philosophy statements, the leader's focus must be on process improvements which meet or exceed stakeholder needs. This is

Quality Model

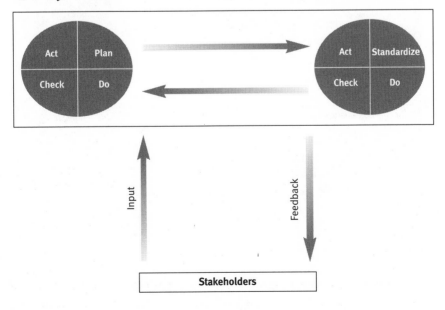

accomplished as reflected in the above Quality Model. Leaders help employees improve and standardize processes to insure ongoing stakeholder satisfaction. Leaders insure that input from stakeholders is the key driving force behind their actions. Also, a critical part of stakeholder satisfaction is providing feedback to the stakeholder about improvements initiated.

Leaders and employees achieve stakeholder satisfaction through new leader roles and the integration of technical processes, social/people processes, and key organization documents such as mission, vision, and values. The integration of these processes and key organization documents is critical to the quality of work life and business success, as shown in the Integrated Leading Process diagram.

This concept is expanded to include stakeholder satisfaction in the Stakeholder Satisfaction Influences diagram. Feedback from stakeholders and business results provide input for improving philosophy and integrating

Integrated Leading Process

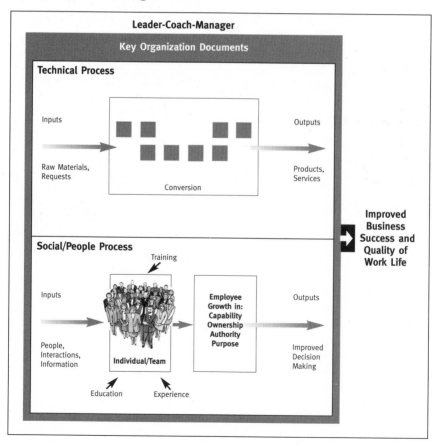

technical and social processes. Improved quality of work life and business success cannot be attained without stakeholder satisfaction.

Stakeholder Satisfaction Influences

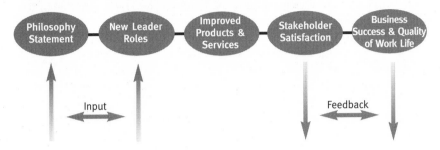

Input   Feedback

SO, WHAT'S THE POINT?
Stakeholder satisfaction is achieved by providing products and services which meet or exceed stakeholder needs. The lack of stakeholder satisfaction causes business decline and loss of jobs. It takes new leader roles to properly blend the organization philosophy and technical/social processes to achieve stakeholder satisfaction.

2. People Are the Potential

Leaders must believe in the potential of their employees (people potential) in order to sustain business success and quality of work life. People potential includes both education and training to enhance employees' capabilities and the recognition of employees' progress, results, and behaviors.

Education and training have made great strides. However, the needs in the workplace continue to outstrip the advances made in education and training. Because of this, some leaders may believe that people are incapable. The reality is people usually rise to the challenge when given the opportunity.

Leaders who believe in people potential must identify how much education and training is needed. This can be accomplished by analyzing current reality and vision and using new leader roles to reach the vision. Typically, organizations in the United States spend less than one half of one percent of their budget on the education and training of employees while Fortune 500 companies will spend an average of three and a half percent of budget. In sharp contrast, high performance organizations (i.e., companies involved in new leader roles and quality systems improvement) spend approximately 7 percent of budget on education and training. What is an appropriate amount for an organization? It depends on the current reality analysis. However, organizations that commit to new leader roles and empowered environments must be prepared to dramatically increase their education and training budgets. We often see organizations dedicating too few resources to education and training when striving for an empowered work environment. Later, this leads to failure and the incorrect perception that the transition journey just does not work. Poor management is, in part, an outcome of insufficient education and training for leaders and employees.

Eastman Chemical Company is an example of an organization investing substantial resources to educate and train leaders in the new leader roles. Newly-appointed, first-level leaders commit four months to full-time education and training. Leaders at the second level and above commit to four hours of education and training every other week for approximately one year. There are over twenty-five courses and numerous books and videos included in the development process.

Leaders normally get what they expect. High expectations create high performance. Low expectations result in low performance. Leaders must have a fundamental belief in the potential of people. Pygmalion, who was a sculptor in Greek mythology, carved a statue of a beautiful woman. Pygmalion fell in love with the statue. He saw great beauty and potential. As the story goes, the Goddess of Love shot an arrow into the heart of the statue and it came to life. The point is one gets what one expects. If leaders treat employees like winners, there is a good likelihood that they will become winners. If employees are treated like failures, they will fail.

The Pygmalion factor was proven in a classic study conducted by Robert Rosenthal and Lenore Jacobson. School children were tested and the results were reported to the teacher. The teacher was told some of the children were spurters (smart) and some were laggards (not as smart). The teacher was not provided accurate information. Subconsciously, this information affected the teacher's behavior towards the children. Because the teacher believed in the perceived capability of certain students, real laggards outperformed real spurters.

As leaders, how do we treat employees? Do we treat them as servants or do we treat them as potential winners? It does make a difference! Expectations, expectations, expectations!

We have frequently asked management audiences the following question: Do you believe employees are capable of doing more than you have let them do or asked them to do in the past? The overwhelming response has been "yes." In fact, we cannot recall a single response to the contrary. If leaders truly believe this, why don't they provide the opportunity for increased capability? Some of the reasons include fear of anarchy, loss of status or perceived worth, and belief in the old paradigm that leaders are supposed to control the workplace. For some leaders, this means sharing power. Contrary to what most leaders may believe, however, sharing power is gaining power because employee loyalty, dedication, and productivity are increased.

Leaders must see employees not as they are, but as they could be. Occasionally, a leader will be disappointed to find that an employee cannot increase his/her capability to assume additional responsibility. However, leaders will find more often that employees will excel or rise to the level of expectations. In today's environment, leaders place the organization at increased risk if they do not believe in the potential of people.

The people potential belief requires that a leader (1) provide sufficient education/training opportunities to enhance employee and leader capabilities, (2) use a leadership style which creates a "want to" attitude, and (3) delegate responsibility to employees consistent with their growth in capability and ownership.

SO, WHAT'S THE POINT?
Leaders must share power and believe in the potential of people. Sharing power is gaining power. Sharing power is essential to new leader roles: no sharing=no new leader roles=decreased power=stagnation.

3. Value is Diversity

People are different. They differ in their opinions, motivations, abilities, preferences, socio-demographics (race, color, creed, and sex), and styles. Differences can add value or become barriers. Differences can add value because diversity normally provides greater or improved creativity, innovation, decision making, and problem solving. Diversity is the foundation for synergy. Differences can be barriers because people may prejudge others, avoid change, keep control, or discriminate.

Diversity, in the positive sense, can contribute to business success and quality of work life. The old saying, "two heads are better than one," is only valid if the people involved truly value diversity and work together effectively.

Opinions are often overlooked as part of the diversity picture. In some organizations, employees are not valued unless they think the same way and share the same ideas as their leaders. This can lead to "straight line thinking" which is thinking with blinders on. As a result, innovative ideas and unique changes to existing programs, services, or products are lost.

On the other hand, some organizations may have so much diversity that they are unable to reach agreement or form a common culture. Therefore, a certain balance of diversity is required to create cooperation and teamwork. Once a decision is reached, those with differing opinions or ideas will need to provide support for the decision. Leaders need to "**challenge up— support down**" in these situations. Leaders should not make comments or take actions which demoralize employees. All concerns and differing opinions should be challenged upward in the organization. Valuing diversity requires that leaders value differing opinions as a way to seek out the best options and ideas for the organization's vision.

SO, WHAT'S THE POINT?
Valuing diversity is critical to unleashing the intellectual capital of leaders and employees. New leader roles require leaders who can appreciate and encourage different ideas and thinking from everyone.

4. Power is Delegation

Leaders must believe in the power of delegation. This belief is compatible with the people potential belief. However, leaders must also know when employees are ready to accept delegation.

An employee must possess capability and ownership before a leader delegates authority. Decision making by employees who lack knowledge, skills, and dedication places the business at significant risk. Employees are at risk when authority is delegated in the absence of capability and/or ownership. The quality of work life is also adversely affected when employees are frustrated or make mistakes. To paraphrase Dr. W. Edwards Deming, if you want to rob employees of their pride of workmanship, ask them to do something they cannot do. This is not fair to the employees, the leader, or the organization. The bottom line is employees should not be given authority without the wherewithal to be successful. Proper delegation by leaders is part of the new leader roles for success.

SO, WHAT'S THE POINT?
Purpose, capability, and ownership must precede delegation of authority. It takes new leader roles to balance risk to the organization and employees while achieving business success and improving the quality of work life.

5. Manage the Journey

Paradigms are the lens we use to view the world. The leader's lens analogy, as outlined in the Leader's Lens diagram, is used to show how the organization's vision can be used to refocus the individual and organization. The leader should be looking through bifocal eyeglasses: the leader looks through the bottom lens at current reality, and through the top lens at the vision for the organization. As with bifocals, you need both near and far-distance lenses to see the whole. The leader plays a key role in shaping the future by helping employees move toward the organization's vision. Leaders always should be asking themselves what is the next logical step consistent with the organization's vision. There are three guiding points that a leader must use: (1) move toward the vision, (2) do not remain at status quo, and (3) make sense to employees (the vision and journey must be considered practical).

Leader's Lens

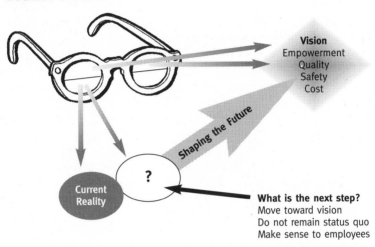

Vision
Empowerment
Quality
Safety
Cost

Shaping the Future

Current Reality

?

What is the next step?
Move toward vision
Do not remain status quo
Make sense to employees

SO, WHAT'S THE POINT?
Manage the journey—see reality and pursue the vision. Meet employees where they are and lead them to the vision. Status quo is not okay.

6. Caring

Most leaders interpret caring as "treat everyone with kid-gloves and everything will be okay," but caring is simply showing people respect and being concerned about them as human beings. Leaders who show employees they care are making good business decisions.

When addressing a teacher's conference, a high school teacher related an incident she experienced on her first job. She was teaching students that were only four years her junior. The teacher knew that a friend of one of her students, Caleb, had been injured in a car accident. One afternoon during class, an announcement was made over the intercom that Caleb's friend had died. Caleb was obviously troubled. The teacher offered and allowed Caleb to leave the classroom. She later joined Caleb in the hall and asked him if there was anything she could do to help him. He responded that she could hug him. Immediately, she thought of all of the reasons why a hug would appear inappropriate. What would other students think? What would the principal or other teachers think? Despite these thoughts, she gave Caleb a hug. At the end of her story, she then made the following point to the teachers: **People don't care how much you know, if they don't know how much you care.** This is also true of leaders.

One employee was having significant personal problems related to his marriage and alcohol consumption. A friend of this employee told the department leader that suicide may be imminent because the telephone at the employee's home was apparently off the hook and the employee had been especially despondent the night before. The leader decided to visit the employee's home.

Upon arrival, the employee invited the leader to sit in his kitchen. They discussed the employee's problems for several hours. When the leader began to leave, he embraced the employee and whispered into the employee's ear. The leader later admitted that he told the employee he loved him. When asked if he was a personal friend, the leader said he had never been to his home or seen him outside of the work setting. He said he wasn't sure why he said that—it just seemed like the right thing to say. The distraught employee returned to work and became one of the leader's strongest supporters. Those leaders who say the soft stuff has no business in business do not understand the power and influence of a caring leader in the workplace.

Caring and showing that care is an essential value, which is consistent with the roles of a leader. In fact, caring is one of a number of attributes which create influential power. Influential power grows when employees increase their respect for the capabilities and influence of a leader. In the modern organization, influential power is stronger than positional power because it does not depend on the title or position of a leader to encourage employees to maximize their discretionary effort.

SO, WHAT'S THE POINT?
Caring about people is critical to the creation of synergistic relationships that help employees grow and leaders become accepted. Influential power is stronger than positional power. Caring is a good business decision in addition to being a needed human response.

7. Face the Consequences
Some psychologists say behavior is solely a function of consequences. This is partially true. Behavior is also a function of values as well as

consequences. History is full of people who have given their lives based on their beliefs or values.

Every behavior has a consequence. Behavior is anything an employee says or does, while consequence is what happens to an employee as a result of a particular behavior. Employees will do what makes sense to them. Thus, it is the responsibility of leaders to provide proper consequences that make sense and which logically relate to the behaviors.

The leader's role is to help employees increase their desire to improve performance. As discussed earlier, discretionary effort is the difference between the individual's minimum and maximum efforts. When employees have a high desire to improve performance, they will go beyond compliance or the minimum level of effort. The effective use of consequences by leaders is a key tool in achieving this result.

There are four basic types of consequences:

- Desirable reinforcement—giving an employee something that is perceived as desirable by that employee;
- Undesirable reinforcement—withholding something perceived as undesirable by that employee;
- Discipline—correcting an employee; and
- Transfer/Termination—removing an employee from their position.

Providing desirable reinforcement increases the likelihood that a behavior will be repeated. Providing discipline increases the likelihood that a behavior will not be repeated. Leaders need to be proactive in the use of desirable reinforcement. However, leaders need to be careful that what is reinforced is indeed the behavior they desire to be repeated.

On the other hand, leaders need to accept the fact that discipline is also an integral role. No leader or employee enjoys discipline but, at times, it is necessary to stop unacceptable behavior. Once the inappropriate behavior is stopped and the appropriate behavior is begun, the leader needs to use desirable reinforcement. Where discipline is ineffective, transfer or termination of an employee may be necessary for the good of the organization.

In addition, providing desirable reinforcement appeals to one of the basic needs of employees. Employees are motivated by several needs as shown below in the Motivational Arenas diagram.

Employees have needs or arenas in the social, emotional, family, spiritual, recreational, mental, and health parts of their lives. Even though the work part of an employee's life is somewhat separate and distinct from these other arenas, it cannot be totally divorced from them. That is the reason why the following diagram is designed with a larger circle, which includes these other motivational arenas, surrounding the smaller work circle.

Motivational Arenas

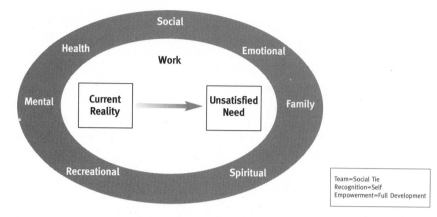

The inner circle of the diagram represents the work arena which is the primary focus of leaders. Leaders must understand each employee's current reality and their unsatisfied needs. In other words, a leader must understand what the employee needs but is not getting from the work arena.

Three specific areas are important to an employee in the work setting and affect an employee's need satisfaction: social ties, sense of self-esteem, and full development. Employees must have a meaningful social tie in the work setting to meet their need to be a part of the greater whole. This is satisfied by the inclusion of the employee as part of a team. Employees also need recognition on the job to meet their personal need. Recognition increases their sense of self-esteem and acknowledges their importance to the organization, like the professional football player who argued he should be allowed to play both defense and offense. In this situation, money was less important to him than being recognized and acknowledged as the best all-around player in the game.

In addition to social ties and feelings of self-esteem, an employee needs full development. In other words, employees want to develop to their fullest because they want to maximize the extent to which they are empowered. Empowerment is important to employees because it meets their need to be the best they can be and gain greater responsibility and control over decisions made within the work setting.

The Motivational Arenas diagram underscores that the leader's focus must be on the following because proper management of consequences is a key factor in influencing these five points:

1. Understanding the current reality and the unsatisfied needs of an employee
2. Social ties provided at work to an employee

3. Self-recognition offered to an employee
4. Empowerment which maximizes an employee's contribution and authority, and
5. Employees' needs as a function of more than just the work arena

SO, WHAT'S THE POINT?
The effective use of consequences by leaders is critical in helping employees grow and shape the future of the organization. Desirable reinforcement causes good performance to be repeated while discipline decreases or stops poor performance.

8. Loyalty is Challenge Up, Support Down

Is it okay for leaders to be negative to employees about company direction? No, no, no, and no! If a leader believes management's direction is wrong, it is appropriate for a leader to seek to understand the situation and attempt to influence the company direction by **challenging up (peers and above) while supporting down**. It is not appropriate to challenge down and demoralize employees by making negative comments about management direction, particularly in the midst of change. Change, alone, provides enough frustration and stress for employees without other complicating factors. Leaders who do not support down should leave their leadership role.

When a leader is challenging down and fails to leave his/her leadership role, the leader's supervisor should remove that leader. There are several reasons for this. A leader, in part, is paid to support the organization's direction and members of higher management. It demoralizes employees when support is not forthcoming and it provides a barrier to change. It is unproductive because people will end up spending more time on internal strife than on getting the job done.

In general, employees must be loyal to the organization; it is a character issue. When employees join an organization, they are committing themselves to making the organization successful. When an employee hurts the organization instead of helping it, he/she has broken the unspoken commitment. The only exception to this rule is where an organization is involved in illegal activity.

Loyalty also applies to members of management. It is inappropriate to belittle, criticize, slander, or assassinate the character of fellow leaders. Such behavior can destroy a leader's credibility with employees more than transgressing any of the other eight beliefs.

Huston was the vice president of sales for a computer manufacturing company. The president of the company announced two days earlier that he believed the company would be sold to another computer company or investment firm. Huston was a long-term employee who felt very strongly that the company could and should compete as a freestanding company. At a meeting of the sales division, a number of employees criticized and questioned the decision of the president. Huston had given a lot of thought to this matter. He realized that his role was to support the president and he responded to the employees by saying that he understood and appreciated their concerns and would relay these to the president. Otherwise, Huston demonstrated support for the president's position by restating the reasons for the sale which were outlined by the president. Huston provided a copy of the reasons cited by the president for this direction. Despite bitter statements made by employees, Huston did not make negative statements about the president. Huston displayed the courage of loyalty instead of the cowardice of abandonment.

The company was not sold as originally suggested and Huston gained his employees' respect for supporting the organization during a difficult time. A number of employees told Huston during a division meeting that it would have been easy for him to make disparaging remarks. Instead, he had shown real character by supporting his supervisor. Following this, Huston's division increased sales well above previous levels and their employee survey results showed marked improvement in leader and employee respect.

SO, WHAT'S THE POINT?
Be loyal to the absent.
Challenge up—support down.

9. Leaders Needback the Feedback

Feedback is providing information about past performance, which will enhance future performance. Leaders need feedback in order to reassess and understand specific situations and available options. Do leaders like to give or receive feedback? For many leaders, the answer is no. However, virtually every improvement comes through feedback. Therefore, leaders need to embrace feedback, not fear it. Feedback is a gift.

Most employees do the right thing if they know the right thing to do. Inappropriate behaviors are usually the result of a scotoma or a blind spot. Feedback plays a key role in the development of appropriate behaviors as shown in the Feedback Purpose diagram below. The left side of the diagram represents the feedback purpose for a leader. Feedback, when asked for or given voluntarily, allows a leader to grow beyond the solid box (current effectiveness box). The dotted-line box represents the leader's growth opportunity in relation to requesting and giving feedback.

Ray was a construction supervisor and reported to Troy, who was president of the construction firm. Ray couldn't understand why they always ran two weeks behind on the site preparation phase of construction. Troy recognized that Ray was struggling with this problem and gave Ray constructive

Feedback Purpose

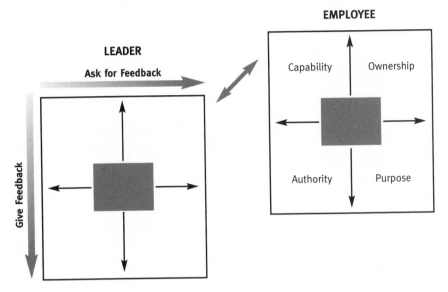

feedback. Troy reviewed the situation with Ray by asking questions about how the preparation phase and related phases were pursued. From the questions, Troy determined that Ray was not planning and ordering materials soon enough at the start of the project. Troy suggested that Ray try a different approach, which worked for Troy in the past. Because of this input, Ray was able to consistently beat the site preparation deadlines in the future. Troy and Ray expanded their effectiveness because of their positive interaction and feedback.

Leaders can also expand their effectiveness boxes by giving feedback to others. Continuing our example, Ray gave constructive feedback to Tim, supervisor for the bricklaying crew. Tim was an expert bricklayer but knew very little about other areas of construction. Ray described to Tim how bricklaying affected the construction project timeline. Tim learned how his project affected the construction company's ability to finish the project ahead of schedule. Ray also asked Tim for feedback regarding what Ray could do to help Tim grow. Tim shared with Ray how he and his crew could decrease the construction time by one week if Ray would work closely with Tim on one specific construction phase. Ray increased the size of both Tim's solid box and his own effectiveness box because of the information he gave and received. This is a win-win situation for the leader and employee.

The right side of the Feedback Purpose diagram represents the feedback purpose for employees. The solid box represents empowerment (an employee's capability, ownership, authority, and purpose). The area between the solid box and the dotted-line box represents the employee's growth opportunity. The diagram shows that employees can expand their capability, ownership, authority, and purpose through giving and receiving constructive feedback. In the example above, Tim was able to decrease his blind spot and increase his effectiveness because of the feedback received from Ray. Because of Tim's expanded knowledge, Ray increased Tim's authority over areas other than bricklaying.

Feedback will affect the four areas in the employee model in different ways. For example, the knowledge Tim received from Ray's feedback may increase his capability but not Tim's ownership of the project. Therefore, the capability part of the solid box may grow while the ownership part of the solid box would remain the same.

Effective management requires a strong belief in feedback from employees and other leaders. Ways to attain constructive feedback include informal and formal methods.

Informal feedback methods may include one-on-one or group interactions. One-on-one interactions between a leader and an employee can be obtained through observation of subtle signals or employee comments. In order to elicit frank comments from employees, leaders must clearly show employees that negative comments will not be met with retribution but with encouragement. In addition, elicited comments can best be gained when a leader depersonalizes the situation. Leaders should state the desire for the organization or the department to improve from constructive comments provided by employees.

Formal feedback mechanisms may include suggestion systems, employee surveys, team feedback (written or verbal), or incentive pay for ideas. Employees will only continue to provide constructive feedback when leaders positively recognize the contribution by employees and action is taken or valid reasons provided for inaction.

SO, WHAT'S THE POINT?
Traditional leaders are quick to provide feedback but not as willing to accept feedback. A growth in the leader's feedback skills is directly proportional to growth in the employee's empowerment. Leaders must both enthusiastically give and receive constructive feedback

MYTH OF THE MARSHMALLOW LEADER

Some leaders think of new leader roles as soft and spongy, like a marshmallow. They see marshmallow leaders as timid or cowardly people. The new roles for leaders are not like the strong, in command leader roles of the traditional organization.

The fact is, new leader roles are a tough job, which requires a tough leader. Four myths surround the new leader roles in a learning organization journey. One myth is that leaders abdicate responsibility; the reality is leaders share responsibility with employees when capability, ownership, and purpose are demonstrated. A second myth is leaders are warm and fuzzy; the reality is leaders care about people but are results-oriented. The third myth is leaders are not passionate but are merely passive team participants; the fact is leaders are assertive and actively involved as team participants. The fourth myth is leaders always agree because they want employees to like them; the reality is leaders engage individuals and teams to ensure good decisions for both business and employees.

SO, WHAT'S THE POINT?
New leader roles are not about leaders avoiding problems or issues. In fact, leaders in a learning organization journey require greater, skillful intervention on the part of the leader than traditional management. The marshmallow leader is a myth!

Own the New Leader Roles

For many leaders, beliefs are like rain—necessary provided no one gets wet. For example, some leaders talk about empowerment but they don't practice empowerment. They don't practice what they preach. Some leaders truly don't believe what they preach. Others don't have the level of ownership required to practice or "walk the talk."

Effective use of the new leader roles in the organization's journey requires effective ownership by leaders. "Ownership" means that a leader behaves as if he or she owned the organization. There are three levels of ownership: politics, knowledge, and commitment. In politics, leaders are just playing the game. They are saying the right thing in front of the right leaders. This means looking good without acting good. This is the weakest level of ownership. For some leaders, this is the initial level of ownership which may lead to knowledge, then commitment. At any rate, it is always dangerous for leaders to talk about a subject when they only have the political level of ownership. Their credibility will suffer because their supervisor and/or employees will recognize their insincerity.

The second level of ownership is knowledge, when leaders begin to understand the issue and are able to discuss its pro's and con's. It is a higher level of ownership than politics, because leaders operate from a more informed position. Some leaders may be at this level of ownership because they are still searching to understand the issue. Some leaders become stuck at the knowledge level because the barriers or doubts are too overpowering. The knowledge level is critical because leaders must have a clear understanding of the issue before the commitment level can truly be achieved.

The third and final level of ownership is commitment. This is when leaders understand the issue and agree with it. At this level, leaders can clearly support the issue because they are convinced it is the right thing to do. The commitment level is the foundation for a learning organization because it creates credibility with employees. The relationship between commitment and business success and quality of work life is shown in the Impact of Leader's Beliefs diagram.

Impact of Leader's Beliefs

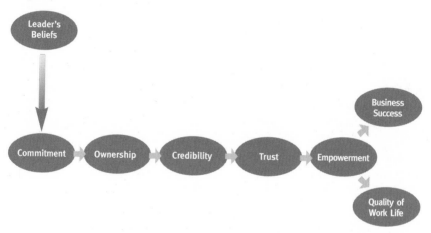

Impact of Leader's Beliefs is an influence diagram underscoring a number of factors, which influence business success and quality of work life. Commitment is the key factor that influences ownership. Ownership influences credibility because employees see it demonstrated daily. In turn, credibility influences the trust others place in leaders. Following credibility, trust is essential for empowerment. Finally, empowerment directly influences business success and quality of work life.

SO, WHAT'S THE POINT?
A leader's belief ultimately affects business success and quality of work life.

Role 1

Role 2

Role 3

Role 4

Role 5

Role 6

Role 7

Role 8

Role 9

Role 10

Role 11

Adopt the
Leader-Coach-Manager Paradigm

Power Gained is Power Given

WHEN THINKING OF new roles for leaders, we reflect on an ancient Chinese proverb:

> If you want one year of prosperity, grow grain.
> If you want ten years of prosperity, grow a tree.
> If you want one hundred years of prosperity, grow people!

For years, leaders have struggled to create and sustain business success. In their struggle, leaders have concentrated on either leading (creating mission, vision, and support systems) or managing (designing processes and organizational systems to implement the vision). Why, then, has it been difficult, if not impossible, for leaders to sustain business success? Sad to say, leaders unknowingly have been using employees only as by-products of their activities. Leaders have not truly recognized that people are the catalyst to achieve mission, vision, systems, and processes. For sustained success in a learning organization, leaders must help people grow by coaching.

Sounds good, but some leaders still ask "why should I coach?" We answer this with a question—are you tired of being a motivational masochist? Leaders have suffered self-inflicted torture trying to motivate employees, grasping at the latest management fad. The reality is leaders do not motivate employees; employees motivate themselves. Therefore, leaders should concentrate on growing employees, on helping employees become self-motivated and personally gratified. Leaders must stop shouldering the unnecessary weight of personal frustration and experience the people business. Any leader can

39

acquire a technologically advanced factory. Any leader can buy a top-notch employee. But, a leader cannot buy hearts and heads. Coaching as an equal, integrated partner with leading and managing is the key to capture hearts and heads. The Leader-Coach-Manager paradigm is about business success . . . successful employees ensuring success for the organization.

This new paradigm emphasizes the point that leaders must lead, coach, and manage in order to prosper as a learning organization. Because most leaders are more familiar with leading and managing, Role 2 will concentrate mostly on coaching. Coaching is distinguished from leading and managing, it is defined, and examples are provided. Leading and managing are briefly defined and integrated with coaching.

COMMAND AND CONTROL MANAGEMENT

The traditional leader uses command and control philosophy and techniques which assume that the leader has, by far, the most knowledge and intelligence. The employee is regarded as "intellectually inferior." This is the essence of the term supervision: leaders have "super-vision" which employees do not possess. As a result, leaders need to tell ("command") employees how to do their job. In addition, because traditional leaders do not trust employees, they create many rules and systems to control employees' behavior. As a result, traditional leaders stifle employees' intellectual input, pride of workmanship and sense of ownership in the organization.

While some organizational experts mention the role of coaching in passing, they either perceive it as merely a small part of leading and managing or they narrowly define the coaching role and relegate it to training duties. Others compare a business coach to a sports coach, but one look at the red-faced, apoplectic, finger-pointing sports coaches suggest that most are still of the old kick-butt, command, and control school.

Before going further, perhaps it's best to look at the notion of coaching and determine what it is and what it isn't. Indeed, the term has been used and misused in so many different ways that we believe an entirely new definition of coaching is needed.

WHAT'S THE DIFFERENCE? ISN'T "COACH" JUST ANOTHER WORD FOR LEADER AND MANAGER?

Many books have been written about leadership and management.

Leading is about creating a vision and helping people make the vision a reality. Leaders focus on systems, changing paradigms, creating corporate culture, and doing the right thing.

Managing is about working on processes within systems and within paradigms to improve the performance of the organization. Leaders focus on the technical or administrative part of the business. They are concerned with how well the production line is keeping up with expected output, the timely provision of services to the customer, and the timely offering of a new product to the customer. Managing is focused on how well one does in doing things right.

The degree to which one leads or manages varies, based on where one is in the organization. A CEO will focus more on leading than will division leaders. A CEO concentrates on processes such as long-term vision and determining the mission of the organization. On the other hand, division leaders spend a greater share of time on managing. The division leader is concerned with doing existing tasks right on a day-to-day basis and implementing new tasks efficiently and effectively. These relationships are outlined in the Leader-Manager Continuum diagram where the "continuum" on the horizontal axis represents the amount of time spent on leading and managing activities by leaders. The vertical axis represents the different management levels within an organization starting with the department leader and ending with the CEO.

Is coaching a part of leading and/or managing? On a number of occasions, we have posed this question to groups of leaders. The quick response is always yes—coaching is a part of leading and managing. After further discussion, however, someone will always point out that he or she never gets asked about the coaching aspects of his or her job except for the required annual performance appraisal or an occasional personnel problem.

Leader-Manager Continuum

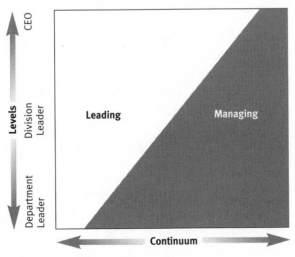

By far, the majority of questions that leaders receive from their supervisors are about the overall status of business operations. Groups we have worked with agree that coaching needs to be separate and distinct from leading and managing. The groups reach this conclusion for two reasons: they realize that coaching is the key to increased productivity and effectiveness; and they understand that coaching is seldom provided when it is given less emphasis than leading and managing. The bottom line is leaders concentrate on processes and systems because they are rewarded for short-term results related to technical matters. Leaders are not directly rewarded for helping others grow through coaching. It is essential that organizations hold leaders accountable for coaching to the same extent they are held accountable for envisioning and implementing systems. Businesses must understand that rewards and accountability for coaching are essential to gain a competitive advantage in the twenty-first century.

Consider the Leader-Manager Journey diagram. A traditional leader will grow the organization from its current reality to the vision which has been defined as concentrating on leading and managing. Leading is concentrating on the right things, while managing is doing the things right. The arrow connecting current reality and vision in part A represents the journey. In a perfect world, leaders would expect a straight line journey from current reality to vision.

Leader-Manager Journey

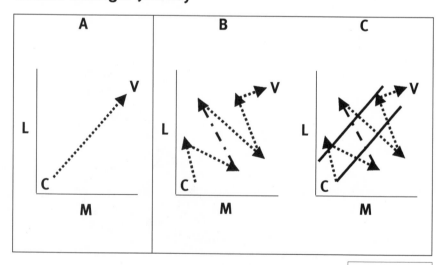

KEY
L=Leading
M=Managing
C=Current Reality
V=Vision

However, leaders have found that during the journey from current reality to the vision, they bounce back and forth trying to implement new programs and efficiently operate existing processes. This bouncing back and forth, represented by part B of the diagram, creates further chaos, frustration, and anxiety.

In part C of the diagram, control limits are placed on the Leader-Manager Journey. The parallel solid lines in part C represent the upper and lower levels for normal variation (control limits) an organization should experience in their journey from current reality to the vision. Where the dashed lines extend beyond the control limits, the process is out of control and requires leader intervention. When the process is out of control, coaching becomes a distant third to leading and managing. Because there is so much going on, people become a secondary focus despite their primary impact on reaching the vision.

The journey from current reality to the vision forces a leader to place a vast amount of time and effort on leading and managing new and existing programs/systems, while people take a secondary focus. This is shown in the Leader-Manager Imbalance diagram. The size of the "L/M" circle (leading/managing) in this diagram represents the focus and time spent on existing and new programs/systems. The size of the "P" circle represents the amount of focus and time spent on people. In a dynamic environment, businesses continuously attain their vision where leaders spend equal effort on people development.

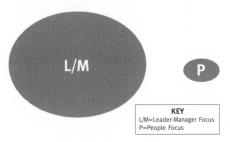

Leader-Manager Imbalance

KEY
L/M=Leader-Manager Focus
P=People Focus

We have walked onto countless floors of manufacturing and service organizations and asked leaders to describe their jobs. The typical answer or response is—"I'm responsible for the production of a certain product or service." Unfortunately, they never say—"I'm responsible for building the capability and ownership of thirty people to produce or create a certain product." The Leader-Manager-Coach Distinguished table outlines the major differences among these three functions.

The Leader-Coach-Manager Balance diagram in part A illustrates what happens when coaching becomes an equal partner with leading and managing. The amount of time and focus in leading and managing will be different at various levels in the organization. The minimal amount of focus and time dedicated to coaching should not vary significantly by organizational level. All levels of leaders should be expected to coach at least one

Leader, Manager, Coach Distinguished

Leader	Manager	Coach
Focus on future	Focus on present	Focus on present and future for people development; deal with what people can be
Provide vision and inspiration	Design processes to implement vision	Develop skills and abilities of people and motivate them to commit to vision and execute work
Lead people	Manage programs, resources	Grow people
Build organizational effectiveness (doing the right things)	Focus on organizational efficiency (doing the right things)	Focus on growth of people's capability, ownership, and authority (doing the right things)
Emphasize shared authority	Emphasize hierarchy	Emphasize learning

third of the time. Part B of the diagram indicates that all three functions (leader, coach, manager) are necessary, but insufficient alone, to achieve the organization's vision. Vision is the common element that connects all three functions.

Eric, a divisional vice president in a chemical company, was on the fast track because of his past accomplishments in sales and marketing. However, he lacked manufacturing experience. For development and career planning purposes, Eric was asked to lead a highly technical manufacturing division with one thousand employees. All leaders in this division possessed greater technical knowledge than Eric. In addition, division employees were experiencing low morale and distrust of management because of many changes that had taken place. Considerable past work focused on leading and managing while there was little or no emphasis on coaching. Eric and the top management team implemented a new leader roles development system during Eric's first year in the division. Eric developed an in-depth personal development plan. The plan focused on coaching 80 percent of his time, working with employees at all divisional levels to identify problems, issues, and successes. The following year, production was at a higher yield than it ever had been. Earnings from operations skyrocketed. Employee morale dramatically improved at all levels. Eric's meteoric journey clearly showed the major impact of effective coaching even when technical knowledge is lacking. In fact, Eric commented that if he possessed technical knowledge, he probably would have spent more time on the technical issues instead of coaching people.

Some leaders say that coaching is a natural part of leading and managing, but this couldn't be farther from reality. Why do we think that leaders suddenly gain coaching expertise once they are anointed to lead others? Would you pick

Leader-Coach-Manager Balance

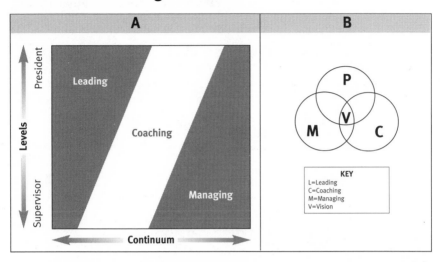

someone from a passenger list and expect him or her to fly an airplane without training and experience as a pilot? Coaching requires as much, if not more, skill and experience as managing and leading. More importantly, over seventy years of history has shown that coaching will not mature in organizations if it is looked upon as a natural part of leading and managing. It is time to stop kidding ourselves. People build organizations, people create and improve products and services, and people drive the financial bottom line.

To use a biological metaphor, the coach is like the brain which provides the body's stimulus to act and nourish the other parts of the body. The leader is the eyes which capture the vision. The manager is the arterial network which keeps the body working. If the brain slows down, the body is sluggish and the vision becomes blurred. If the brain stops functioning, the body is clinically dead.

SO, WHAT'S THE POINT?
Organizations succeed because leaders embrace leading, coaching, and managing. New roles and skills are required to maximize the benefit which can be obtained from coaching.

THE FOUR P's OF COACHING

Coaching is an ongoing, principle-centered, focused process using specific roles to help each employee grow in his/her capabilities, ownership,

authority, and purpose to improve business success and quality of work life.
To be successful, leaders must focus on the four coaching P's outlined in the
following Coaching Definition:

1. Process—an ongoing journey with specified roles, tools, techniques, and
   initiatives
2. People—a belief and trust in people's capabilities to learn and grow,
   take ownership for their part of the organization's business, and be
   responsible for their decisions while focused on the organization's
   purpose
3. Product—an enhanced quality of work life and increased business
   success
4. Principles—the values, beliefs, and practices which balance concerns
   for people and business

Coaching Definition

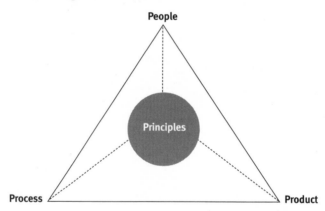

First P: Process

Coaching is a process that leaders do every day. Coaching is a relentless,
monomaniacal mind-set to achieve excellence through people, not just products or systems. Coaches treat people not as they are, but as they can be. In
a word, coaches are H.O.G.'s: they **H**elp **O**thers **G**row.

Elaine had been a successful president of a printing company. She was
informed by the head of personnel that several department leaders had
complained about her lack of support and the meager amount of training
they had been provided. Elaine decided to pursue a one-week training
program. Following the training, Elaine proudly announced to all leaders in
her company that she was setting aside each Friday as her coaching day to

help improve leader's skills and provide increased support. While setting Fridays aside was better than doing nothing, it was not the same as looking at each situation, every day, as a coaching opportunity. Elaine failed to understand that coaching is an every-day, moment-to-moment opportunity. It is an eyeball-to-eyeball and toe-to-toe proactive process.

Coaching: Not Just Another Name for Empowerment

The growth of people is at the heart of coaching. Coaching is the process of helping others grow through the use of specific roles and competencies. Empowerment is the natural outcome of effective coaching; it is only a part of coaching. Coaching requires that the leader identifies whether the employee has the capability to do the job and if the employee has demonstrated a strong ownership to do the job. If the employee has capability and ownership focused on the organization's purpose, then the leader should delegate the job and provide proper authority. This interrelationship of capability, ownership, purpose, and assumption of additional authority completes the empowerment cycle. It is coaching that starts the growth process cycle again on a new or broader defined task so that an employee's boundary is forever expanded. This relationship is ongoing and limitless as shown in the New Roles-Empowerment Relationship diagram.

The growth cycle, shown in part A of the diagram, includes four steps: increase capability (C), achieve ownership (O), and provide authority or delegate if capability and ownership exist (A) with a purpose (P). Empowerment is the recognition of capability and ownership.

New Roles-Empowerment Relationship

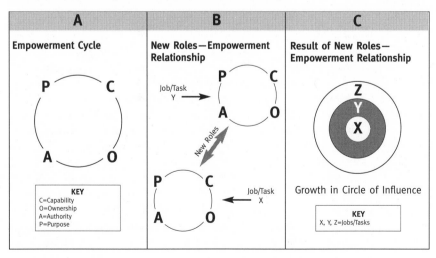

The relationship of coaching and empowerment is outlined in part B of the diagram. The empowerment cycle shown in part A is enhanced with coaching. Coaching builds capability (C), ownership (O), and authority (A) with a purpose (P) through application of the new leader roles. These new roles are required to expand the boundary of the job (or task) from Job/Task X to Job/Task Y. Empowerment focuses within the circle of influence where an employee has the ability to make an impact. The facade of empowerment is that once delegation takes place the leader's job is complete. Coaching focuses within the current circle of influence, such as Job/Task X, to help employees increase their capability, ownership, and authority with a purpose. Coaching also focuses on cheerleading and support as the employee performs Job/Task X. In addition, coaching increases the employee's circle of influence through increased capability and ownership. This is shown where coaching helps the employee grow from Job/Task X to Job/Task Y.

The end result of coaching-empowerment is shown in part C of the diagram. The employee's circle of influence covers not only Job/Task X but also Job/Task Y because of the coaching-empowerment relationship. The diagram also reflects that the employee is beginning to focus on being empowered in Job/Task Z. Basically, the circle of influence or boundary has doubled for the employee and he/she is working toward tripling that circle of influence.

Coaching requires understanding the capabilities of each employee, adopting numerous roles and skills to maximize the employee's growth, and recognizing the proper integration of organizational and people needs.

Some leaders may see empowerment as the latest in a long line of management fads. It is seen by some as a way to decrease the number of management positions while delegating responsibility downward in the organization.

This issue recently arose in a large manufacturing organization. Most of the department leaders were of the opinion that the purpose of empowerment was to eliminate their jobs, and rumors about the president's intent were running through the company. Not surprisingly, these leaders were opposed to change. The president of the company was not fully aware of the breadth and depth of the rumors. When he heard of the rumors, he decided to use a leadership meeting to explain "his side of the story." During the meeting, he addressed the subject openly and honestly, using data and his vision of empowerment. It became apparent that the purpose of empowerment was to increase the capability, ownership, and authority of everyone—not eliminate leaders.

When this growth in maturity occurs, the need for fewer leaders becomes an operational necessity. The president said that a ratio of one leader for every six employees was not the "right place" to be, nor did he think that a one to fifty ratio was right either. The right number would vary, based on factors such as how well employees had been coached, technology involved, safety considerations, and the maturity of the employees. The president went on to say that for those leaders whose positions were eliminated, coaching was an organizational commitment to develop their skills to take on remaining jobs within the organization. In other words, an indirect outcome of empowerment was the elimination of a number of management positions. However, coaching would be used to help the affected leaders grow into remaining jobs. It is amazing what a little open, honest, sincere, and personal communication can do to squelch demoralizing rumors.

To some employees, empowerment means doing his/her own thing while the leader stays in the office and out of the way. The theory is that employees will become empowered through trial and error. This does not result in empowerment; it results in chaos. To some employees, empowerment means having more to do in their job for the same pay. However, jobs must continue to change and grow or else employees should be paid less. Thus, many employees welcome empowerment practices because these practices allow them to maintain or enhance their level of pay. The added benefit is that employees should be more satisfied because they are gaining greater control and input in the decision-making processes.

"High Tech" and "High Touch"

Today's advanced technology produces a startling number of changes in the workplace. Employees need to understand these changes and the reasons for them. Thus, the leader's job includes the delicate integration of people processes and technical processes. The leader must spend a vast amount of time educating or training employees in both processes.

In a teaching hospital, discussions among leaders and employees centered upon the role change from a traditional leader to Leader-Coach-Manager. Some employees were concerned that senior management would no longer be available to provide guidance when it was needed. Others said they felt this was "more talk and no walk" by the senior management. Startling changes were needed in this organization to make the point. Bob, a senior leader, created a revised organization chart with the employees positioned at the top of the chart and his position on the bottom. Bob then rearranged his office, removed his executive desk, and replaced it with a couch, chairs, and a round worktable. He began spending more time coaching by using the new roles of a leader, especially the communication role. It is interesting how employees began to understand and appreciate the change. They began talking about the changes and the difficulty Bob faced in making the change. Almost overnight, they began to see that their journey and Bob's journey were very similar.

"High Tech"

Quality management is based on the principle that everything we do is a process. Most employees recognize and understand the technical part of

Technical Processes

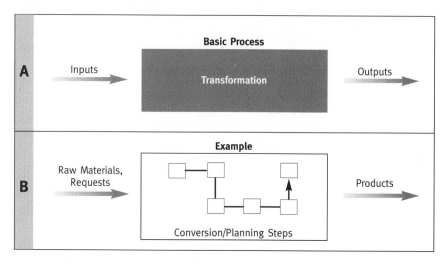

their jobs and see it as a process. As shown in part A of the Technical Processes diagram, process includes inputs (material coming into the work area), transformation (doing something to the inputs to add value), and outputs (final product produced that goes to someone inside or outside the organization). The manager part of Leader-Coach-Manager is focused on the technical processes.

Part B of the Technical Processes diagram provides a manufacturing and services example. A manufacturer utilizes raw materials (inputs from suppliers) and transforms the raw material to create a finished product (output), such as an automobile. In a travel agency, the input may be a request for vacation alternatives in the Caribbean. This may result in the transformation or creation of information on the Caribbean. The output is basically the provision of information in the form of brochures and other literature.

The quality management approach is based on the concept that everyone has a customer or they don't have a job. It emphasizes the continual improvement of the technical process (high tech) to assure business success.

"High Touch"

The social or people process (high touch) is just as important as the technical process. After all, who runs the technical process? People. As cold-hearted as it may first appear, the people side of the business is also a process. The people process has inputs, transformation, and outputs as shown in the Social/People Process diagram.

Social/People Process

The inputs in the process are the people interactions and information. The transformation includes such steps as training and capability building of individuals and creation of teams. Coaching creates the transformation by building or increasing employee capability, ownership, authority, and purpose. The output is improved decision making.

Don was a sales leader of three salespeople for an automobile dealership. The three salespeople became embroiled in a disagreement about how new customers were equitably allocated among them. When Don became aware of the problem (input), he recognized that he needed to use the conflict resolution skills he was previously taught. Don called a meeting with the three salespeople to discuss the problem. Don used the opportunity to employ the conflict resolution model and train the three salespeople to use it (transformation). The issue was resolved through use of a revolving customer assignment system. The salespeople were pleased because the conflict was quickly and equitably resolved. The end results (output) were resolution of the problem and increased capability.

Organizations have both technical processes and social/people processes, which are heavily influenced and affected by coaching. Where coaching is appropriately and effectively applied, the likelihood of business success (financial and operational) is increased. In addition, employees will have an improved quality of work life and a higher satisfaction level because their job provides a challenge, offers individual and team contribution, and provides valued rewards for their efforts.

Coaching creates the social/people transformation and integrates the technical and social/people processes. This is done through use of the new leader roles.

SO, WHAT'S THE POINT?
True organizational effectiveness is derived from a balance of high tech and high touch. The Leader-Coach-Manager paradigm is the missing link to achieve high tech and high touch outcomes.

Second P: People

Coaching is about people. The leader's job is to enable employees to increase their capability through enhanced knowledge and skills. The leader works with employees in such a way that they take ownership of the task or assignment. In other words, the employees must take responsibility and personal pride for their own tasks or projects. The ultimate goal of the leader's job is to continually help people develop enough knowledge and skills to do and expand the job with little or no input from the leader except for direction, recognition, and encouragement.

Thus, four ingredients are needed for the leader's focus on people:

1. **Capability**—Leaders help employees obtain knowledge and skills necessary to complete the technical and social requirements within their area

2. **Ownership**—Leaders determine whether or not employees have the proper understanding, involvement, commitment, and initiative relative to their area

3. **Authority**—Leaders give employees the formal power to act and be both accountable and responsible for their own actions within their expanded area

4. **Purpose**—Leaders pursue tasks with a specific focus or goal in mind that is consistent with the mission, vision, values, and strategies

Employees should possess certain knowledge, skills, and abilities prior to delegation. In other words, a certain level of capability and ownership needs to precede authority. Why? How would you like to live in a community where the local nuclear power plant company has empowered an employee to take responsibility for a hazardous process without the adequate skills, knowledge, and ownership to avoid a catastrophe?

Knowledge, skills, and ownership should exist before increasing the level of risk or authority for a new job, task, or process. Otherwise, the employee will be at risk and/or the business will be placed at risk. This point is illustrated in the Managing Risk diagram which shows the relationship between capability and authority, assuming the employee takes ownership and has a clear purpose.

It is not an either/or situation. It is critical that the risk be managed. Authority should be increased consistent with demonstrated capability and ownership. When capability is high and authority is low, the employee is at risk (i.e., frustrated). When authority is high and capability is low, the business is at risk.

Managing Risk

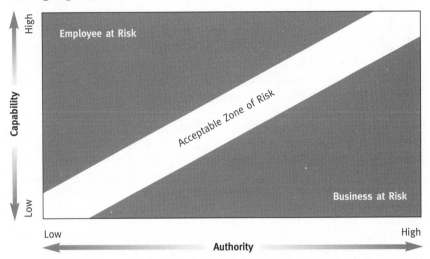

Note: Assumes Purpose and Ownership are present

Many leaders are concerned. Pursuit of an empowered work force takes them out of their comfort zone and places them in their fear of failure zone. As a result, they may become defensive, overly cautious or, worst case, immobile. Other leaders may see it as the program of the month or a passing trend. Therefore, they only see a need to pay lip service to it until it passes into oblivion.

Despite these fears, empowerment is very important and necessary. It can dramatically increase the organization's business success and the quality of work life for its employees. It is a basic foundation for the development of employees to increase productivity and enhance value. We are often asked a controversial question—can empowerment occur without coaching? Yes, we have seen a few employees who have grown in areas of capability and ownership without coaching. Some employees have a very strong inner drive to learn, increase their skills, and take on additional responsibilities. In situations like this, the leader is merely recognizing self-initiated achievement by the employee when authority is delegated.

However, such employees are quite rare. Most need the leader-employee relationship where they are full partners in their own personal developmental process. Coaching is essentially running alongside employees asking how they can be helped and helping them when appropriate.

SO, WHAT'S THE POINT?
The end result of the coaching-empowerment relationship is understanding purpose and having increased capability, ownership, and authority so that employees will be in a better position to improve quality in their areas of responsibility. Normally, empowerment will not occur without effective coaching. Leaders have a choice—either build or destroy the framework for an empowered workforce.

Third P: Product

A product is the end result of a process. In technical processes, raw material is transformed into some output or result. In social/people processes, people development is transformed into intellectual capital.

Coaching is a process focused on an end result: business success (financial) and quality of work life (people). Business success is the achievement of a return on capital that is greater than the cost of capital.

People success is achieved when a return on intellectual capital (i.e., investment in people) is greater than the cost of developing that intellectual capital. For example, the long-term difference between an increase in business sales and a decrease in expenses should be greater in value than the cost of developing coaches.

The financial rewards from coaching are reaped by individuals as well as organizations. For example, a leader receives empowerment training to take on additional responsibilities and provide greater input into business planning. This change creates more compensation to the leader because of additional responsibilities. There is also greater personal satisfaction for the leader because of the expanded opportunities for decision making and input. This is referred to as quality of work life.

The organization reaps financial rewards from coaching because of faster cycle time, maximized resource effectiveness, and increased employee capability and ownership.

At a candy manufacturing plant, employees were not allowed to run a jelly bean line until management inspected the machine setup. In other words, employees were not productive for thirty to sixty minutes during each shift. Following implementation of a Leader-Coach-Manager development program, employees were expected to run the jelly bean line without inspection because they were trained and empowered to review the machine setup. The manufacturer saw immediate results. Jelly bean orders were filled in 6 percent less time. This increased the number of orders processed by each shift and increased revenue and net income to the company.

The Leader-Coach-Manager paradigm also leads to business success because of increased staff productivity. Leader-Coach-Manager expands the abilities of employees and increases responsibilities for problem identification and resolution. In an automobile manufacturing plant, employees could not stop the assembly line without management approval if a problem was discovered. If wrong parts were used or defective parts were being assembled, employees continued to assemble automobiles until a leader shut down the assembly line. This increased the number of defective automobiles and rework required on defective units. Following the implementation of coaching and empowerment, employees could stop the assembly line if they found an error. This saved valuable time and rework for the automobile manufacturer and decreased labor expenses.

In addition to faster cycle time and increased staff productivity, business success is increased because employees enhance their job skills and organizational commitment where coaching is implemented. Coaching spreads responsibility over a greater number of employees. Employees are challenged to learn new skills and take responsibility for more tasks. This also increases the type of information available to employees which enhances their appreciation for what it takes to succeed in business.

A large retail organization had a formal suggestion system where it provided compensation for suggestions made by employees. The suggestion system was discarded because management decided it should be considered part of the employee's job and thus no additional compensation should be necessary. Following this change, the number of suggestions submitted decreased by over 90 percent. The organization's bottom line decreased while expenses began to rise. Shortly after, the company developed a coaching development process. A part of the process included coaching skills training for leaders. Richard, who was a leader at one of the major retail units which was experiencing declining financial results, received the training and dramatically improved his listening skills. He methodically began his communications with any employee by carefully listening, searching for the employee's perceived problem, feelings about the situation, perceived solution, and support needed from management. In the past, Richard would have spent little time listening to employees, and instead would have offered a painstaking description of the solution to the problem. Because of Richard's transformation, the company saw a dramatic increase in revenues and net income from Richard's retail unit. At a team meeting attended by the CEO, Richard shared with the group that the number of suggestions and suggestions implemented had increased by 800 percent. Employees stated that they were motivated to provide suggestions because Richard seemed more genuinely interested in their ideas and suggestions. Richard added that his improved listening skills had also proven helpful in his relationship with his teenage daughter. For the first time ever, they were able to discuss issues, understand each other's point of view, and resolve problems. The end result was a win-win for Richard, the company, and his daughter.

SO, WHAT'S THE POINT?
The focus of all organizations should be to improve business success and quality of work life of all employees. If either element is out of focus, both the organization and people are at risk. Investment in financial capital and intellectual capital is a necessity for success. (Return on financial capital + Return on intellectual capital > cost of capital.)

Fourth P: Principles

Underlying the four P's of coaching are five coaching principles. The principles are consistent with the purpose of coaching which is to Help Others Grow.

First, everyone deserves to be treated with respect. Leaders who fail to respect employees will fail to coach. Coaching is primarily based on influential power and credibility. Positional power is secondary. In other words, influence is more effective than the title or position held by a leader. The behaviors most of us were taught as children still apply: listen and try to understand other points of view, maintain self-esteem, be courteous, apologize when you make a mistake, keep your word, and don't talk bad about people not in your presence.

Second, most employees want and need help from leaders. A management team was faced with a difficult, financial investment decision which was very important to the organization's future. The team actively tried to resolve the issue by using appropriate problem-solving techniques but they had trouble admitting to each other that they lacked confidence and expertise in addressing this particular problem. Following the meeting, one of the team members asked to meet with their senior vice president. During the meeting, the team member admitted that they were not an empowered team. They needed ideas and guidance because they didn't feel comfortable in going ahead without the senior vice president's support. They really didn't understand all of the issues surrounding the problem.

Some may say this team wasn't really empowered. However, one indicator of effective coaching is knowing when to seek guidance or help. The team in this case was empowered and recognized the need for additional coaching.

Third, employees want to grow personally and professionally. As many researchers have found, there is no evidence that America has a poor work ethic. Rather, lack of organizational support and inspiration are to blame for poor teamwork, role conflict, and other failures. Most people will do the right thing, if they know the right thing to do.

We recently flew to North Carolina to attend a business planning session. Following the meeting, we were scheduled to travel to the airport by taxicab. However, the taxicab driver never arrived because he was involved in an accident. One of the off-duty bellboys, Jeff, became aware of our problem. He immediately offered to drive us to the airport in his personal car so we would not miss our flight. He quickly placed an infant car seat in the trunk of his car and drove the car to the front portico of the hotel to pick us up. We very much appreciated Jeff's willingness to help, and offered to pay him for the inconvenience. Jeff could have easily taken the money; however, he declined. In fact, he apologized for our inconvenience, even though the hotel was not at fault for the situation. There are many Jeffs in this world. Some are only in need of further coaching to shine.

Fourth, coaches Help Others Grow. They are H.O.G.s. Leaders who want personal recognition for work accomplishments will have a difficult time being an effective coach. Coaches must be interested in encouraging, recognizing, and rewarding the progress, behaviors, and results of others. Continued business success is likely where leaders build the capability of employees consistent with the organization's mission and vision. Coaches clearly recognize the development of people as a key part of their responsibility.

Finally, everyone within an organization is a coach. Most employees regard their immediate supervisor as their only coach in the organization. But, their supervisor's supervisor, even the president of the organization, are all coaches too. In fact, everyone needs a coach. Yet, very few people have received training on the subject of coaching. For those who studied business courses in college, it is most likely that their education was based on the traditional or transactional leader model which emphasized command and control. Coaching, as discussed in this book, is a relatively new subject. While the main focus addresses those in management roles, the information in this book can be applied to both leaders and all other employees as well. Everybody in an organization coaches. It takes everyone to help people grow, not just the leader. Ghandi said, "Life is one indivisible whole." Several years ago, we were training leaders involved in a Leader-Coach-Manager program. We covered a wide range of coaching topics related to quality, interpersonal communication, empowerment, counseling, and work design. Jim was a member of this particular team. Approximately two years later, a presentation was made to obtain approval for the use of a formal development system throughout the plant. Jim was asked to participate and identify, from his point of view, the merits of the program. Jim made several positive comments. He graphically described how the program changed his entire life, including examples of improved personal relationships with family, friends, and employees. His comments surprised most people in the room, because Jim was considered a "bull in the woods" kind of leader. As we looked around the room, several of the very business-oriented leaders were teary-eyed. Helping Others Grow can truly add to the quality of one's work and personal life. After all, coaches are in the people-helping business. Helping people grow helps the business grow.

SO, WHAT'S THE POINT?
Traditional leaders use rules for decision making. Leader-Coach-Managers are focused on principles as guides to respect and value the capability and potential of people.

FROM BOSSING TO COACHING—FROM BOSSTHINK TO COACHTHINK

While many organizations acknowledge that coaching might be a good thing to try, most have no clear idea what is involved. When asked for specific guidance, the typical response is "well you know . . . just go out there and work closely with employees."

The first step toward being an effective Leader-Coach-Manager, then, is to determine exactly what it is that Leader-Coach-Managers do. The change from traditional management to new leader roles in a learning organization is not incremental or natural. It is a major paradigm shift, as shown in the Changing Roles diagram, from an organization driven by a traditional leader-centered base to an employee-centered one.

Changing Roles

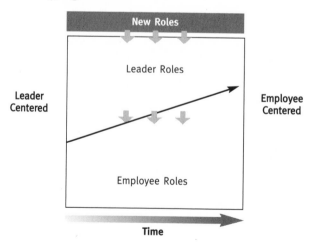

Coaching involves a complete reversal of roles whereby employees assume increasing capabilities and responsibilities. The leader assists with their personal development and encourages their increasing participation and commitment to both their own personal growth and the growth of the organization. Some of the past leader tasks will be taken on by employees because their roles have expanded.

Specific differences between bosses and coaches are outlined in the Boss to Coach Role Changes table by comparing the respective roles.

Boss to Coach Role Changes

From Boss	To Leader-Coach-Manager
Supervisor/director	Empowerer/leader
Rules	Principles
Experience	Educator/trainer
Reactive	Proactive
Positional power	Influence/credibility
Process control	Process improvement
Task/product centered	Process centered
Status quo	Initiate/manage change
Authoritative	Participative
Compliance	Ownership/commitment
Technical focus	Process and people focus
Individualist	Team member
Insensitive	Empathic
Product orientation	Stakeholder orientation
Achieve numbers	Satisfy stakeholders
People are means to achieving goal	People are critical resources
Avoid failure at all costs	Learn and build from failures
Avoid career risks	Take career risks

The table summarily identifies what effective leaders or Leader-Coach-Managers do. However, before they change their actions, they must completely change their way of thinking. A change in thinking leads to a change in behavior which leads to a change in results.

Leaders don't have to know all the answers, but they must be effective in asking questions. We repeat, leaders don't have to know all the answers. Having all the answers implies a command and control "boss" style which demands compliance by the employee. Living with the questions requires that leaders use questioning techniques and participative coaching styles. This combination will ultimately encourage ownership from employees. Gaining ownership from employees requires **CoachThink**.

BossThink demands that "you do as I say" and the only satisfactory response is compliance. CoachThink, on the other hand, asks "what do you

Boss Think to Coach Think

Boss Think	Coach Think
(Compliance—"Do As I Say!")	(Ownership—"What Do You Think?")
"Pick up the rags in the hallway and put them in the dumpster."	How can I get employees to take ownership of housekeeping?
"Okay, I have had enough of the negative comments. We're going to stick to the agenda."	"It seems like many of you have several serious concerns. Perhaps we need to set aside today's agenda and resolve the concerns."
"Empowerment is one of the principles of our company policy. We're going to work toward empowerment whether you're in agreement or not."	How can I more clearly explain our empowerment vision to gain their ownership and support?
"We need to respond to the customer's demands. I will provide the action plan and tell each of you how to respond. I will monitor this plan to make sure the action steps are being adhered to."	"As you know, the customer's demands are changing as shown in the survey research we have shared with you. I am interested in your interpretation of the data and development of an action plan that identifies overall goals, tasks, responsibilities, and timetables for completion. Most of you recently had hands-on training with respect to action-plan development. However, since this is new to many of you, I have provided some samples of plan formulas previously developed by employees in other parts of our organization. If you have any questions or issues that require feedback, please let me know. I am excited by this opportunity and very much look forward to your thoughts."

think" and the satisfactory response is open discussion, personal examination, and willingness to accept responsibility. The shift from BossThink to CoachThink is a shift from "I say" to "you think."

SO, WHAT'S THE POINT?
Changing roles essentially means the transfer of authority to employees who understand purpose and have demonstrated ownership. This is difficult or perhaps impossible to achieve without CoachThink. The transformation is a critical part of the empowerment journey. It takes effective coaching.

OWNING THE BUFFET BAR—READINESS TO BE COACHED: FEELING THE HEAT VS. SEEING THE LIGHT

Coaching is focused on employees "taking ownership" of their jobs. Employees take ownership when they perform a task because they are strongly committed to their job, not because they need to meet the minimum expectations of management. In other words, when employees "own" their job, they perform certain tasks, not because they are told to perform them, but because they genuinely want to do a good job. In order for employees to take ownership of their jobs, leaders must coach, not boss.

Debra is a restaurant employee responsible for the buffet area. She cleans the buffet area, restocks it, and periodically checks it as instructed. However, Debra will not normally help customers identify the buffet items or provide feedback to management on possible new items of interest to customers because these tasks are not required to meet the minimum job performance. Stella, owner of the buffet restaurant, keeps an eagle eye on Debra and constantly tells her what to do, leaving little incentive for Debra to take ownership. Stella is wedded to the command and control "boss" technique, and Debra has no choice but to comply.

Normally, compliance is the maximum performance level when command and control is used as exemplified by Debra in the salad bar example. Some employees may go beyond compliance because of their personal values—they are truly a gift to the organization.

If the leader is coaching, the performance level of employees should routinely exceed compliance and move toward ownership. The range between compliance and ownership is frequently referred to as discretionary effort. This could be the difference between giving 65 percent (compliance) and 110 percent (ownership) to the organization. There are two basic ways to get people to produce in an organization. One is to feel the heat, the other is to see the light. Those employees who see the light have ownership.

Some people do not want to be coached; they want to be told what to do. If leaders do not at least try to coach these employees, then the likelihood of employees going beyond the compliance level is minuscule. Coaching in these situations will provide some percentage of success. Success, to a great extent, boils down to whether an employee is ready and willing to be coached.

How can a leader identify the readiness level of the employee to be coached? This is outlined in the Readiness diagram. If an employee is able to do the work and has taken ownership, that employee has capability and ownership. This is the highest level of readiness to be coached, which is the upper left quadrant of the diagram. The challenge for a leader in this situation is to provide the employee with the appropriate level of authority to do the job. The leader becomes a cheerleader and manages the boundaries. In other words, the leader encourages and provides desirable feedback. At the same time, the leader needs to monitor and assess the employee's performance to assure authority is expanded consistent with the employee's future growth in capability and ownership.

Let's revisit the story about Debra and Stella and the buffet. Stella recently attended a seminar on coaching styles. Following a self-assessment

Readiness

Willing

Able   Unable

Unwilling

exercise, Stella suddenly realized that she was more a boss than a coach. She also realized that the coaching function must be used before she could accurately assess whether her employees were willing and able to perform their job. Stella decided to try this new coaching style with Debra.

The following week, Stella approached Debra as she was preparing to set up the buffet area. Stella told Debra that she had been thinking about their working relationship. Stella realized that she was telling Debra in detail how to do her job. Stella also recognized that this must be frustrating for Debra; it must stifle her creativity, growth, and self-esteem. In the future, Stella agreed to start asking more questions about Debra's thoughts and ideas and give fewer commands. Stella asked for Debra's help. In addition, Stella asked Debra to explain her job expectations. In other words, what did Debra see as the major parts of her job and how could the two of them better design Debra's job to meet customer needs and Debra's work interests.

Debra was both surprised and skeptical. She tested Stella by telling Stella that she was a good boss and didn't see the need for the change.

During the seminar, Stella had been forewarned that employees may not readily embrace coaching. Stella responded by talking about her management style and realizing how that could be negatively affecting Debra's performance. Confessing her discomfort with the new leader roles, Stella asked for Debra's support and commitment.

Debra finally agreed to try Stella's new approach but she remained skeptical about Stella's motivation. Debra offered her thoughts about the job including a suggestion to use identification cards for each buffet item to assist customers in their food selections. This was an excellent idea which showed Stella that Debra was thinking about her job and how to improve it.

Stella recognized that Debra was still skeptical about coaching. It was evident from Debra's continued hesitation to support Stella in her coaching journey, and it showed in her body language (her arms were folded on her chest and she leaned back on her heels as she listened). Because of this, Stella knew that it was important to give desirable reinforcement to Debra for the suggestions she provided.

The next day, Stella provided the identification cards to Debra for the buffet items and praised her for the suggestion. Later that same day, Stella asked how Debra's day was progressing and if there were any issues they needed to discuss.

It was clear from observation that Debra owned her job and had the skills to perform it. Debra kept the buffet restocked with food without any suggestions from Stella. The customers were now commenting on the fast and courteous service. These comments provided desirable reinforcement to Stella that coaching did make the ownership difference. Stella shared these positive comments with Debra to reinforce her new behavior. Because of Stella's actions, Debra became the most productive and customer-oriented employee in the restaurant. Debra was now in the upper left-hand quadrant of the Readiness diagram which required a basic level of coaching from Stella. At this level of readiness, Stella must show support for Debra by specifically identifying what she is doing well and praising her for it. Stella must continue to communicate with Debra on a regular basis using questions to understand if Debra needs additional education or training, boundary management, or other support from Stella to perform her job. If an employee is in one of the other quadrants in the Readiness diagram, the leader needs to help the employee grow to the upper left quadrant. For the employee who is in the upper right hand quadrant (ownership), the leader needs to concentrate on the development of knowledge and skills to improve the employee's ability to perform his/her job. The leader needs to create "capability plus."

Stella recently hired a cook, Craig, who had some experience working in a local diner. From the first day on the job, Craig was willing to help other employees and take on odd jobs such as garbage and clean-up detail. However, it became apparent from customer feedback and employee suggestions that Craig did not have sufficient cooking skills.

Using periodic observation of Craig's work and employee feedback, Stella assessed the situation and carefully approached Craig. She told Craig that she was pleased with his performance because he was timely, thorough, and customer oriented. She added that his enthusiasm was infectious. Because of his accomplishments, Stella offered to create several opportunities for Craig to expand his skills.

Craig was asked to work with the senior cook on staff. The senior cook was asked to help Craig improve his skills and productivity. This was received positively by the senior cook because he was recognized for his superior skills.

Stella also asked Craig to participate in the "cook rounds." The lead cooks would periodically walk through the restaurant offering pleasantries to the customers and gaining feedback on food preparation and presentation. Because of Craig's customer orientation, he was received positively by the customers. Craig, in turn, gained a greater sensitivity regarding proper preparation of the food. After several weeks, progress reports showed that Craig had increased his capability to the desired level and maintained his enthusiasm and willingness to do the job. Stella and the other employees had helped Craig grow from the "ownership" quadrant to the "capability and ownership" quadrant in the Readiness diagram.

An employee in the lower left hand quadrant of the Readiness diagram (capability) needs to concentrate on ownership which includes focus and basic beliefs. The employee needs to understand, first, why it is important to change and, then, to identify his/her role in that change journey.

Stella hired Janice as a hostess for the dinner shift. Janice had excellent communication, presentation, and conflict resolution skills which she gained from her previous experience with two other four star restaurants. After several weeks, Stella became aware of employee complaints about Janice. Complaints indicated that Janice would not help out in a crisis unless it was specifically part of her job. Also, she was sporadically late to work.

Stella had an informal dinner with Janice following the closing of the restaurant. During her discussion with Janice, Stella asked how Janice liked her job and what she thought of it. Janice responded that it was a job that kept bread on her table. From additional questions, Stella was able to discover that Janice enjoyed her job but did not understand the team concept required to run the restaurant. The restaurant philosophy that each employee had internal partners and external customers was foreign to Janice.

Stella approached the team problem by reviewing the restaurant's mission, vision, and values statements with Janice a second time. She emphasized the relationship of these statements to serving the needs of internal partners and external customers. Stella also stated that being on time was very important and tardiness would not be tolerated.

The meeting with Janice went well; Janice stated that she wanted to be the best hostess possible. Recognizing that Janice would not improve unless she adopted the principle of internal partners and external customers, Stella asked a long-term employee and assistant manager to spend time with Janice and look for situations to involve Janice in the support of other employees. Initially, Janice was resistant and would not help others, but through continued encouragement to support others and the assistant manager's role modeling of support to the internal partners,

Janice finally began supporting the needs of the waitresses and cooks. The waitresses recognized Janice's support by providing positive comments to Janice and her supervisor and assisting Janice with customer seating on busy evenings. Janice's pride in customer satisfaction, which Stella recognized and built upon, helped Janice understand the importance of the team concept and internal partner satisfaction. It took at least six weeks for Janice to move from the "capability" quadrant to the "capability and ownership" quadrant in the Readiness diagram but Stella found the effort was worthwhile because she ultimately had a capable and willing employee.

For employees in the lower right hand quadrant of the Readiness diagram, both ownership and capability are missing. These employees are the least likely to attain the desired ownership and capability level. In most cases, these employees should be transferred to an area where they will either grow or be terminated.

The transfer or termination of employees is consistent with coaching. Some believe a coach is a "soft" leader who is kind to everyone and does not terminate employees. In fact, terminating employees, where appropriate, is a necessary and essential part of coaching.

Stella hired a waitress, Patti, for the lunch shift. Patti had previous experience and needed the work to pay her college-related expenses. After two weeks, the other waitresses and cooks complained about Patti's inability to order from the computer menu, pick up orders in a timely manner, and complete her fair share of the work. Stella spent time individually with the cooks and waitresses to observe what was creating the problems, how Patti might work more effectively, and how to resolve the matter. Stella found that some of Patti's tables were being waited on by other waitresses because customers were waiting too long for Patti to take their orders. Because of this, waitresses complained about being overworked.

The employee responses, customer survey responses, and Stella's observation of Patti's work confirmed that Patti wasn't able to perform the work and didn't seem to care. Stella met with Patti to discuss her perception of Patti's work and commitment to the job. Stella began by asking Patti how she thought she was doing. Patti responded that her work was going well.

Stella offered comments from customers and internal partners. Without mentioning any employee names, Stella discussed the specific problem areas. Patti denied there was a problem and did not exhibit any concern. Stella specifically outlined the job expectations and the review process to be followed. One week later, Patti's work was still unacceptable. Stella recognized that Patti was not capable of or willing to do the work. Patti was terminated. One week following Patti's last day of work, the customer surveys dramatically improved and waitress complaints ceased.

SO, WHAT'S THE POINT?
Assessment of employee readiness is an essential part of coaching. Employees who have capability and ownership should be provided commensurate authority. Employees who do not have and cannot or will not obtain capability and ownership should be transferred or terminated. Coaching, in part, is focused on helping employees grow in ownership and capability. Coaching helps employees see the light.

ROLES AND FUNCTIONS

The Leader-Coach-Manager paradigm is used by leaders to pursue organization and personal success. As shown in the Relationship of Roles to Functions diagram, the three functions are related and overlap because leading and managing work through employees (coaching) to accomplish organization success. In other words, coaching must be used to effectively lead or manage.

The Relationship of Roles to Functions diagram also shows (through the horizontal arrow) that the new leader roles are used to make the Leader-Coach-Manager paradigm a practical reality. For example, the Create a New Mindset role is just as important to leading as it is to coaching and managing. Employees must take ownership of the vision (lead) as well as the systems and processes (manage).

Relationship of Roles to Functions

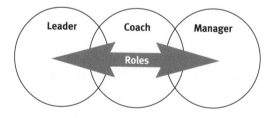

Where leaders adopt the Leader-Coach-Managers paradigm, they will find greater personal rewards. Leader-Coach-Manager shifts part of the responsibility for success from leaders to employees recognizing the interdependence of leaders and employees. Leaders feel less stressed out or overburdened because they are not the only people shouldering responsibility. Employees are less stressed out because they have greater input and control over their job and environment. Leaders also develop a greater sense of accomplishment because they see employees grow and receive desirable feedback from empowered employees. For most leaders who experience this transition, their work becomes more meaningful and enjoyable. There is a similar outcome for employees for similar reasons. Essentially, both leaders and employees add soul to their work.

SO, WHAT'S THE POINT?
Coaching is an equal partner with leading and managing. The Leader-Coach-Manager paradigm is foundational to attaining competitive advantage.

DEVELOP YOUR LEADER STYLES

A Wardrobe for All Seasons

IN THE 1960s, Gary Lewis and the Playboys were frequently heard on the radio singing about the girl "who's just my style." People were "groovy" in the 1960s, if they had the right style. By the late 1980s, people were "bad," if they had the right style.

Leaders also have distinctive styles and must understand the styles they use to interact with employees. A leader's style is the distinctive way he or she behaves in a given situation. Leader styles are what employees see, as opposed to what they hear. Style usually has a greater affect upon employees' perceptions than any eloquent speech given by a leader. An old saying summarizes this best—"Actions speak louder than words."

This role concentrates on styles required of leaders. Some of the questions addressed include:

- Why are styles so important?
- Why do leaders have different styles?
- Do values affect style?
- Where do styles come from?
- What different styles should leaders be aware of?
- Is there one style that is right for all leaders?

IS LEADER STYLE IMPORTANT?

Growth in individual and team effectiveness is greatly affected by leader styles. Styles are important because they are foundational to the success of employees.

68

Terry acquired a fledgling office supply company with ten employees, a life-long dream of his. During the first year of operation, he spent most of his time trying to gain business from several local companies that showed strong potential for business growth. Following months of hard work, one of these companies, a growing, regional, managed care firm, asked Terry to provide all the supplies and forms needed for their new managed care plans. They needed a major campaign for use with their sales agents located in a three-state area. The company needed special printed forms, checklists, and product description sheets in addition to pens, pencils, stationery, and three-ring binders.

Terry could provide all of the materials needed except for printing which could be coordinated with a local printer. The biggest decision for Terry was how to prepare for this major project. Since Terry was personally committed to coordinate another major project for a new client, he knew he would need to assign this project to one of his senior vice presidents. Terry had two very competent leaders offering very different leader styles. Russ was a strong supporter of empowerment while Joan heavily favored telling employees what to do and how to accomplish their tasks. Which style would be most effective for completion of this project? Terry envisioned how each of the leaders would pursue this project and the outcome.

Joan the Teller

Joan contacted the company and assured them that the project would be completed on time and that she would handle all communication with them. Prior to calling a meeting with the three other team members, Joan created a detailed task list which painstakingly identified the discrete tasks of each member. The list even included information regarding how each member would pursue their assigned task.

During the team meeting, Joan did most of the talking—telling each member exactly what was expected and how she wanted the various tasks completed. Joan asked only one question: do you understand what you're to do? It was clear to the team members that Joan did not want input because she kept emphasizing that she had everything under control and she was assigned to this all-important project. Because of her style, the team members didn't share with Joan any concerns about the printing schedule or the expected delivery on the printed pens and pencils. Future team meetings were scheduled for Monday, Wednesday, and Friday for the next four weeks. Joan closed the meeting saying that the team would complete this important project on time or else heads would roll. Joan checked every hour of the day with each team member to make sure each and every detail was followed as she had outlined. After a few days, the team members recognized that this was Joan's project and it had to be done her way. They reacted to the style by doing only what was directed. Many times, the project came to a screeching halt because team members would not make even the most basic decisions.

Joan seemed to revel in this while the project moved even slower.

The customer was initially pleased with the progress because Joan seemed to know each and every discrete detail. However, they began to lose confidence in the company when small order changes could not be handled. The team members would not handle the change orders until Joan specifically revised their directions and clearly described how their tasks were to be handled. Critical time was lost and the customer perceived the office supply company as being anything but customer-friendly.

Russ the Empowerer

Russ began the project by reviewing the capabilities of each team member assigned to the project. He then scheduled a meeting with the managed care company and the team to review the project and his company's plan of action. Prior to meeting with the managed care company, the team met to review the general timeline and major deliverables expected by the customer.

Russ asked each team member to offer suggestions regarding the best way to handle the project and assign the work. At first, the group offered minimal response. Russ responded to the silence by sharing with the team how important this project was to the office supply company and to each of their jobs. This seemed to jettison the group. They began to share numerous suggestions. Russ wrote down each of the suggestions without critiquing them. Later, the group reviewed and critiqued the responses and agreed upon a production plan, responsible parties for each major component of the plan, and timelines. Each team member was expected to complete a plan of action for each component. The team members met later in the week to review their plans, revise the master plans and components, and schedule weekly meetings to review the project status and any major issues. Russ ended the meeting with a short motivational speech. He related a story about NASA's research which showed that a team effort was more productive than one person, except in a crisis where time did not allow for team input. He ended the meeting with the guarantee that the team would receive a pizza party if they could beat the project deadline.

The meeting between the customer and the team went exceptionally well. Each team member quickly reviewed their expected production schedule and areas requiring additional customer input. The managed care company was impressed that such a small company had a strong, capable team to handle this project. The company became even more impressed when their changes to the order were easily integrated into the plan by each area.

During the project, Russ informally and periodically contacted each of the team members asking if they needed any assistance or were facing a critical issue. He used open-ended questions to provide opportunity for each team member to address problems without Russ' direct involvement.

If issues were identified, Russ would ask questions to see if the team members were able to solve the problem. Team members responded to this style by taking ownership of the project, providing improvements on the project, and offering suggestions for enhanced customer satisfaction.

The team completed the project one-half week in advance of the expected deadline. The office supply company had a satisfied customer, and a satisfied team enjoyed their pizza.

Terry the Coach

Terry selected Russ for the managed care company project. Just as he expected, Russ and his team delivered the product ahead of schedule and increased their commitment to the office supply company. Terry also assigned Joan to work with Russ on another project. Terry was undertaking an opportunity to transition Joan from a good technician to a good Leader-Coach-Manager through toe-to-toe, nose-to-nose experiences. The latest word about Joan is that she is making the journey from a telling to an empowering style.

Leader styles have a positive or negative impact on employees. In the above story, the most effective leader style was empowerment. The empowering style increased input, improved decision making, and created an enhanced outcome. The telling style, on the other hand, dramatically limited the amount of input, increased the response time, and decreased employee ownership of the project. Let's face it, why would employees be willing to risk severe criticism if they know the leader wants to control decision making?

Leader style integrates social and technical processes and makes empowerment effective. Without the proper leader style, teamwork is adversely affected. Leader styles bridge the gap between employees' current situations and their future goals as shown below.

As noted in this role, there are different styles. Some leader styles are more effective in certain situations than others. Leader styles are important and do contribute to the success or failure of employees which, in turn, affects business success and quality of work life.

LEADERS ARE DIFFERENT

Leaders are different in many ways and, not surprisingly, their styles also differ. Leader styles are affected by personal preferences, influences from a leader's supervisor and employees, training and education, work experiences, communication skills, race, and gender. Basically, there are many factors that affect leader styles.

Some leaders focus their energies inward on their world of thoughts and feelings while some focus outward on people and things. Their preferences may also include an orientation toward detail and decisions by logic versus feelings.

Leaders are heavily influenced by the style of a supervisor or others they use as role models. Typically, leaders that report to dictatorial supervisors tend to imitate the dictatorial style. Leaders are also affected by employee attitudes and morale. Whether employees are unionized or nonunionized, the type of work they are asked to do can have an affect on leaders.

Some leaders progress through the ranks without the benefit of any college courses while others are highly educated. Similar to education and training, leader's work experiences will vary: some leaders will have had many past employers while others will have few other experiences outside of their present organization. Communication skills will differ among leaders because of verbal and written skills and charismatic aspects.

In terms of race and gender, employees can have built-in biases and can express these in actions and words. The expressions will have an influence on the leader's style.

Despite attempts by many organizations to separate work life from personal life, leaders are affected by, and are products of, their personal and work lives. Preferences, personalities, and behaviors are complicated subjects.

In addition, there are many facets to our lives. These include health, wealth, family, friends, education, work, recreation, spiritual meaning, emotional levels, and physical well-being. Situations which impact one part of our life often affect another part. For example, when things are not going well at work, it usually adversely affects family life, and vice versa. Or, if the leader's health is failing, it can affect job performance. Leaders must understand what influences their style and how their style impacts those around them.

It is also important to recognize that leader styles are learned. Leaders change styles when they understand that certain styles are more appropriate than others and a gap exists between their present and preferred or appropriate leader styles.

This point became very clear when Kathy became president of a division of a regional health care system. In her past job as vice president for patient care, Kathy used the dictatorial style with employees. She would provide employees with detailed descriptions of problems, specific tasks to be performed to remedy the problem, and expected feedback to provide to her once the tasks were completed. Despite the limitations of this style, division financial results remained positive. However, the division experienced a high turn-over rate which could be partially attributable to her dictatorial style.

When Kathy assumed the position of president of the hospital division, she uncharacteristically started using a more open, participative, and supportive style. Employees were asked to give their opinions regarding priority projects and Kathy intentionally avoided telling employees how to perform the tasks. Kathy used questions to understand whether employees understood the problems, the alternative solutions, and the desired outcomes. Upon completion of the projects, Kathy made sure she first emphasized a positive accomplishment of the employee prior to addressing any shortcomings. The results were astounding! The hospital division, which had a high employee turnover rate and lackluster financial results, started showing a growing bottom line and stable employment levels. Employee surveys showed increased levels of job satisfaction. Kathy was asked why she changed her style and what effect that had on employees and financial performance. Kathy admitted she gradually realized how much her management style affected people in her previous position.

The turning point came when she reviewed a report which involved the development and implementation of a new unit for patients too sick to go home but too well to receive traditional hospital care. The initial performance report for the new service indicated high employee performance and job satisfaction in addition to excellent financial results. The reasons listed for success included a more empowering management style. When Kathy thought about it, she had not been able to pay much attention to the new project because of cross-training efforts taking place in another area. In fact, she had been more hands-off in her management style than she usually was. She also realized that the pace of change and broad area of responsibilities required the use of an empowering style. When Kathy took the new job, she decided to test whether a more empowering style could make a difference. It did!

SO, WHAT'S THE POINT?
Understanding and continually learning about leader styles to improve personal effectiveness is an ongoing journey. It is a journey that must be taken by leaders who are interested in enhancing overall organizational effectiveness and personal satisfaction.

WHAT EFFECT DO VALUES HAVE ON STYLE?

Leaders' behaviors are heavily influenced by their values. Successful leaders possess a balance of values associated with people (quality of work life) and business outcomes (business success). However, some leaders may tend to be more sensitive to financial results than quality of work life. Other leaders may place a greater value on people. Values may lead the leader to prefer one style versus another.

Mary Ann was a stellar leader in the credit union who was well liked by her employees. She addressed problems by looking at how she could improve the employees' job satisfaction. Mary Ann firmly believed that a happy staff would be a productive staff. During a three month period, Mary Ann's loan department showed major decreases in loans from prior years. When Mary Ann's supervisor investigated the situation, she found that Mary Ann had allowed her employees to change major processes in the unit because they wanted to make their jobs easier. The changes made it more difficult for customers to use the credit union's loan services. Many disgruntled customers no longer used the credit union for loans; loan interest revenue dramatically declined. Mary Ann's dependence on one style created a financial nightmare for the credit union. Mary Ann valued quality of work life much more than business success. Mary Ann's supervisor was able to underscore the problem by using customer feedback to show the nature of the problem. Mary Ann recognized how her values may negatively affect job performance and changed her approach toward employees.

SO, WHAT'S THE POINT?
Styles are a reflection of a leader's personal or business values. Inappropriate styles can create bad results.

FIVE MAJOR LEADER S.T.Y.L.E.S

There are five major leader styles: **S**idestepping, **T**elling, **Y**o-yoing, **L**iking, and **E**mpowering. They are shown in the Leader STYLEs diagram.

Leader styles are based on managerial beliefs. Leaders will normally focus on either business success or people. Some leaders may use a combination of styles. However, most leaders will tend to exhibit one of these styles at a time. For simplicity, we will address the five leader styles as separate and distinct.

Leader STYLEs

S	Sidestepping
T	Telling
Y	Yo-yoing
L	Liking
E	Empowering

Choice of STYLE

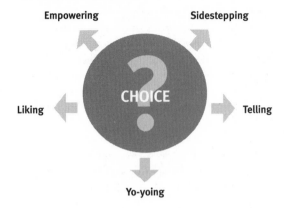

Empowering   Sidestepping

Liking   CHOICE   Telling

Yo-yoing

CHOICE OF STYLE

Style is a matter of choice. Leaders may select from many styles to deal with an issue or relationship. As shown in the Choice of STYLEs diagram, the direction that leaders follow is a function of their choice.

Sidestepping Style

Some leaders do not value relationships with people or business success. They focus more on indifference or avoidance of unnecessary risks. This leader style is sidestepping. Leaders using the sidestepping style have essentially retired on the job. They don't choose to focus on business success or people. This style is not necessarily predominant in the older leader ranks. Sidestepping is the worst style, bar none, from an organizational effectiveness perspective. These leaders do just enough to get by and may consume their day with "busy work." They typically do not show any enthusiasm or support for resolving issues related to people or business success. Too often, they don't have time to show enthusiasm because they are too busy trying to avoid decisions or responsibilities.

Jack was a division leader and twenty-year employee in an automotive parts manufacturing firm. He made a point of periodically walking around the plant to exchange gossip. The firm had taken on a major contract for a new automobile model and was behind production schedules. The addition of a second shift and weekend work became necessary. Part of Jack's job was to oversee the tooling staff which kept the machinery working. As problems arose, Jack was either not available or unresponsive to the problem. Most often, he would respond to a question by saying he would give them an answer at a later time (which never happened). As production fell further behind, machinery repairs increased. Jack's employees were unable to gain direction or support from Jack on how to deal with the increased failures. In other areas of the firm, employees talked negatively about the tooling employees because they were viewed as lazy and unresponsive. In fact, tooling was working harder and going nowhere faster. Jack's supervisor initially thought that there was a problem with the tooling staff. In order to test this theory, Jack's supervisor increased the amount of time spent in the tooling area. In addition, he would ask open questions of Jack and the tooling staff about how they were dealing with problems. At first, the tooling staff provided vague answers and tried to avoid questions. Jack seemed confused as to why the staff was unable to perform properly. Finally, Jack's supervisor saw that the staff was lost but did not want to blame Jack. As a result, Jack was given very clear job expectations and training on problem-solving techniques. In the end, Jack even sidestepped directives provided by upper management. The end result was termination.

Frankly, it is best that leaders like Jack be transferred or terminated. They detract from the mission and vision of the organization and may project a negative attitude to other employees. Normally, they will not buy into the new leader roles, won't understand the concept, and won't assume additional responsibilities. When it comes to decision making, sidestepping is used to avoid taking ownership of an issue or a decision. Sidesteppers often leave the problem for others. And if others take the problem, sidestepping is perpetuated.

Telling Style

Some leaders value only business success. They command and control and focus primarily on quantifiable results and/or productivity. They pay little attention to the people aspect of the business and emphasize task completion by closely monitoring employees' behaviors. This leader style is "telling." In its purest form, this style is typified by the leader who looks at the financial bottom line as the only true indicator of organization success. Leaders using the telling style choose to focus on business success. Employees are told what to do, how to do it, and are expected to follow orders. Some have referred to this leader style as "my way or the highway." There are some situations where the telling style is appropriate. These are reviewed later in this section.

The principle reasons leaders exhibit a telling style are (a) they believe they need to know all of the answers and (b) they believe they know all of the answers. How sad! This may achieve short-term business success. However, the long-term picture is usually dismal because of poor worker relationships and its adverse effect on productivity. The telling style, used solely and consistently, is definitely counterproductive to establishing a high performance, empowering environment.

The telling style was used frequently by Claire, a department leader of courier employees in a laboratory services company. Employees were expected to pick up and deliver lab specimens to the main laboratory for batch runs. Detailed schedules and constant communication via hand-held telephones were used to insure compliance. As the company grew in geographic area and market share, Claire continued to use the telling style and required this approach by all of her supervisors. Customer satisfaction decreased. A quick survey showed that the couriers became so dependent on the telling style they were unable or unwilling to make basic decisions to deal with customer problems in the field. The telling style—which appeared to make passing grades early on—was a major stumbling block to expansion plans.

Following careful examination of the situation, Claire's supervisor recognized an empowering style was more appropriate in Claire's situation. Claire's supervisor dealt with the problem early on by involving Claire in problem identification and reviews of customer survey results. The supervisor focused on how to meet customer requirements, rather than Claire's personal style problem. Questions were used to gain feedback from Claire to clearly define the problem. In addition, Claire was taught how to improve her interpersonal effectiveness by changing her style. She moved away from a telling style as a result and found she had time to work on new technological advances which improved the lab specimen delivery systems. The company improved on its' customer satisfaction, increased its market share, and enhanced its bottom line. In addition, Claire found her job to be less stressful and more rewarding when she realized that she didn't personally need to have all the answers and that her employees had knowledge, experience, and good ideas too.

In certain situations, leaders prefer the telling style because it is a short-term, quick resolution to a specific task or problem. In fact, while leaders may believe in the employees' capability and knowledge, they may find themselves in situations where there is minimal time to deal with the issues without giving detailed direction. In some situations, this may be an appropriate style. This is especially true when quick action is required, coaching is needed but cannot be provided in a timely manner, or the decision has a high level of risk associated with it.

Miles was CEO of a growing managed care company. He preached that employees must take responsibility and initiative wherever reasonable. Miles selected Denise to serve as vice president for planning and asked her to lead the efforts of the board planning committee. Despite his firm commitment to employee initiative, Miles repeatedly took center stage at the planning committee meetings and answered questions that were more appropriate for Denise. After two frustrating and disappointing years, Denise handed in her resignation leaving to join a firm as head of managed care operations. In her new position, Denise talked about the lessons of management she learned from her earlier job. She underscored the importance of employee initiative.

Agnes, an inexperienced but competent quality management director, was strongly moved by Denise's message. Taking the message to heart, Agnes attempted to handle a very explosive and potentially litigious situation with a disgruntled physician. Denise saw that the situation was out of hand and could lead to serious legal liability for the company. Denise quickly intervened and worked closely with Agnes to create a plan of action to handle the physician. Immediately following this, Denise spent more than two hours with Agnes explaining her perception of the situation, fear for Agnes' safety, and the role of leaders. At first, Agnes was angry with Denise because she didn't "walk the talk." This subsided as Denise talked about her support role and the right time to grow on the job. Agnes began to see that Denise intervened and used the telling style in that one particular situation because it was in the best interest of the company and Agnes. Denise had not taken on the bad habits of her past boss, Miles.

Yo-yoing Style

Have you ever carefully watched a yo-yo in action? The yo-yo goes in several directions, never coming to rest. Sometimes, the yo-yo may go in one direction more than another.

The yo-yoing leader style mimics the toy's movement. Leaders use this style see-sawing between a focus on business success and people. It occurs when a leader tries to do a little bit related to people and a little bit related to business success, providing little consistency in the handling of issues. For example, a leader may attempt to achieve a political compromise with an employee because this will have little effect upon finances. Later, that same situation may be handled differently because the personal repercussions are small but the financial negative outcome may be greater.

In certain situations, yo-yoing may be acceptable when the issue and its resolution don't have a major adverse effect on the organization. However, some leaders consistently operate on the basis that it is best to give a little and take a little. On one issue, for example, an employee may lose. On a later issue, the score is evened by allowing that employee to win. Oftentimes, no one is getting what is believed to be best. Therefore, employees may only extend minimal effort on the job in such situations. This style is acceptable in decision making when there is a minimal amount of potential business loss or harm to people. Leaders attempt to "keep it between the ditches" by minimizing risk.

The president of a national food distribution firm was planning to promote his son to a vice presidency position because of growing pressure from family members. Most employees thought the son was not the top candidate for the position. The son always bounced back and forth on issues. Because of this, employees had no clear expectation of the company direction. Instead, many thought that Kay should receive the promotion because of her success in building sales for the company. The president promoted his son despite the negative comments shared by others. Once the acrimony became too great, the president appointed Kay to a newly developed executive vice president role. From the start, it was evident that Kay and the president's son did not respect each other. They did not communicate with each other and avoided any cooperation or support where it was reasonable to expect such. Business financial results plummeted as teamwork dwindled and communication slowed throughout the organization. The president finally addressed the problem by asking Kay to leave the organization. Kay left but problems persisted because of employee dissatisfaction with the yo-yoing style of the president and Kay's abrupt firing. In this situation, yo-yoing was not an effective style because the risks were too high from the start. However, in other situations, yo-yoing may be perfectly acceptable. Leaders can use the yo-yoing style to the benefit of an organization but it requires a keen sense of people issues and business risks.

Liking Style

Some leaders focus heavily on relationships with people and pay little or no attention to business success. They are overly concerned about pleasing people and being well liked. This leader style is "liking." Leaders using a liking style choose people as their focus. This style might create a happy workplace in the short-term. However, in the long-term, decision making based on "going along with the crowd" may have a devastating effect on people due to business problems, wrong culture for the environment, or, worse yet, business failure.

Liking can be one of the most difficult styles to diagnose because employees may cover up failures or problems for the likable leader. Given sufficient time, the problems will normally rise to the surface when employees can no longer carry the weight for the leader who is unable to do the job.

The liking style can have a devastating effect on the long-term viability of the organization. The underlying theme of liking is that leaders can succeed if they are kind but incompetent.

The principle concern with liking is that leaders do not have to think. Their focus is to go along with employees in order to be accepted by them. The principle reason for leaders using this style is insecurity or a desire to be wanted and appreciated.

The liking style was exhibited by the chief operating officer of a regional fast food chain. Vicki used to tell management they should not accept anything but hard work and excellence from their employees. She even went to the point of speaking out at administrative meetings about firing employees who would not carry their weight or add value to the organization. All the time, Vicki allowed two directors to remain on the job despite their lack of performance and periodic incompetence. When other senior leaders brought their performance into question, Vicki would be very protective and defensive over concerns expressed by the other leaders. Because the CEO would not take action, dedicated employees became disenchanted. They saw that performance was not rewarded. Reward was related to friendship. Decision making based on the liking style can adversely impact business results and employee morale because it is related to who you know, not what you do on the job.

Empowering Style

The empowering leader style is a balanced focus on people involvement and business success. In order to attain the proper blend, leaders are working collaboratively with employees to achieve the objectives of a particular project and ultimately the organization's vision and goals. Notice, this is a proper blend, not a compromise between people and business success. When compared to the yo-yoing style, empowering is a proactive blend of people and business results while yo-yoing is a reactive style that vacillates between people and business results.

When using the empowering style, leaders fully involve people in studying, identifying, deciding, and implementing business focused decisions. This style exemplifies participation, honesty, trust, teamwork, diversity, and learning. The overall intent is to maximize synergy.

The empowering style was exhibited when Dana, a senior vice president in a plastics development firm, was asked by his CEO to travel from the Midwest to California in order to resolve a problem with a key account. The plastics company had long been the primary supplier of plastic molds to a large computer manufacturer. Because of some difficulties with mold configurations, the computer manufacturer, their biggest client, was considering switching most of their business to a major competitor. Dana had been instructed by his CEO to solve the problem and gain long term commitment from the manufacturer. In his previous work, Dana had gained the respect of the manufacturer and proved he could resolve difficult problems. When Dana arrived at the California plant he worked with their technical people, identified their needs and wants, and recommended solutions. It became obvious that several days of free development time would be needed to rectify the problem, satisfy the manufacturer, and maintain harmonious working relationships. Dana provided the client free development work in addition to free delivery of the new molds. When Dana returned home, he updated the CEO. The CEO congratulated Dana on his successful trip and complimented him for making a quick decision that saved their biggest account. The CEO and Dana used empowering styles because they recognized that the problem required a quick decision in order to satisfy the customer's needs, both technical and social. Dana's knowledge that this CEO would support his decision and actions reinforced his willingness to take a reasonable risk.

The empowering style is not a "soft" style. Leaders with an empowering style are attempting to enhance the capability and commitment of employees and add value to the organization. Empowering leaders hold employees responsible for their decisions and actions, unlike the liking style. However, mistakes based on reasonable risk taken are treated as learning opportunities.

The principle reason leaders use an empowering style is it's consistent with their fundamental beliefs in the capability of people and their potential effect on business success. As discussed earlier, there are three levels of ownership associated with a key issue. These three levels are politics, knowledge, and commitment. Leaders must be at the commitment level of ownership to effectively practice an empowering leader style.

The principal concern is that some leaders will try to fake an empowering style because they are at the politics or knowledge level of ownership. This can result in frustration and confusion for employees and loss of respect for a leader. There is an old saying to the effect that it is better to have tried and failed than to never have tried at all. This does not apply to empowering style. This style is best used when leaders have attained the highest level of ownership and are committed to its success.

SO, WHAT'S THE POINT?
Style is a matter of choice. Where leaders do not choose either business success or people, they will fail. Where leaders choose either business success or people, they will have limited effectiveness. Leaders who choose to focus on both business success and people will maximize effectiveness.

BUSINESS IN A BLENDER:
BUSINESS SUCCESS AND PEOPLE

A leader must have a proper blend focusing on business success and people. To focus solely on business success is to risk the respect and ownership of people. To focus solely on people is to risk financial ruin.

Sidestepping does not focus either on people or business success. Telling, on the other hand, is singularly focused upon business success. Yoyoing goes a little bit in both directions but is erratic and lacks consistency. Liking is only focused on people, and decisions are made based on the perceived desires and interests of the people affected by the decision.

The empowering style is equally focused on people and business success in an interactive, consistent manner. In other words, empowering style is a two-way connection, an equal blend of people and business success.

WHAT IS THE PREFERRED STYLE?

Generally speaking, empowering is the preferred style because it focuses on both, people and business success, while ensuring interaction to grow and change as needed. Even though the empowering style is preferred, not all organizations or leaders are ready to adopt such a style.

A CEO of a small organization was determined to use an empowering style soon after he joined the company. In the past, employees of this organization were managed in a command and control (telling) manner. They expected to be told what to do and how to proceed. When the new CEO started out using the empowering style, employees were confused and scared. They were fearful of making a mistake. They were not prepared to take on the responsibilities required when their leader used an empowering style. The CEO was surprised to find that the employees did not openly embrace the empowering style. He initially failed to recognize that empowering style took the employees out of their former cocoon or comfort zone.

An empowering style requires maturity on the part of both leaders and employees. There needs to be a proper focus and values understood by all, support by leaders, and capability and support from employees in order to effectively use the empowering style. In other words, the empowering style best fits when employees clearly understand their roles, have the necessary skills, and establish a trusting work relationship with the leader. If the empowering style is used when the leader and/or employees are not ready, the organization will quickly revert back to an old or more comfortable style. In the case outlined above, employees reacted by performing as if they were either in a telling or sidestepping style environment.

In certain situations, leaders, particularly under pressure, may revert to the telling style because they are more familiar and comfortable with that style. Once this reversion takes place, it becomes even more difficult to attain an empowering style in the organization because leaders lose credibility in the eyes of employees and fall back into the past behavior of command and control.

The continuous sidestepping leader style should normally be avoided. Sidestepping basically characterizes a state of hopelessness and a lack of focus, ownership, and self-confidence. Leaders who constantly sidestep issues do not want to think and take responsibility. It is a lose-lose mindset. The leader loses because he or she is viewed as incompetent and/or lazy. The organization and employees lose because decisions are not being made.

The liking leader style, where it is constantly used, should also be avoided. Leaders using this style are involved in playing the political game or merely want to "belong to the group." Real thinking about key issues is not involved. The primary thinking is finding out where everyone is on an issue or problem in order to know which decision or side to take. This is a lose-win mindset. It is okay for others to decide and get their way. The leader and organization lose because decisions are focused only on pleasing employees and not based on business success and quality of work life.

The yo-yoing leader style is appropriate in certain decisions where the issue and its resolution won't have a major adverse effect on the organization. Leaders who use this style consider both the impact on people and on business success. This style is best used in situations where employees know their limitations. In other words, employees understand what they know and what they are good at. With the yo-yoing style, leaders are interested in obtaining a common ground but avoiding taking on an employee's responsibilities. A key concern with this type of decision making is ownership. Very little support will occur where few or none of the decision makers are getting what they truly believe to be the best answer. It can become a combination of either a win-lose or lose-win mindset unless leaders carefully use this style.

The telling leader style is appropriate in certain situations primarily related to urgency or safety. Oftentimes, leaders using this style are primarily focused on business results. They think about decisions to be made but place more emphasis upon business success than people. This unbalanced thought process leads to blind spots which can result in poor people and business success ramifications. It is a win-lose mindset. It represents the "I am the boss" mentality and "I get paid to be right."

The empowering leader style is appropriate in all important situations if leaders and employees are knowledgeable and skillful in decision-making processes. Empowering style is important when commitment of employees and the quality of the decision is of high importance. Otherwise, urgency (timing) can be a key consideration in determining which style is most appropriate. Decisions made using the sidestepping, liking, yo-yoing, and telling styles should be looked upon as learning opportunities. Leaders should analyze their prior decision-making processes to learn how to be more effective the next time an important situation occurs.

EFFECTIVE STYLES—IS THE EMPOWERING STYLE ALWAYS RIGHT?

Day-to-Day Effectiveness

Should a leader use an empowering style all of the time? On the surface, the answer to the question would appear to be "yes." However, from a practical, day-to-day, work point of view, it isn't reasonable. Other styles may better fit the situation at that moment. For example, it is reasonable to use the liking style when a people-based decision does not affect business success. A senior hospital leader may decide not to reorganize the director of medical records position to that of a manager of medical records. Even though it would otherwise be appropriate, this change would negatively affect the entire attitude of department employees during an important transition from manual to computerized patient medical records. In this case, it may be best for long term purposes to create harmony and not reorganize.

Short term, the telling style may be more appropriate when employees are not following safety rules which could have a disastrous effect upon the life and limb of team members and the public. When imminent danger faces employees and/or the public, the telling style is necessary. Once the danger has been resolved, it then is appropriate to use an empowering style to build employee ownership of safety rules. The yo-yoing style also may be more appropriate than an empowering style where employees do not appreciate what they don't know or they cannot adapt well to the empowering style.

Overall, the empowering style is preferred. But leaders need to carefully deviate from this style if a situation requires it and does not destroy the long-term credibility associated with new leader roles and empowerment. This balance is more of an art than a science. Where leaders deviate from empowerment, they must communicate effectively for employees to recognize why empowerment was not followed in the particular situation. Otherwise, management credibility could suffer. Leaders must carefully judge every situation and weigh the consequences of alternative actions. None of the styles will be effective in the absence of thorough knowledge, understanding, and caring of people and business—this is fundamental.

Organization-wide Effectiveness

When considering overall effectiveness of the organization, it is necessary to look at each of the styles as outlined in the Styles Effectiveness diagram.

The diagram is designed based on observed experiences and leader input from numerous workshops. The sidestepping style is the lowest in organization effectiveness because there is no focus. Typically, the sidestepping style creates a string of avoided decisions. In most cases, employees will readily perceive the leader as avoiding his or her leadership role.

The telling style has been very effective for organizations in the past because it allowed them to move quickly and to control the organization. As environments change and organizations need to be proactive in the marketplace, the telling style tends to decrease in its relative level of effectiveness.

The telling style does not rank as high as yo-yoing or empowering because it fails to involve or engage others in the decision-making process. In other words, the "buy-in" or sense of ownership that comes with yo-yoing and empowering styles is lacking.

Yo-yoing is, generally speaking, an effective style. Yo-yoing allows employees to get involved and influence decision making. A possible problem with yo-yoing is that employees may not have a strong indication of the basic direction to take on various issues because the leader makes decisions in a perceived erratic manner with little, if any, continuity from one decision to another. In other words, past management decisions do not provide any pattern or consistency which would provide a pattern or trend for others to follow. Because of this, employees may feel compelled to defer decisions. Leaders can avoid this perception problem where yo-yoing is used by explaining the reasons for their decisions. These explanations should provide the logic for employees to understand that decisions are not made in an erratic manner.

The liking style, on the other hand, is lower in effectiveness than all styles except for sidestepping. Liking tends to have a short-term,

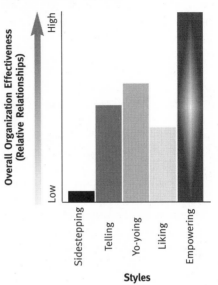

Style Effectiveness

high effectiveness rating, but overall is woefully lacking because leaders are focused on quality of work life while business success suffers.

The empowering style is normally the most effective style overall for the organization because it includes a well-balanced concern for people and business success. This style has a long-term effect on building a team environment while concentrating on a positive bottom line. However, as we stated above, empowerment is not always the best style for a given situation.

A large, financial corporation hired Whitney to take over the sales responsibilities previously performed by another vice president, Daryl. Whitney made a few mistakes in judgment alienating several large clients. He did not follow the reasonable commitments made by Daryl. Whitney's decisions created some adverse impact, both personal and professional for Daryl. As a result, Daryl felt that his integrity was being unfairly questioned by the disgusted clients. Something needed to be done to address the issue. Daryl considered several options.

One option would be to do nothing because a face-to-face discussion would probably be involved, and would create a high level of risk (i.e., sidestepping). However, this approach was unacceptable because it failed to address the negative client reaction.

A second option would be to meet with Whitney and confront him, eyeball-to-eyeball, telling him to back off or he would be dealt with in a very direct manner (i.e., telling). This approach was ill advised in this situation because the two executives needed to develop a harmonious work relationship.

A third option would be to give a little and take a little, recognizing that the world is full of compromise (i.e., yo-yoing). This would provide some safe and secure progress in dealing with the problem. However, this style failed to address both the people and business issues related to the problem. The clients needed to be addressed and the two executives required very open and honest discussions with each other on this issue if they were to develop any long-term working relationship.

The fourth option would be to give in to whatever Whitney wanted because he was new and had a strong personality (i.e., liking). After all, Daryl may be reporting to him one day. This may be a safe solution for the individual but not for the organization. The clients concerns would not be adequately addressed and the two executives would not have formed a well-balanced working relationship.

Another option would be to meet with Whitney and openly and honestly discuss the issue (i.e., empowering). The intent here is to understand each other and agree on alternative(s) which would be good for the clients, the organization, others impacted by the conflict, and the two executives. The empowering option was the most viable approach when trying to make a decision based on principles because it fully addressed the concerns of all parties affected by the issue. The other alternatives failed to address both the client issues and the long-term working relationships of the two executives. The empowering approach was, in fact, used in this situation.

Whitney was invited to go to lunch by Daryl. The luncheon discussions centered on perceptions and what was best for the clients and the organization. Daryl recognized early in the conversation that Whitney had a strong allegiance to client service but was "caught in a corner" by his own decision and could not figure out how to change the situation while saving face. Daryl offered his assistance and some suggestions on how to resolve the situation with minimal risk to the organization and Whitney. Daryl made sure that his offer of assistance was not seen as "you owe me one." He was able to accomplish this by stating that they both needed to find a solution to the problem because they were both negatively affected. Whitney used one of the alternatives that was offered and called on the past vice president for assistance. The client relations improved and sales from these accounts rebounded. To this day, the two executives have a strong working relationship which has dramatically improved the business success and team environment of the organization.

SO, WHAT'S THE POINT?
Leader styles directly affect culture. The empowering leader style offers the greatest opportunity to positively affect individual and organization effectiveness.

Role 1
Role 2
Role 3
Role 4
Role 5
Role 6
Role 7
Role 8
Role 9
Role 10
Role 11

DEVELOP EMPLOYEES

A Mind Is a Parachute— It Works Best When Fully Opened

CONTINUOUS IMPROVEMENT IS essential for organizations to survive. Constant innovation will be required to remain competitive in the future. Pricing, technology, or cost alone will not sustain organizations in the future. Leaders and employees who can constantly change will be the key. Their minds must be open to the concept of change and new roles. Change is the norm, no longer the exception. As a result, leaders and employees must reinvent their roles to remain competitive.

This role will focus on developing employees to insure that the organization can continue to change aided by the dynamic roles of leaders and employees. Two problems will be explored that most organizations encounter where continuous improvement is pursued—learned helplessness and employee blind spots. The tools and skills to overcome these two problems are outlined. Finally, a six step model is provided, which is referred to as The Change Journey, to develop employees effectively and efficiently.

WHERE IS YOUR CENTER?

Employees must be willing and able to carry out coordinator roles which are small chunks of the traditional leader's responsibilities. Coordinator roles include such tasks as scheduling vacations, monitoring quality measures, and creating work assignments. Employees must also give constructive feedback to leaders and other employees; for example, performance appraisal input.

The focus on changing roles is illustrated in the Boss to Employee Centered diagram. This diagram reflects the interdependence among employees as a result of their expanding roles. It also underscores the changing roles of leaders as they shift from Boss to Leader-Coach-Manager. The diagram shows that Boss-Centered organizations place employees in narrowly defined silos. In Employee-Centered organizations, employees work in broadly defined roles where their responsibilities include their traditional roles and some responsibilities of a leader. Employee-Centered organizations have less narrowly defined employee roles because such organizations realize the necessity of employees growing and taking on additional responsibilities.

Boss to Employee Centered

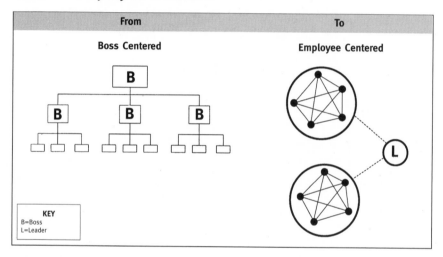

Experience has shown the employee-centered approach is difficult to implement because it requires a major paradigm shift for both leaders and employees. It is especially difficult for employees to change because they have learned to be helpless and insecure under traditional management. In addition, employees have blind spots that make it difficult for them to properly assess self and the work environment. This role provides the "how to" component for successfully changing the roles of employees.

EMPLOY CHANGE, DON'T EMPLOY THE PAST

Leader and employee roles must be changed to better meet customer needs, reduce operational costs, increase employee morale and productivity, and provide an improved environment for empowerment to flourish. When employees are truly empowered, they are better able to meet customer needs in a timely, cost effective, and quality manner because bureaucracy is minimized or eliminated.

A good case in point happened to Jennifer, a nurse and leader of an occupational medicine clinic serving businesses in an industrial park. In the past, she was expected to provide sufficient staff to meet the needs of business clients within set time frames and operate the clinic. While providing care to an injured worker, Jennifer overheard the injured worker comment that back injuries were a growing problem for a number of area employers because employees did not understand how to properly lift raw materials and finished products. This was not the first time Jennifer heard such a remark. She checked the records and found an increasing trend of back injuries. Jennifer immediately followed proper procedure for her organization and informed her off-site supervisor of the need and interest in providing a back safety school. Three months later, Jennifer received word that management felt it was a good idea and should be developed. It was too late! A competing clinic had heard the same opportunity from one of their employees and quickly developed a back safety school. Jennifer was disappointed and concerned that management did not appreciate employee feedback and could not respond to grasp opportunities.

The net result was the loss of substantial revenue. Jennifer's organization failed to recognize the need to change her role to compete in a fast moving environment. What should Jennifer's supervisor have done? He should have used a development process, which is outlined in the second part of this role, to expand Jennifer's role and skills. Jennifer should have received training in product development which would have encouraged her to take the necessary action on her own, create the proposal, and gain commitment from her organization in a timely manner. Instead, the organization operated in a traditional manner and missed an opportunity to serve their customers. Jennifer's organization employed the past instead of employing change.

Leader roles within an organization have an obvious effect on the cost of doing business. Where employees become responsible for some of the traditional leader tasks, fewer leaders are required. In addition to the obvious salary and benefit costs saved from fewer leaders, facilities and supplies costs are decreased. The more leaders an organization has, the more space the organization requires. The greater the space required, the greater the facilities cost. The greater the number of leaders, the greater the consumption of supplies for such things as paper clips, staples, paper, and computer disks.

If the number of leaders is reduced, employees will generally spend less time reporting. This creates added capacity for employees to take on other work because leaders will not have sufficient time to use command

and control behavior. Also, many employees will find working in an empowering environment personally rewarding.

A word of caution. It is easy to become excited and to mindlessly pursue downsized management. Studies show that downsizing alone has minimal long-term effect on operating costs. A *Money Magazine* study showed that a 10 percent reduction in employment caused only an average reduction of 1.5 percent in operating costs. Management downsizing should be a long-term effect, not the primary goal.

A last word of caution: downsizing is not the time to dump on employees. The transitioning of roles should be pursued in a logical, evolutionary way, once employees have demonstrated capability and taken ownership of their new roles. An organization must provide training to ease the employee's transition.

Doug, a salesman, was becoming demoralized despite his organization's verbal commitment to new leader roles and empowerment. The organization had committed to training employees to take on greater responsibility. Senior management stated that some of the management roles would no longer be needed following the initial development phase. Despite the numerous hours of training and development for the role transition, Doug did not see a major change in his job because he continued to spend countless hours every month filling out sales reports for his supervisor and attending ineffective department meetings. In his frustration, Doug submitted a suggestion to his supervisor which identified how many more clients he could call on and the increased revenue dollars he could generate by changing report requirements and applying some of the report writing and departmental meeting time to increased sales calls. The idea was rejected without an explanation. Needless to say, Doug felt demoralized and betrayed by the organization.

Subsequently, the vice president for Doug's division requested that everyone submit productivity improvement ideas. Doug submitted the same idea he had submitted before. The vice president adopted Doug's idea, promoted Doug to a group leader position, and eliminated the leader's position in Doug's area. Doug's area was now reporting to another leader who was responsible for two areas. We asked the vice president why the leader's position in Doug's area was eliminated. His answer was visionary. He said that there was less need for supervision in a changed environment after initial training of employees took place and employee responsibilities were increased. However, he did not decrease the number of leaders during the initial training and development of employees. He realized that employee development required a vast amount of leader support to transition successfully. He added that remaining leaders were selected based, in part, on who embraced change. The selection process insured that continued employee development would be emphasized. Those leaders will lead the organization into the future, not into the past.

SO, WHAT'S THE POINT?
Changing roles of leaders and employees is not optional; it is essential for competitive advantage. Leader support is required to properly transition roles. Otherwise, employees may become disillusioned and react to the transition process rather than proactively pursue improvement opportunities.

CHANGEVISION—WHEN EMPLOYEES ARE LIKE DEER CAUGHT IN HEADLIGHTS

On the surface, most employees appear very interested in being self-directed. However, the reverse is usually true. We recently spoke at a conference where a large number of companies were represented. On the first conference day, speakers were singing the praises of self-directed teams and empowerment. On the second day, we stated that employees have been hostile toward self-directed teams and empowerment. The audience gave resounding applause and related their similar experiences. They confessed that self-directed teams and coaching/empowerment were not easy.

Why? One key reason is something called learned helplessness. Learned helplessness is where previous experiences have conditioned employees to believe they cannot improve upon or change their situation and, if they do make an effort, the consequences will be undesirable. We have also heard it referred to as a deer caught in the headlights, unable to act, lost, and certainly fearful.

For the past eight years, Caroline served as the account executive for a cellular telephone service company. When she initially took the job, she aggressively pursued sales opportunities. Each time she did this, her supervisor chastised her for not depending on directives from the home office. After several times, Caroline only pursued the directives provided from the home office.

During the last eighteen months, Caroline experienced increased competition as a competing firm used their empowered sales staff to increase their market share. Because of the lost market share, Caroline's company terminated all middle management positions including Caroline's supervisor. Following the staffing cuts, Caroline was encouraged to pursue market sales opportunities. Because she had learned over the years that she could not create and implement effective sales strategy, she asked and waited for home office direction. As she waited, her company lost more than 50 percent market share to the new entrants in the market. Caroline's new supervisor terminated her because she was unable to learn how to function in the new environment.

Just like Caroline, employees and leaders focus on the past, unless they learn to live out of their imaginations (instead of their past). Organizations cannot have significant breakthroughs until their employees and leaders learn to think of "what can be." In addition, organizations cannot implement a long-term employee development process until leaders have helped employees overcome learned helplessness. **ChangeVision** is critical because it penetrates the invisible wall of learned helplessness!

ChangeVision is the daily process used by leaders to transition employees toward taking greater responsibility on the job and leaving behind learned helplessness by use of imagination, visioning, employee involvement, and goal development. ChangeVision must be used before the employee development process can be successfully implemented.

ChangeVision is the ability to define alternatives through imagination, instead of dwelling in the past. ChangeVision should be used to overcome learned helplessness in such areas as people relationships, process focus, quality plans, and definitions of business success. For example, employees may expect only a 3 percent bottom line because they have been unable to do any better in the past. With ChangeVision, leaders help employees consider what they can accomplish, such as an 8 percent margin. ChangeVision helps employees to think out of the box.

ChangeVision is not only the ability to imagine, but also the ability to share that vision with employees in a convincing and meaningful way. ChangeVision normally requires repeated presentations of the vision (at least four to five times) before employees understand. It is helpful to construct a picture or model of the vision to use with employees. Many times, a picture or model will mean more to employees than mere words. In addition to the picture or model, employees must relate the vision to their own situation. Otherwise, employees will not be convinced that change is necessary or even possible.

We can recount the number of times we have asked our children to change their behavior. Oftentimes, we would emphasize how a certain change would affect others. We failed to create a picture that was meaningful to our children and would make a case for change. Our children did not change. And to make matters worse, we misdiagnosed the situation as our children's lack of interest in making the change.

A good example of this took place when Gail called Rick to attend the senior prom. Rick knew he wasn't going to go with her to the prom but delayed giving her a response because he didn't want to face her disappointment. Two days before the prom, Rick told Gail he wouldn't attend the prom. By then, Gail had purchased a gown and shoes. Rick's father stressed that this placed Gail in a difficult situation because she had no alternatives left at such a late date and she had spent hard-earned money in preparation for the event. Rick was not moved by this appeal. Rick's father should have emphasized to him that this situation would be known by his friends and would negatively reflect on their relationship with him. Rick's father should have emphasized the risk of damage instead of the losses faced by Gail. The point of this story is that a leader needs to talk about the impact of the situation on the employee, not the impact on others. Parent-child relationships are very similar to leader-employee relationships in this regard.

ChangeVision also requires employee involvement and responsibility for visioning. Employees must be involved in visioning because it is part of the ownership quotient. Also, employees can add an important perspective that will strengthen the vision.

ChangeVision includes the use of goals as part of that vision. However, a word of caution is in order. Goal setting can limit potential. For example, a goal could be set to make an improvement of 10 percent when, in fact, the organization could reach an improvement of 40 percent. One way to avoid this problem is to analyze data before setting goals.

ChangeVision uses goals not as walls but as windows of opportunity to positively reinforce employees for their behaviors, progress, and results, which form the basis for business success. Goals provide team opportunities to celebrate a newfound ability to overcome learned helplessness.

CHANGEVISION—JOURNEY

Think of a journey. Let's suppose that employees have never been outside of their own hometown. They will feel vulnerable and very hesitant to journey forth. They will not make the trip unless they see the need and understand how it will affect their situation positively. The ChangeVision table (p. 289) provides the four basic steps (map the journey, begin the journey, share the ride, and complete the journey) required for leaders to help employees overcome learned helplessness.

Map the Journey

Leaders must use imagination and create a picture of the present and where they and employees need to be in the future. Leaders must initiate visioning because of learned helplessness. The initial journeys should be relatively easy to accomplish especially when the organization faces significant levels of learned helplessness. The map provides a picture of the journey from the present to the future. The map must provide a shared vision that includes the vision's relationship to the needs and interests of employees.

Begin the Journey

Leaders should literally draw pictures of the journey. Leaders must consistently repeat the reasons for the journey and the vision, while relating this specifically to the employees' changing roles and frame of reference. Leaders must continuously communicate, role model, and encourage employees to make the change. Leaders' expectations will build employees' confidence.

Share the Ride

After senior leaders initiate the vision, the vision is further shared with other leaders and employees to gain additional perspectives and acceptance of the vision. This is called "visioning." Employees will start to understand that they can have an effect upon the organization, unlike learned helplessness. Leaders can engage employees in visioning by use of questions (see Communicate Effectively role). During the journey, employees must be reinforced for their progress. This will further instill confidence to overcome learned helplessness.

Complete the Journey

ChangeVision has goals and measures for the journey. With ChangeVision, goals and measures allow leaders and employees to know when they have arrived to complete the journey. Celebration is appropriate, especially when the journey was the first such journey as a Leader-Coach-Manager or was a difficult journey. Desirable reinforcement must be used throughout the journey to help form new habits.

A good example of ChangeVision took place in a medium-sized food warehousing and marketing company. The company had operated for years under a command and control (telling) management style. Because of increased competition and changing product needs, management decided it was time to leave command and control management behind.

Management decided employee input and response to customer needs was important to the company's survival. Robert, who was responsible for the order department, wholeheartedly bought into the change and tried to train employees to become customer service representatives concentrating on customer needs and warehouse solutions. However, his department was largely made up of employees with more than twenty years of experience as order takers. They were unwilling to change from order takers to customer representatives. Many of them explained that they did not feel comfortable in the new role because they had tried to expand their roles in the past only to be ridiculed by the past president and other departments.

Following some education from the president, Robert realized that his employees were saying they had learned helplessness. Robert decided to take a few small steps instead of a major leap. Employees could understand small progress steps, but not all. Robert decided to concentrate on one product line to develop a customer orientation. The journey started with Robert's vision of an Italian line of products supported by product information modules included in the company's computer order entry software. Robert created a drawing showing the company offering information in addition to products. He then added a picture of the customer that included a list of their interests such as flavor, texture, and color of product. He pasted pictures of their product line on an easel pad and listed several different options. A computer was drawn on the picture along with product description information that would be of interest to customers based on recent survey research. During Robert's presentation, he emphasized that their department depended on customer loyalty and meeting customer needs. He made sure they understood how their paycheck was affected by customer decisions. If customers left to use another warehouse, the number of order takers would decrease. His last picture included a long line drawn from the present (order takers) to the future (customer service).

Robert started with a vision and proceeded to develop it using pictures that dealt with employees' needs and roles. When employees began asking questions about the vision, Robert used that as an opportunity to ask employees how the vision could be improved. Soon, employees were participating in shared visioning. Before they finished the session, Robert had repeated the revised vision at least four times. The final step included goal setting through shared visioning. The outcome was a commitment by order department employees to use a computerized, Italian food product information program. After several months, employees saw a dramatic rise in Italian food related orders and asked that the entire system be upgraded to include information on all products. Together, Robert and employees had overcome learned helplessness and earned commitment from their customers through ChangeVision.

SO, WHAT'S THE POINT?
It is natural for leaders and employees to be concerned about change. ChangeVision directly impacts employees' understanding of new possibilities and helps them overcome learned helplessness. Learned helplessness must be overcome in order to effectively change roles.

EMPLOYEE SCOTOMAS—BLIND IN BOTH EYES

Earlier in this book, leaders were recognized as having scotomas or blind spots, which we referred to as **Coachotomas**. Similarly, employees have a number of scotomas which may adversely affect their ability to deal with role transitions. Scotomas differ from learned helplessness in that blind spots are formed from a lack of certain experiences or information, or from a bias based on a past experience which affected their present actions. Learned helpless-ness, on the other hand, is a belief that it is useless to act or dangerous to act. Leaders and employees exhibit both scotomas and learned helplessness.

Let's face it: change is not pretty or orderly. It is largely ill-defined, messy, and menacing. Change creates many questions and fewer answers. In addi-tion, change tends to increase anxiety. Employees who fared well in the past expect they will lose ground, while employees who suffered in the past expect they will suffer even more. Remember, traditional management created a very routine world overshadowed with periodic, small increments of change. New leader roles, on the other hand, is all about continuous change with just a few brief periods of tranquility thrown in for good measure.

Why do leaders need to deal with employee scotomas? Scotomas can limit employees' ability to see beyond the present. Scotomas are barriers. In many cases, scotomas will be the focus until a leader adequately addresses the issue. From experiences of a number of organizations in various industries, we have identified several common scotomas affecting employees. Comments are provided in order to better define the situation and a preferred leader's response to the scotoma is also included.

Scotomas

Scotoma 1:
"I have always followed orders so I will continue to do so in the future."

Comments:
Even if you are working in an organization that is not officially pursuing empowerment, it is possible to go beyond job expectations. A perception of a barrier may be a greater impediment than reality. Many leaders appre-ciate proactive employees even when they are not officially pursuing empowerment. Generally, employees will not grow faster than their leader.

Leader Response:
"Unfortunately, you have probably been asked to follow orders in the past. Our organization cannot continue to be successful with that mode of operation. Things are changing too fast. I need your help. You are too valu-able not to be a part of the team which manages the change."

Scotoma 2:
"This isn't my job; you're expecting me to do things that my boss used to do."

Comments:
Typical, traditional job descriptions and human resource organizations did not permit employees to work outside of their described job. This may have created a mindset that one can only do the job as previously and rigidly

defined. In empowered organizations, employees do not have this mindset because they are proactive and are not limited by their previous experiences. Employees need to be proactive in perfecting the flow of work. They need to ask what they can do for their company. This is the absolute minimum employees can do for their company and take up any visioning slack for their leader. Think! It is the employee's job not because someone is trying to take advantage of team members, but rather, it is an operational necessity in order to survive.

Leader Response:

"Our organization must change to remain competitive. Your job must change or else your job may not exist. Roles must change from being leader-centered to team-centered. Because of all this change, I now must do things that were previously done by my leader. The definition of average performance five years ago would be significantly below what it is today. The bar of expectations is rising every day. I would like to relate a story I heard. When the sun rises on the Amazon, the leopard knows that he must move faster than the slowest monkey or he will starve. The monkey knows when he wakes up that he must move faster than the fastest leopard or he will die. The moral of the story is when the sun comes up, you'd better be running. Leaders help employees run longer and faster than ever before."

Scotoma 3:

"Are you going to pay me extra for doing that?"

Comments:

This scotoma raises the issue whether the employee is committed to the organization. The ownership issue may seem naive, but the reality is that we believe in the hereafter. The hereafter is if you're not here after what the organization is here after, then the company will be here after you're gone. This may be tough language, but it underscores that employees must buy into continual improvement as well as quality of work life. In the long run, if employees are being asked to do significantly more, compensation systems should be redesigned to support work redesign or reengineering.

Leader Response:

"Not now. The reality is everyone's job must be more productive in order for the pay to remain the same. If your job responsibilities did not increase, your pay would be decreased. It is true that we must continually search for improved support systems that are compatible with the increase in responsibilities for our job. There is absolutely no intention to take advantage of you. I also work according to these realities."

Scotoma 4:
"This is just a plan to get rid of a bunch of employees."

Comments:

In the long term, this will probably be the natural result of a well-empowered organization. The intent is to empower employees (that is increase ownership, capability, and authority focused on purpose) to improve business success and quality of work life. It is a recognition that quality improvement is best attained through decision making at the level closest to the work and customer. In essence, what is good for the business long term should be best for employees. Many organizations attempt to minimize any adverse impact on leaders and employees resulting from empowerment-related change.

Leader Response:

"The management team spends an enormous amount of time trying to minimize adverse impact upon employees. The intent is definitely not to get rid of people. The intent is to remain competitive for the survival of the organization. Every reasonable effort is made to balance the focus on business success and the impact on people."

BRUSHSTROKING

How should a leader deal with employee scotomas? The approach is different from ChangeVision. Employee scotomas develop when employees are prisoners of their own experiences and leaders must help employees stretch beyond their blind spots and accept new paradigms. **Brushstroking** is a process to overcome blind spots. Like a professional portrait photographer who uses the brushstroking technique to blot out blemishes, leaders must brushstroke out negative experiences that are stored in employee minds. Brushstroking is a six step process:

1. Identify employee behaviors that are barriers to change. Leaders should use observation and informal discussion with employees to identify the situation. Later when problem solving in a formal setting with employees, leaders must test whether the behavior is accurately described. Leaders should state that it is his or her "perception that . . . "
2. Determine the rationale for employee behavior. Identify whether the rationale is based on observation, second-hand information, beliefs, and/or assumptions. The rationale can be identified from both informal discussions and individual or team meetings through proper use of questions instead of accusations (question types are covered in the Communicate Effectively role)

3. Determine appropriate behavior and logic and relate that to the observed behavior. The interests, needs, and concerns of employees should be considered in developing the logic. What is important to employees and relates to their perceptions?

4. Explain to employees what consequences are likely if the observed behavior is continued. Never use threatening language. Identify whether the observed behavior is good for the community, customers, organization, work team, and employee (CCOWE). Compare consequences from the desired behavior with consequences of the observed behavior. For example, state whether the desired behavior is good for the individual and the community, and compare that with the observed behavior and its impact on the community

5. Enhance credibility by discussing situations where similar change was required. The four points above should be clearly outlined. It may be helpful to ask an external party, who has experienced a similar change in a similar setting, to share their experiences with the individual or the team. This is necessary when a major change is required to avoid a major, negative financial outcome. Also, it may be helpful to visit other organizations to help change the brushstrokes of employees. When the issue is large in scope or breadth and employees perceive the change as major, leaders should expect that change will take substantial time to attain

6. Finally, it is necessary to determine if a change in behavior has occurred. Does the employee agree a problem exists and a change in behavior is needed? If so, leaders should provide desirable reinforcement for the demonstrated behavior. If not, consequences need to be revisited to determine appropriate action

Brushstroking was used in a division within a teaching hospital when the hospital decided to pursue an empowering environment. The hospital published its values which were developed through the efforts of employees, leaders, physicians, and board members. Following this, senior leaders received feedback from middle management via a written employee survey. One division's results indicated growing hostility. Following the first meeting to review the results, Brushstroking was identified as a process to pinpoint issues affecting change. Informal conversations with division employees indicated that a number of them were becoming less team oriented. Lack of empowerment was initially cited as the reason for this trend.

At the next meeting, division employees agreed to follow the first four Brushstroking steps. The purpose of Brushstroking was explained as a way for everyone to understand the issues and reach resolution. Each Brushstroking step was reviewed. Employees were then asked to identify behaviors that were barriers to change. The major issues identified by the employees were growing hostility among the leader and employees,

empowerment and appropriate support, and role modeling of empowerment by senior leaders.

   One employee said that when the organization adopted the mission, vision,
and values, which specifically included empowerment, he expected his leader
would stay in his office and not bother him. Another employee was more
specific and stated that he should only need to meet with his leader once every
three months. During the other months, he would provide a monthly report
which briefly listed his accomplishments for that time period. Otherwise, the
leader should not bother him. Both employees agreed that their leader did not
"buy into empowerment" because their expectations were not being met. The
meeting was becoming increasingly tense. The leader, by design, did not
respond to the perceptions of these employees. This would only serve to
increase the level of hostility in the room and possibly create perceptions that
the leader was defensive when criticism was offered. Instead, the leader in
question asked the rest of the group how they perceived the situation. One
employee offered that she did not expect the leader to disappear or to stay out
of her space and did not see the leader's behavior as negatively as others.
Another employee asked what a reasonable definition of empowerment should
be. The leader responded by asking the group if individual definitions of
empowerment were the rationale for behaviors displayed by the leader and
employees. Most employees agreed while several employees felt strongly that
their expectations were consistent with the definition of empowerment.

   The leader asked each employee to consider whether the rationale for
behaviors shown was based on observation, beliefs, second hand information,
or assumptions. Employee feedback showed that some employees had a definition of empowerment which appeared similar to abdication. These
employees assumed their definition was ironclad and without question.
Other employees added that they had discussed this issue with others or read
several books trying to discover a reasonable definition of empowerment.
What they found was no clear definition. Most of the employees agreed that
the rationale was based on individual assumptions. The group agreed that a
definition of empowerment must be created and "bought into by all."

   Following a short meeting break, the leader offered a definition of
empowerment that the division might use. Empowerment was differenti-
ated from abdication. The definition was related to employee needs (e.g.,
perform the job with minimal interference, receive appropriate communication so as to be aware of project status). The definition included employee
capability and ownership before authority is delegated from the leader to the
employee. Just as important, the employees agreed that empowerment
required increased visibility from the leader. They agreed that the leader's
role should include the use of questions to make sure the employee understands the purpose and has the capability, ownership, and authority required
for the task or project. The employees were able to agree upon these points

because the leader kept turning the questions back to them asking what was needed to create a successful, efficient, and effective workplace.

The group used CCOWE to identify whether this empowerment definition was good for community, customers, organization, work team, and employees. They agreed it was good for the community and customers because it protected them from incapable employees. This was a good definition for the organization because it balanced the interests of leaders and employees and gave each group a better-defined boundary. They agreed it was a good definition for the work team because it rewarded capability and ownership with both greater freedom and responsibility. Finally, the group agreed that this was a good definition for employees because it provided a clear definition and fair expectations. From this exercise, the employees agreed that they had gone beyond their own point of interest to include consideration of the needs and interests of the organization and others.

Now that the issue was well defined and resolved, the group discussed what the consequences should be for employees who did not follow this course. The leader asked the employees if they had any expectations they would like to share along with their rationale. The employees and leader agreed that punishment would be used as a last resort. The leader agreed to discuss his perceptions with the employee when he first saw behavior that was inconsistent with their agreed behavior. The second time this employee showed the unacceptable behavior he would provide a verbal warning to the employee in addition to coaching on the issue. A third infraction would require discipline by the leader including a personal report.

The leader agreed to work on several behavioral issues: use face-to-face communication instead of handwritten notes when dealing with the empowerment issue and an employee, hold monthly meetings with employees and discuss progress on the issue of empowerment, and create clear definitions of projects and expected feedback points for employees in order to minimize the potential for perceived anarchy. The employees agreed to improve upon several methods of communication for project updates (including voice mail, e-mail, face-to-face meetings, and use of personal goals and objectives for the year) and to provide periodic report on these. An outside consultant was also used in a division retreat to work with the group and develop an agreed upon work environment. The consultant was selected because he came from an organization that experienced similar problems with similar cultural issues. Empowerment and the changing roles of senior leaders and division leaders were the focus of the later meetings.

The Brushstroking process minimized chaos and strife. Employees appreciated the diverse opinions and adopted a process to deal with conflict. The employees began to monitor themselves and provide constructive criticism to their fellow employees. Some employees did not agree with the empowerment definition adopted by the majority of employees and left the division to seek a different environment. The end result was an improvement in the internal employee survey and team productivity.

SO, WHAT'S THE POINT?
Everyone has scotomas, including employees. If scotomas represent barriers to business success, they must be challenged. It takes Brushstroking to help employees identify and deal with issues resulting from scotomas.

THE CHANGE JOURNEY TO DEVELOP EMPLOYEES

An organization is comprised of individuals. One important way to develop the organization is to improve each individual's skills and knowledge. Empowerment requires the development of all employees, not just leaders. If an organization is unwilling to commit to extensive, long term training, the transition must be reassessed because the journey is doomed to failure.

The Change Journey for Employee Development diagram reflects six actions for the development of employees: create shared vision, assess current reality, communicate current performance, provide resources, manage boundaries, and reassess and provide feedback. In addition to these actions, it may be necessary to reassess and revise support systems such as the organization's personnel performance system. The existing support systems may be based on traditional methods of management and reward the wrong type of behavior.

Change Journey for Employee Development

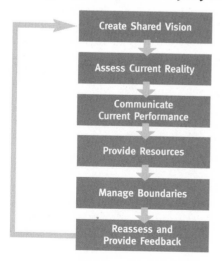

CREATE SHARED VISION—CHANGE THE GAME, DON'T LOSE YOUR JOB

Creating a shared vision does not mean simply telling employees what the vision is. It means involving them in the development of that vision. Why? It will increase ownership by employees. When employees care enough about an issue, they will seek to improve their understanding. Increased understanding leads to greater openness. When each employee is open, it creates greater openness within the team and ultimately the organization. Team openness results in greater team understanding and caring. Unity is the end result. Unity does not mean all employees think or act the same. Unity is respecting and valuing differences. Respecting and valuing differences is essential to achieve consensus.

The vision challenge reminds us of David, a salesman with a financial firm. David had grown comfortable with the level of sales success in the past and did not believe that he and his team needed to increase their level of productivity. He even went so far as to keep copies of favorable e-mails from other leaders to him in order to support his complacency. David's supervisor was fully aware of the situation. The supervisor started working on the problem by speaking with David about the changes in the environment and how the past levels of success would no longer bring future success. David agreed that times had changed. However, he did not understand why he would fall short of success if he continued to use the same efforts.

The supervisor used internal customer results and data regarding the changed external environment to analyze the issue. Success is often a perception. David's internal customers no longer perceived David as being successful in selling their services and related this in the anonymous written survey coordinated by the personnel department. Their expectations had changed in response to the market changes. They now expected a higher ratio of sales to sales calls than before, because they felt the company and their products had successfully matured to that point.

Following the use of the internal survey results, senior management brought in a sales leader from a more advanced market to share his experiences with David and his team. He carefully recounted the similarities with David's market and how they were successful with a certain approach. He then proceeded to tell David how they failed over time because the nature of the game had changed quickly. Financial services were now available through many channels including department stores, banks, and telemarketing. In the past, a company could be successful if they offered only a few products. Now, customers expected a company to provide a broad array of products and services or "one stop shopping." The old tools no longer worked. The presenter challenged David and his staff to beat the changing market and reemphasize their sales leadership. A short time following this presentation, David and his team developed a new sales development plan. They added contracts with banks and a telemarketing program to sell the products. They increased the number of products by entering into agreements with other firms that offered the missing products. The net result was increased sales. David changed the game instead of losing his job.

ASSESS CURRENT REALITY—WHAT PLANET ARE WE ON ANYWAY?

This step in the process involves a review of current job descriptions. The desired job description must be designed to fit the organization's vision. This should be mutually developed by leaders and employees and reviewed by a representative from the human resources area. The current job description then should be compared to the desired job description and a transition plan created in order to close any gap. This should be done annually in a fast-changing company or industry and every two or three years in most companies or industries.

A local telephone company merged with a regional communication firm and reorganized its services including the adoption of a Leader-Coach-Manager environment. Sam was a leader of linemen who repaired telephone lines and installed new lines. The employees in his area became very frustrated because they were being asked to accomplish tasks that were foreign to them. At one department meeting, a lineman complained that he didn't understand what was going on and didn't feel like he even knew what planet they were on. Sam realized that the frustration developed because their existing job descriptions no longer applied to the new expectations. However, no one had revised the old job description nor had they discussed this with employees. Sam used The Change Journey in order to help the linemen grow. When it came to job descriptions, Sam met individually with each lineman to explain the change and the reasons for change, and then showed how the change affected the job description. They then reviewed the job description line-by-line. Changes were made to reflect the new job expectations while the personnel department reviewed the changes for consistency with policies and systems. Sam and each employee agreed upon the progress needed to transition from the old job description to the new. The end result was improvement in employee morale and communications. The employees felt they had contributed input to make the transition. Sam came to better understand the work concerns of each employee. Both felt they were finally back on earth—on the same planet.

COMMUNICATE CURRENT PERFORMANCE—
THIS ISN'T KANSAS ANYMORE, TOTO!

This step deals with assessing the employee's transition performance from the old job description to the new job description. Employees must be positively reinforced (for example, through a verbal or written thank you to the individual and by group recognition of efforts) when progress is made toward the new job description. Also, leaders must intervene where employees have not progressed toward the new job description. The key here is not to punish, but to correct the situation. Leaders must be specific about inappropriate behaviors and appropriate behaviors. Leaders also must be clear about the rationale behind the appropriate behavior, offer an opportunity to demonstrate the appropriate behavior, and provide feedback.

It is important for leaders to determine where employees are in this process. Leaders should adapt their own behaviors to the employees' points of progress. This approach is outlined in the Change Behaviors diagram.

The Change Behaviors diagram first requires consideration of the current reality. What is the present situation? Where are the employees at in their development? Second, the leader needs to consider where the employees need to be. This is the target for the development of individuals and teams.

Change Behaviors

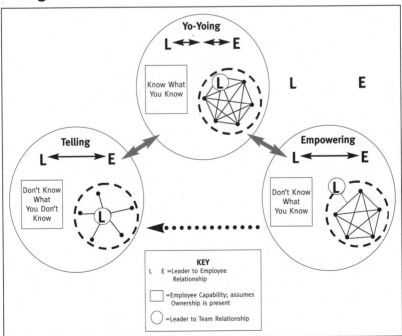

Once the current reality and empowerment zone have been considered, the leader must assess the stage of development for each of the employees. There are three stages of development as shown in the Change Behaviors diagram: Don't Know What You Don't Know, Know What You Know, and Don't Know What You Know. Where an employee exhibits Don't Know What You Don't Know behavior, a leader should use the telling behavior. Where a team exhibits this same behavior, the leader needs to be using the telling behavior as well. Graphically, the relationship of the leader to the employee and team are outlined in the telling circle shown in the diagram. Where an employee and/or team exhibit behavior associated with Know What You Know, a leader should use the yo-yoing behavior. Where the Don't Know What You Know behavior is shown by an employee and/or team, an empowering behavior is appropriate for a leader to use in interactions.

The best way to understand and apply the Change Behaviors diagram is to review each of the stages of individual development and review a case example. Keep in mind it is normal for employees and teams to exhibit each of the three behaviors at some point in time during the work relationship. That is why it is important for leaders to recognize the stages of development for employees and teams.

The telling change behavior is a correct behavior where an employee doesn't know what he or she doesn't know. Telling means that a leader will do more directing and make most of the decisions. Telling includes making a good case for change and providing it in a clear, concise, and convincing manner. There is a minimal amount of employee participation at this point.

Jeanine is a vice president of a large wellness and fitness company. She did not realize and would not admit that she did not understand how to prepare the employees for empowerment. Jeanine's supervisor knew that Jeanine did not understand and was not aware of her performance gap. Jeanine's supervisor figured this out by asking open-ended questions on the subject of empowerment and appropriate approaches to implement empowerment. In addition, Jeanine's supervisor carefully watched interactions among Jeanine and her employee's.

Jeanine's supervisor told or directed Jeanine regarding the preparation of employees for empowerment. In this situation, Jeanine was not alone. Other senior leaders did not have an understanding of empowerment and techniques to develop such skills. Therefore, the appropriate team interaction is represented by the wheel located in the diagram directly beneath "telling." Because the team did not know about empowerment and how to approach it, the leader must take center stage and "tell" the individuals on the team how to prepare for empowerment, implement the plan, respond to issues, questions, and problems, and assess their progress in the empowerment journey.

In this situation, the president of the company held several meetings with management. During the first meeting, the president defined empowerment and what affect it had on their job and employees. Next, the purpose of empowerment was carefully outlined and related to their individual jobs. During the second meeting, the president led the meeting and helped to describe a plan to implement empowerment. The president made sure that issues were identified with involvement from the leaders. It was important to have the leaders involved in the plan. Otherwise, they would be less likely to take ownership of the plan. Because management did not recognize their lack of empowerment skills, the president needed to protect their self-esteem while educating them on the subject. The telling behavior was used without confronting the leaders with their lack of empowerment knowledge and capabilities. This was accomplished through the input opportunities and avoidance of any direct comments regarding their capabilities.

At the end of the second meeting, the president discussed the implementation phase providing detailed descriptions. Finally, the assessment stage was outlined and what was expected of management. The empowerment program was successful for the wellness and fitness company because the president recognized the stage of development and used the appropriate behavior.

The second stage of individual development is "Know What You Know." Employees are highly participative in decision making at this stage and provide suggestions for improvements. Leaders are no longer at the center of the activity or team. Employees share some of the traditional leader functions. For example, employees share responsibility for training, labor and vacation scheduling, safety, and quality measures. At the yo-yoing stage, employees demonstrate high capability and ownership on a consistent basis.

Larry, a divisional leader for a food manufacturer, had been working with a team of food product leaders for several years. From his interactions with the group and assessment of their progress, he realized they were a maturing team. They knew what they knew and understood what they didn't know. When a new quality plan was unveiled by the corporate office, Larry knew that the group had the knowledge and skills to handle this project. He turned the project over to the team offering his support as needed. Larry attended the first team meeting that was held to discuss the plan of action for rolling out the quality plan in their division. Larry was very quiet during the meeting offering comments when the group asked questions directed toward him or a clarification was needed regarding the intent of the organization's quality plan. At future meetings, Larry's role, to an outside observer, appeared to be a team member instead of a division leader. The group very ably implemented the quality plan in their division because the yo-yoing behavior was effective.

The interaction required for the yo-yoing change behavior is shown in the diagram. The leader becomes more of a part of the team as indicated by the letter "L," which is a part of the circle of employees. The leader is no longer at the center of the team as was the case in the telling stage.

The third stage in the Change Behaviors diagram is reached when employees Don't Know What You Know. In this stage, employees know so much about the situation they can't fully describe everything they know even if they were asked. At this stage, employees are truly empowered because they have capability, ownership, and authority with a purpose. Employees assume a broader span of responsibilities while the leader assumes a greater span as well. At this stage, the leader may be given responsibility for more than one team because teams at this stage are more self-directing. Unfortunately, typical behavior exhibited by many organizations is to jump from the telling stage to the empowerment stage bypassing the yo-yoing stage. In these situations, employees are not at a stage of maturity to be truly self directing. This normally results in frustration for both leaders and employees. Additionally, the organization is at risk.

David was a leader of a health care products distribution center. He had been using teams for over eight years, advancing from the telling behavior to empowering behavior. Because teams had used their extensive education and training to become truly empowered teams, David gave his teams most of the day-to-day responsibilities previously provided by leaders. The leaders were assigned to oversee a greater number of teams and pursue company expansion projects. Leaders served more as boundary managers addressing the friction or overlap that may arise from team activities. The empowering stage created a new world for their division. They were able to adapt faster to changing market forces and offer new services and products to their customers.

In the empowering stage, leaders are operating outside of the team circle as shown in the Change Behaviors diagram. Leaders work on projects previously pursued by their supervisor and on boundary management for their teams.

Leaders must determine where each employee is in the Change Behavior Model relative to each major element of the employee's job. Leaders and employees should mutually identify goals and objectives to move to the empowering stage. This assessment needs to be communicated clearly to each employee, along with the leader's commitment to help employees grow.

The most perplexing thing for leaders who use the Change Behaviors Model is the use of different behaviors for different situations. We have heard many leaders say that they thought they should exhibit only one type of behavior where they took on the new leader roles. This seems to be a carry-over from traditional command and control management which was focused on one type of behavior. When leaders apply the Change Behaviors Model, they find that it is more sensible to adapt their behavior to specific situations rather than apply the single behavior of command and control management. This became crystal clear to Carol, a regional leader of a supermarket chain. She was trying to be supportive and follow the new company policy by empowering employees. The company expected leaders to delegate more responsibilities to employees but failed to train leaders and employees on techniques to accomplish this. In support of the company policy, Carol became less visible and decreased her communications with employees. The result was a sharp decrease in employee productivity and morale.

At first, Carol thought this must be due to empowerment; her employees were trying to take advantage of less structure. Then, she talked with her supervisor who explained that she might not be providing the right type of support. Carol's supervisor helped her understand where the employees were on the Change Behavior Model by asking questions about each employee and how Carol approached specific situations. Carol drew a simple diagram to identify where each employee was in his or her under-standing and skills related to empowerment. Each employee seemed to fit within the first box. Like a flash of lightning, Carol recognized that the problem was not the employees but the approach she used. They still needed the telling style but she had jumped to the empowering style.

Carol was both embarrassed and dejected to find that she had been following the wrong course. Carol's supervisor shared with her a story about another senior leader who made the same mistake and suffered the same reaction. He stopped and smiled. He was that leader. Carol's super-visor likened the situation to Dorothy and Toto crashing down into the Land of Oz. Dorothy had to change her behavior because she was no longer in Kansas; she needed to interact based on the needs and perceptions of the Munchkins. Like Dorothy, Carol required further training to understand how to use appropriate change behaviors. He promised to support Carol by using available resources to further develop her skills in empowerment. He accomplished this by asking specific questions each week about employee behavior and how Carol was handling their behavior. He also provided materials and videos for Carol and her employees to use. At future meetings, Carol's supervisor would set aside part of their meeting time to discuss the materials she had read or the videos she had watched. They would discuss how she had used the key points from these materials to improve her skills and employee development levels. The supervisor interspersed humor during their conversation in order to ease Carol's anxiety about making the new leader roles transition. He periodically offered constructive comments to help her adjust to use of the Change Behavior Model.

PROVIDE RESOURCES—PENNIES FROM HEAVEN

Resources, such as money, educational tools, personnel, and a visible Leader-Coach-Manager presence, are required to move employees along the development process. Resources should be a major concern and focus of leaders using the Change Behaviors Model. Leaders and employees must agree upon needed resources and how they are to be provided.

Employees deserve a competent, caring, readily available leader presence. It is unfair to ask people to do something and not provide necessary support. To paraphrase Dr. Deming, if you want to destroy people, ask them to do something they cannot do and rob them of their pride of workmanship.

Francis was a regional leader for a financial firm. Part of her responsibilities was to be a team leader for a project focused on updating an existing customer satisfaction survey system. The team decided a major redesign of the system was needed in order to meet the objectives outlined by senior management. Because the firm was going through a major cost reduction effort and monies were very difficult to come by, Francis and other team members became disillusioned because they thought they would fail to accomplish the objectives. Francis decided to approach her senior vice president to discuss the issue. The senior vice president found monies from another part of the organization to redesign the system. The senior vice president stated that it was wrong to ask employees to pursue a major project and not provide necessary resources. Francis and the team members celebrated the successful redesign by holding a party for senior management paid from team member contributions. They used balloons that included their theme "pennies from heaven." Senior management was moved because they had never received such positive feedback and everyone was placed in a win-win situation.

MANAGE BOUNDARIES—THAT'S NOT A HILL FOR A CLIMBER

The Change Behavior Model emphasized the importance of managing boundaries when teams and/or individuals reach the yo-yoing and empowering stages. Leaders must be able to understand boundaries and how to manage boundaries as teams progress.

A boundary is an imaginary line or border that surrounds team members or an actual circle of responsibility for specific tasks that surrounds team members and separates them from other parts of the organization. A management team of a division has a boundary that separates them from another divisional team. A departmental team which consists of supervisors from that area has a boundary which separates its activities and interests from other departments. The concept of a boundary is best outlined in the empowering stage the Change Behavior Model. Each team has a boundary or an imaginary line of authority which may overlap with another team's boundary. Where team boundaries overlap, there is a common concern, interest, or activity which may require the involvement of their respective leader to remove barriers or minimize conflict.

Because boundary management is critical to the success of leaders and employees, we have dedicated a role to this subject. Suffice it to say here, that leaders must become adept at boundary management in all three Change Behavior stages—telling, yo-yoing, and empowering.

REASSESS AND PROVIDE FEEDBACK

Reassessment is the purposeful review by both leaders and employees of progress made toward established goals and objectives. If good progress has been made, leaders should use desirable reinforcement. If progress is less than satisfactory, leaders must decide on the best method to correct the situation. Feedback itself is a critical step and reviewed in detail in the Communicate Effectively role. This role provides the tips and skill sets to apply to this stage.

SO, WHAT'S THE POINT?
Employees cannot develop in a vacuum. Employee development requires a readily available leader presence by one who possesses knowledge, skill, and ownership to help others grow. Employee development is not a one time intervention, it is an ongoing process.

Role 5

Role 6
Role 7
Role 8
Role 9
Role 10
Role 11

CLARIFY EMPLOYEE
EXPECTATIONS

Drive Without a
Rearview Mirror

DOLPHINS ARE THOUGHT to be one of the most intelligent animals on earth—possibly second only to human beings. They perform complex tasks and communicate with humans and with their own species.

At the Oceana complex, once located in Sandusky, Ohio's Cedar Point Amusement Park, dolphins were trained to perform feats once thought possible only by human beings. They played catch with a volleyball over a net and waved at the crowd with their fins. We learned from their trainers that dolphins are able to reach these levels of achievement because of two principles. First, clear expectations are set for the dolphins. Second, desirable reinforcement is used when the expectations are met. If a dolphin fails to perform as requested, there is no scolding or reprimand.

Human beings are clearly superior to dolphins in a number of ways, but leaders could learn a few lessons from our seaworthy friends. One lesson is leaders must create clear expectations for employees. Without clear expectations, employees will not understand their roles. Without a clear understanding of what is expected, employees will not succeed. Clear communication of expectations is critical!

There are nine general expectations leaders must communicate to employees to create an effective environment. Employees must:

1. Understand what new leader roles and empowerment are and are not
2. Be willing to grow and be empowered
3. Proactively pursue coaching and empowerment of self and other employees

4. Understand, support, and carry out the expectations the organization has defined for employees
5. First look upon others favorably
6. Learn, learn, learn
7. Understand and improve the Big O (larger organization)
8. Maintain or enhance quality during times of significant change
9. Help the leader grow

UNDERSTAND WHAT NEW LEADER ROLES AND EMPOWERMENT ARE AND ARE NOT

Many employees and leaders alike have a misunderstanding of new leader roles and empowerment. Because of their perceptions, employees expect leaders will leave them alone and allow them to do whatever they wish.

This is not empowerment—it is anarchy. Leaders, on the other hand, expect they only need to teach or talk to employees in order to apply the new leader roles. This is merely talking the talk and not walking the walk. New leader roles involve much more than just teaching or talking.

The problem has been compounded by numerous definitions of empowerment offered in books, journals, and videos, confusing leaders and employees instead of helping them. Most definitions are just narrowly defined additions to the traditional leader, emphasizing communication skills. Because of this misunderstanding, leaders should not be surprised to find that employees are confused by the marketplace rhetoric.

If leaders expect employees to understand the new leader roles, leaders must carefully explain the new concepts. The "case for change" or the reason for new roles needs to be underscored. The "case for change" must be clearly related to the employee's situation. If an employee fails to see the need for change, they will not adapt to the new leader roles. Whenever drawings or diagrams can be used, the concept will be clearer to many employees.

The definition of Leader-Coach-Manager functions and the roles need to be clearly stated and related to everyone in the organization. These definitions provided in this book may need to be revised to be more meaningful to employees in their culture. The definitions, when presented, should be divided into small phrases. This approach provides employees with the opportunity to understand each component of the definition.

After defining Leader-Coach-Manager functions and roles, empowerment needs to be defined. Without a common definition of empowerment, confusion will continue. Without an agreed upon definition of empowerment, employees may use this opportunity to emphasize their personal definition of empowerment (which is closely related to anarchy). If leaders can effectively use the new leader roles, the "E" word, empowerment, does not need to be used. The "E" word disappears.

Employee expectations needed to be communicated at a large hospital in the Southeast because it was pursuing a new direction utilizing new leader roles, empowerment, and self-directed work groups. Ted, the director for case managers, had responsibility for eight nurses. The case managers were expected to review the patient's record upon admission, develop a plan for their discharge, identify the need for use of resources not identified in the record, and work closely with physicians to maximize patients' outcomes. Case managers were also expected to work with nurses and clinical staff, from such areas as laboratory, pharmacy, and radiology, to enhance the efficiency and effectiveness of treatment through coordination of efforts. The case managers had received basic training for work groups and empowerment but implementation had started on only one patient unit in the hospital.

Despite the training case managers had regarding empowerment and work groups, Ted was apprehensive about working with them on new leader roles and empowerment. Ted was more comfortable with command and control management than his new leader roles.

Ted called a meeting of the case managers stating the purpose of the meeting was to discuss his role and work groups. Ted began the meeting emphasizing that his role as leader had changed as well as their role as case managers. He expressed his discomfort and nervousness because of this major change.

Ted then described the need for work groups. He emphasized the need for quicker patient service and more efficient care because of increased pressures on health care costs as evidenced by decreasing reimbursement from payers. He underscored the fact that other hospitals were encountering the same change. This was important because it told the staff that everyone in the industry had to deal with change. Following this, he recounted the empowerment and work group education provided to all case managers which would allow them to work with less guidance from Ted. Ted provided a specific example—clinical pathways.

Clinical pathways had recently been implemented at the hospital. Clinical pathways were outlines of day-by-day, expected patient care for specific types of cases. Clinical pathways were intended to create the basic expectations for care provided to the patient and decrease the wide variation in cost of care and quality for like patients. With this tool, case managers understood the basic expectations for patients who were on a clinical pathway. Because the journey was clearly outlined, less guidance was needed.

Ted talked at length about the concept of his new role and how it related to the case managers. He asked for their support as he tried his best to support their efforts in their new role.

Ted asked if he could share with the group definitions of Leader-Coach-Manager that had been developed by a group of hospital employees. Ted wrote the Leader-Coach-Manager definitions on a flip chart and explained the definitions, providing opportunity for case managers to discuss the meaning of these. If case managers did not freely offer comments regarding a phrase, Ted used questions to increase communication. What does this mean to you, how is this different from what you have been used to, how does this affect your job, and how does this affect your relationship to your leader?

When Ted was finished with the definitions, he asked them to compare that with the organization's empowerment definition. Once again, Ted engaged the case managers in discussion, dissecting the empowerment definition phrase-by-phrase. He engaged the staff by asking questions. What does this mean to you, what does this mean to our organization, how does this become part of what we do, how difficult is this to implement and how does this compare to Leader-Coach-Manager? At the end of the meeting, Ted checked to see whether the group understood the definitions, empowerment, and the relationship of these concepts by asking questions. The answers provided by the case managers clearly showed they under-stood the concepts. They could clearly describe the concepts and provide specific examples when asked by Ted.

Despite Ted's anxiety related to his new leader roles, he was a success. His success was due to several factors:

1. The group shared common definitions and role expectations
2. They all understood the reason for role changes and they accepted it
3. Ted had asked for their help in making the transition just as he had asked them to make the transition
4. Ted and the case managers entered into a win-win relationship. The case managers gained autonomy while Ted expanded his area of influence
5. Ted and the case managers continued their communications as they pursued work groups, empowerment, and new roles

A final word of advice that Ted and others have learned—new leader roles must come first. This advice runs counter to the approach taken by many organizations. Most start with empowerment just as the hospital in the above story. However, confusion will increase within the management ranks where new leader roles follow the "E" word. Confusion is inevitable because empowerment transfers responsibilities from leaders to employees leaving leaders with no clear role expectations. When this happens, many leaders may stop emphasizing empowerment because they cannot see how it fits their role. In place of empowerment, leaders may resort to command and control management which destroys the empowerment fabric. Or, leaders may result to abdication or anarchy, leaving employees to fend for themselves as they use empowerment.

BE WILLING TO GROW AND BE EMPOWERED

An employee must want help before a leader can be effective in the new leader roles. Otherwise, a leader will be ignored. Some unwilling employees have even been vengeful where a leader attempts to use the new leader roles.

This became clear for Susan when she hired a new employee for a consulting firm. The new consultant showed a strong knowledge base, good interaction skills, and a stated desire to work as part of the team. However, he never embraced the new leader roles and empowerment. Whenever Susan attempted to provide some support, he would ignore her advice, acting as if she wasn't present. Initially, Susan tried different ways to approach him, thinking her style was at fault. Several months later, the problem remained despite her efforts to change the situation. Susan continued to take responsibility for the lack of ownership on his part. She repeatedly had discussions with him about the problem, sharing her perception that he was unwilling to accept input. Susan went to great lengths to explain situations while maintaining his self-esteem. Each time, he gave Susan the same verbal support. However, his actions clearly showed that he was not going to be a team member. He continued to use information as his power base, sharing information only when he perceived it would further strengthen his personal position within the organization. The other members of his work group began to complain about his lack of team effort.

Needless to say, Susan was frustrated. She felt like she had failed. Susan shared these perceptions with the president of the firm. The president posed the following questions: What are the roles and responsibilities of an employee? What is your role and responsibility as a leader? Did you provide a clear sense of expectations? Were those expectations reasonable? Did the employee take responsibility for his own actions or inactions? From this exercise, Susan realized that the employee did not take responsibility for his actions. The problem was not Susan. She finally resolved the issue by allowing him to leave the organization. It took her eighteen months to learn the lesson that employees must be willing to accept the new leader roles and empowerment. If an employee isn't willing despite repeated efforts of management, a leader must recognize it early on and make the necessary personnel changes. The longer it takes to recognize this, the employee may have a demoralizing impact on the whole team.

In Susan's situation, she thought the new employee would embrace the new leader roles and empowerment because he verbally committed to it during the interview. How then can a leader determine if a candidate is willing to adapt? In an interview, it is helpful to use past behavior of the candidate as a guide.

Candidates should be asked questions about past situations where they were confronted with a similar situation and how they reacted. Inquire about past experiences in empowered environments and ask questions about how the person dealt with the changes. Ask for examples where they had to adapt in such an environment and actions taken by the candidate. If a candidate indicates that he or she did not embrace this change, other candidates should be pursued.

How can a leader tell if employees will adapt in an organization that is transitioning to new leader roles and empowerment? The first step is to create a "case for change." In other words, leaders must tell employees "why" they need to accept the change. If this does not result in positive feedback from an employee, there is likely to be difficulty in making the transition.

Barry was the president of a physician practice with over one hundred physicians. He was trained to work with leaders and help them transition to new leader roles and empowerment. Barry spearheaded training for a group of leaders to work with teams. The leaders were not excited and really doubted the need. They had shared these feelings with Barry prior to the meeting. Barry knew he had to present a convincing case for change.

Barry began the meeting by stating the obvious—some leaders may not believe in new leader roles and empowerment or see the need for it. Some were surprised to hear Barry admit that he initially didn't accept the change. He asked that the leaders at least keep an open mind.

Barry began by asking the group to help examine how leaders have developed over time. He started with a chart listing four columns. The first column was titled "type of organization." The next column was "time period." The third column header was "information," while the fourth column was titled "education."

Barry took the group through a total of four time periods asking the group to fill in each column. When the group was finished, the chart looked similar to the Case for Change in Management table provided below.

Barry explained that organizations during the industrial revolution were thought of as machines. Therefore, organizations in the 1800's were "mechanistic." Education levels remained low and the change in the amount of information was relatively low. Following World War I, organizations needed more capital than the individual owners or families could provide. This increased emphasis upon external investment in technology to help the organization grow. Because of the emphasis upon growth, organizations were looked upon as organisms. The rise of large organizations and professional leaders took place during this time period, while the amount of information doubled every thirty years and education levels slowly increased from earlier time periods.

Automation forced organizations to become more complex and dynamic following World War II. The importance of capital in the previous time period gave way to the importance of people and knowledge. Organizations were looked upon as social systems. Information expanded rapidly with the amount of information doubling every three years. The level of education increased dramatically as exemplified by the fact that over 80 percent of all people who had Ph.D.s were alive in 1990.

Barry inquired about what type of management was used in the 1800s and early 1900s. The group agreed that a military type of management or command and control management was used during the 1800s and into the 1900s. The group agreed with Barry that the changes in information and capability of employees required a different type of leader.

The group discussed the issues raised by Barry. They agreed that the environment had changed so dramatically that it was impossible to effectively practice traditional management. They also agreed that they couldn't know all the answers because the universe of knowledge had exploded. At this point, Barry offered the definitions for the Leader-Coach-Manager functions and contrasted them. The group agreed that coaching must be emphasized to the same extent as leading and managing.

Because of this session, the group appreciated "why" they needed to change. However, Barry needed to pursue other actions as well. Barry recognized that he was trying to develop "leader influence," which is outlined in the Leader Influence diagram: explaining the case for change, character modeling, relationship building, and teaching. Barry had effectively explained the case for change. He also needed to model good character and build relationships. In fact, Barry provided character modeling by being honest, keeping promises, and showing sincerity and maturity before, during, and following the training session.

Barry effectively built relationships with members of the group through use of genuine listening skills, respect for others which builds self-esteem, and caring for individuals. During the training session, Barry listened to the leaders and provided feedback to them to show his level of understanding. The group members were treated in a manner that developed

Case for Change in Management

Type of Organization	Time Period	Information	Education
Farming	1700s	>100 years	Low
Mechanistic	1800s–early 1900s	50–80 years	Low
Organism	Post World War I	30 years	Low to medium
Social system	Post World War II	In 1990, every three years; by 2000, every two years	High level of education. In 1960, 16 percent of adults over 25 were college educated; over 45 percent by 1990. Eighty percent of all Ph.D.s ever born were alive in 1990.

Leader Influence

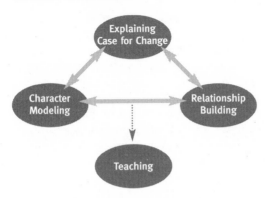

their self-esteem. Finally, Barry showed that he truly cared about what each individual thought and felt on the subject as evidenced by his request for feedback and his genuine listening.

Explaining the case for change, character modeling, and relationship building were prerequisites before Barry could pursue further teaching relative to coaching. Too often, leaders start with teaching. Employees will not accept education and grow as much as possible until the first three components of the model have been achieved.

The group was willing to grow because Barry had taken the time and carefully provided facts which created a logical case for change. Barry made sure that the case for change was developed through the involvement of the group. He proved to them that he had the character to be trusted and he developed a relationship with each of them. Later, the group used this case for change to explain their transition to employees. Their success depended upon their ability to make the case for change, show good character, build relationships, and teach employees.

PROACTIVELY PURSUE COACHING AND EMPOWERMENT OF SELF AND OTHER EMPLOYEES

Proactive pursuit means making decisions and taking actions based on beliefs and values. Why should leaders and employees prefer value-based decisions? Value-based decision making means that an employee selects from alternatives using their beliefs. Values are based on the impact choices have upon self-esteem and growth opportunities for employees. Otherwise, decisions become unpredictable. Inevitably, this creates fear in the workplace.

A northeastern university library staff adopted work groups to improve service to students and faculty and enhance the quality of work life for employees. Frank was a member of the work group responsible for computer-aided learning resources at the library. He and his group were expected to make a decision about the purchase of self-guided history software. Frank did not like the department head for history because they had become embroiled in a heated argument in the past. Because of this, Frank decided to oppose any ideas the history department would offer. The other members of the work group became aware of the conflict between the department head and Frank because of comments Frank made during discussions.

Frank was responsible for researching available software and making the purchase recommendation to the work group. The work group had selected Frank for this job because he was the most knowledgeable person in the liberal arts. In his recommendation to the work group, Frank selected the software that was the least acceptable to the history department. The work group asked Frank for additional reasons why the history department's recommendation should not be pursued. Frank's response was clearly based on emotions because his reasons were weak at best.

The work group selected the software package that was recommended by the history department. Because the work group and Frank's supervisor saw Frank as unpredictable and emotional in his decision making, Frank was passed over for future lead assignments. He failed to gain the respect of the work group. Despite countless efforts by work group members to help Frank make the transition to a values-based decision approach, they failed. Frank left the university because he felt that his opinions were not appreciated.

The bottom line of this section is that each employee needs to do whatever it takes to convince oneself that the pursuit of coaching and empowerment is best for the organization and other employees. Each employee's commitment to coaching and empowerment must be based on values, not emotions. Employees must see the value of coaching and empowerment for themselves, their leader, and the organization.

It is amazing to see organizations with better resources and stronger personnel than other organizations struggling to keep up with their competitors. These situations are reminiscent of a fishing story. A leader-turned-fisherman, Reese, tried hard every year to win the fishing tournament at his family reunion.

Similar to every other year, Reese was embarrassed by his showing. He caught tree limbs, old boots, and seaweed, but no fish. As he drove home from the reunion, he decided it was time to give up fishing—he was a failure. When he stopped at an old country store, he tossed his fishing pole in the trashcan before filling up his gas tank. When he went inside the store to pay for the gasoline, he spotted a weatherworn, old salt of a fisherman sitting beside a barrel filled with ice and soda bottles. The old fisherman had a pail full of fish sitting at his feet.

Reese walked across the room and struck up a conversation with the fisherman. He told the old fisherman about his less than stellar fishing expeditions, year after year.

The fisherman quietly looked across the room as if staring into the eyes of a guardian angel. The old man carefully weighed each and every word Reese poured forth. Finally, in desperation, Reese asked the old fisherman what his problem was.

Nodding ever so slowly, the old fisherman said, "You think that fishing is science. Not the case. Art, son, art. Just keep a sharp hook, steady line, and focus. Focus. Everyone gets the same number of bites. If you're focused on the right thing, you'll bring them in." With that, the fisherman reached down and gave Reese the pail of fish.

Reese rose, placed the pail firmly in his hand, and walked toward the door. The old fisherman, without looking over his shoulder, called to Reese, "And you won't catch fish with your pole in the trashcan."

Reese retrieved his fishing pole. He won the family reunion fishing contest the next year. Reese told the above story to all who would listen and he ended with the moral of the story: Telling is for today; empowering is for a lifetime.

Coaching and empowerment are like this story. Command for a day, Lead-Coach-Manage for a lifetime. Managing is telling employees what to do. Coaching is teaching employees how to do it. Without the proper focus, it is impossible to catch the fish that is biting. Coaching and empowerment make the difference between a good organization and an excellent organization. Leaders and employees must equally understand and proactively pursue coaching and empowerment. Leaders and employees must understand this in their heads and their hearts.

UNDERSTAND, SUPPORT, AND CARRY OUT EXPECTATIONS THE ORGANIZATION HAS FOR EMPLOYEES

Employees do not operate in a vacuum. The attitudes, behaviors, and work results of each employee affects other employees and the organization as a whole, either positively or negatively. All employees need to be aligned with the expectations of the organization. Otherwise, they will be counterproductive—they will not add value to the organization.

Employees must understand the expectations the organization has for them. Employees must clearly understand the answers to the following questions: What does the organization expect each employee will do to add value to the organization? How does the organization expect each employee will add value to the organization? What does the organization expect employees will do to carry out these expectations?

Oftentimes, leaders expect that employees know what they are supposed to do on the job because each employee has a job description. The problem is that the pace of change has exceeded the ability of leaders to provide clear and up-to-date definitions of the job. Also, job descriptions are becoming broader in scope and more vague because employees are expected to do more and expand their boundaries. Leaders must continuously communicate job expectations; employees must understand these expectations and use them on the job.

Jack was hired by a healthcare management firm to lead the care management program for their company. In addition to his product and process development responsibilities, Jack was supposed to supervise the staff of registered nurses (case managers) who managed workers compensation cases for client employers. The registered nurses would work with physicians and other clinical staff members involved in diagnosing and treating employees injured on the job to identify the most efficient way to treat employees and return them to work.

Following a couple of weeks on the job, Jack noticed there was growing friction among the case managers. Jack asked questions about what each case manager was doing and ways to improve their job and productivity. Several case managers told Jack that everyone would improve their productivity if three of the nurses were made to do their work. As Jack pried deeper, he found that three case managers were not working the full forty hours per week and dumping tasks for their own case work on other case managers.

This had been going on despite the knowledge of Jack's predecessor. Employees understood that it was a problem, but leadership was unwilling to set clear expectations for the three case managers as well as the others.

Jack called a meeting of all case managers for the purpose of setting clear expectations as their new leader. In preparation for the meeting, Jack outlined the expectations the organization had for the case managers using information from the company booklet and his conversations with each of the nurses.

The meeting began with Jack talking about the importance of expectations. He explained that job expectations are important because they clearly send a signal to each employee about what is expected on the job. Since Jack was new to this position, he talked about expectations he had of each case manager. He discussed how case managers should add value to the organization. It was emphasized repeatedly that case managers are paid a wage and provided good benefits because of the value they provide to the organization. The employee wins because of the wages paid to him or her. The organization wins because it has received increased value for the wages paid out. However, if the expectations of the employee are not met, it becomes a win-lose situation. The employee wins because he or she is paid a wage. However, the organization loses because it is paying wages for value that was not received. Not only is that situation bad for the organization, it is bad for other employees.

He went on to outline the expectations the organization had for the case managers. When he was finished, Jack asked the employees about each of the expectations. He was able to gauge whether employees understood the expectations by the feedback he received from them. Relative to one expectation, Jack specifically asked the employees to recount what they understood was expected of them. He did this because he did not feel they clearly understood the point. Following a few questions, all case managers agreed to pursue win-win relationships.

The following week Jack approached each nurse informally to gain feedback regarding the meeting and whether the information had changed the behaviors of the three nurses. He was pleased to find that two of the three nurses were no longer dumping work on other nurses. Over the next several weeks, the third nurse resigned.

Jack had made it clear that expectations must be understood and supported by each employee. The third nurse had decided she was not willing to meet those expectations and needed to pursue other employment. One month later, the remaining nurses had increased their productivity and attitudes improved because a win-win situation had been established.

Once employees understand what is expected of them on the job, they will need to understand how to meet those expectations. This is especially critical where the organization has added new leader roles and empowerment to the work environment. In this case, employees need to understand and support the different way leaders and employees are expected to interact. Employees must support the idea that they are taking on more responsibilities while leaders are changing their support behaviors. Otherwise, it will be difficult for a leader to effectively develop and support an employee.

A furniture manufacturer company implemented work groups and adopted new leader roles. Sally was a vice president who had come up through the ranks. She knew that the employees would support work groups and new leader roles if they clearly understood why they needed to change and how this affected the way they worked.

Sally asked the president of the company to meet with a group of leaders from her areas of responsibility and explain the reason for the change to work groups and new leader roles. The president shared the case for change with the employees which was similar to the approach laid out in the above section, "Be Willing to Grow and Be Empowered." However, the president related the case for change specifically to their job by emphasizing the need to increase finishing turnaround times and decrease costs. Work groups and new leader roles were underscored as the way to increase employee responsibility for the work and expand Sally's responsibilities to cover additional areas of work.

Finally, the president talked about how this was a win for employees because it gave them more input about how to do the work and a win for the company because it would increase productivity while decreasing costs. Sally showed her support for the transition by talking about her nervousness, understanding of the reasons for change, and her commitment to make the transition.

The initial response to the meeting was positive; however, employees were concerned that this was a program to dump responsibility on them and diminish Sally's support for their area. Expecting this reaction, Sally had scheduled the work group training to take place immediately following the meeting with the president.

Expectations and skills for work groups were outlined and discussed during the training sessions. Sally joined the group training sessions to interact and agree to expectations for support from her. At the end of the session each employee and Sally signed a document outlining how they would work together in the new environment.

After several months into the transition, the group was doing well. The employees made the transition because Sally took the time to share why they needed to change. And everyone took the time and made the commitment to change in a specific way. The employees understood the expectations. And—probably most important—management asked them for their commitment.

FIRST LOOK UPON OTHERS FAVORABLY

Too often, leaders negatively interpret employee actions or inactions when they could just as easily be interpreted in a more positive light. This is a trait that is too often shared by employees. Leaders' actions are often interpreted negatively by employees when the opposite may be true. For example, a leader may greet a group of employees in the morning. One employee might say, "This is going to be a tough day. Did you see how he had very little to say to us today?" The fact of the matter may be that the leader was preoccupied with a problem. Or, the greeting was the same as always. The only difference was an employee's interpretation.

With change, employees need to give leaders the benefit of the doubt. Employees need to recognize that leaders generally want to do what is right. Leaders don't always know what is right. Mistakes will be made during the transition to new leader roles and employee support is necessary. A leader may even have a momentary relapse toward control and command management. Employees need to trust leaders.

Both leaders and employees should first look upon others favorably. In other words, they need to view the other's actions or behaviors in a more favorable light.

Nicholas was a new employee hired in the product development area of a healthcare company. He had been given responsibility for a project that required several support staff. Nicholas had scheduled an important Monday meeting with outside clients. The meeting would determine whether the project would continue or be terminated. When the morning of the important meeting arrived, Nicholas was nowhere to be found. Worse yet, the agendas for the meeting and the report could not be found.

One of the support staff complained that the junior whiz kid had let them down. Another employee looked at the situation differently wondering whether his old car wouldn't start or whether it broke down.

Another employee arrived to let the group know Nicholas' mother was severely injured in an automobile accident in California. Nicholas left a message for the group before he raced to the airport to catch a flight to California. He left the materials where the group could find them in time for the meeting.

The meeting went on and the product was approved for development. For Nicholas, the news was less heartening when he reached California. His mother had died just a few hours before he reached the hospital.

When he arrived back home, the support staff showed their appreciation for Nicholas' efforts to support them during a difficult time. From that day forward, Nicholas was respected as a leader. More important, staff members learned that they needed to judge a person favorably instead of jumping to negative conclusions.

LEARN, LEARN, LEARN

Organizations are like plants: they grow when properly nourished. Employees are like plants, too. Employees grow and add value to organizations where learning is clearly expected and opportunities are provided. Employees must expect they will be challenged by a learning organization.

What is a learning organization and what does it have to do with employees? A learning organization is one that provides resources to employees to support their continued growth in skills and knowledge and where leaders encourage, support, and model learning, creativity, and innovation. In a learning organization, each employee has a responsibility to learn, grow, and add value to the rest of the organization through his or her expanded knowledge and skills. An employee must be open-minded, ready to shift paradigms, and committed to being objective. Otherwise, an employee is through learning, and the organization is through. Competitive advantage is the ability of an organization to outlearn the competition.

Employees bring value to an organization because of their ability to learn, not just the knowledge they hold. The ability to learn is more important long term than knowledge because the work-world is changing rapidly. What was learned five years ago is largely out-dated.

An organization will need to use various methods and approaches to expand employees' knowledge and skills. Various methods and approaches are required because employees will respond differently to learning opportunities.

If learning is important for continued success, how is a commitment to learning instilled in all employees? A case must be made for such a commitment. Such was the situation for Terry, who purchased a publishing firm that had been very popular and prosperous in the 1970s and 1980s. The firm suffered financial losses and dwindling readership following the 1980s because it failed to adapt to the market. From conversations Terry had with individual employees, part of the problem seemed to be a lack of innovation and learning. As he probed deeper, Terry found the firm had not offered learning opportunities to employees. The employees became stagnant and ideas stale.

Terry carefully explained to the employees gathered at their first operations meeting that without growth in knowledge and skills, the organization would not survive. Terry then shared with them the organization's financial trends which were very dismal. He followed the firm's financial trends with information about the industry leaders. The information clearly showed the importance of several factors including a commitment to learning resources.

Terry told the employees that if the organization survived, it would take a commitment on everyone's part. It would require a commitment to learning. The publishing firm would have to learn how to succeed in a changing industry. Before the meeting ended, Terry asked for their commitment to this goal.

The employees were visibly shaken by his comments. One employee, who worked over twenty-five years for the company, stood up and said he wasn't going to let the company fail. He said he would make the commitment if Terry made the commitment.

Terry thanked him for his support. One by one, employees nodded. The organization made a major commitment to learning resources in addition to new product development. The learning opportunities were carefully planned to coincide with opportunities for employees to use the new skills and knowledge. For mid-level leaders, Terry required them to use their new knowledge by teaching the material to their direct reports. He had learned that there was no better way to understand and apply new knowledge and skills than to teach the material. Terry's firm faced a steep uphill battle but they have turned the corner because they were willing to learn, learn, learn.

UNDERSTAND AND IMPROVE THE BIG O
(LARGER ORGANIZATION)

Leonard, a novice hunter, went small game hunting late in the afternoon. He decided to try a new hunting ground in a forest that was unfamiliar to him. After two hours of hunting, Leonard was tired, thirsty, and lost. He had wandered deeper into the forest and lost track of the path he had followed. At first, he casually tried to find his path to retrace his steps. As dusk began to descend, Leonard started to panic, hastily looking for a familiar tree or stump.

Leonard was lost, cold, and weary. He lay down to rest, fearing the worst. Seven hours later, Leonard was found asleep by a farm-boy. The boy led Leonard to the edge of the forest. To Leonard's astonishment, only two hundred yards away from where Leonard slept, stood a shopping center complete with a convenience store, laundry, and video rental shop. All the time, Leonard was on the edge of civilization but without his bearings.

Too often, leaders and employees are lost in the organization's forest. They are unable to understand how their area and roles fit within the overall organization. Despite this problem, few might see the need to understand the fit of their area and roles to the overall organization.

In a changed environment where new leader roles and empowerment thrive, both leaders and employees must understand and appreciate how their areas and roles fit within the overall organization. The overall organization is referred to here as the "Big O." The employees' area within the organization is referred to as the "Little o." Without this level of understanding, leaders, employees, and organizations are unaligned. They are out of sync. Leaders, employees, and organizations are like three arrows pointing in different directions. Without the appropriate alignment, it is purely coincidental if leaders and employees improve the organization.

How do leaders facilitate this understanding? Two elements are needed: mission/vision and strategic initiatives of the organization. The sharing of an organization's mission and vision is a good place to start. These statements should provide employees with a basic foundation for understanding the organization and its direction. It is also important to share with all employees the basic strategic direction or initiatives of the organization and the reasons for this journey.

The expectation that employees will improve the "Big O" is the recognition that jobs should only exist where they add value to the organization. If a job does not add value to the organization, leaders should strongly question the need for that position. This expectation can be emphasized where organizations create critical success factors and expect that all employees will show how their efforts have contributed to these factors. In other words, an organization may create an expectation that it will increase overall productivity by 5 percent over a one year period. All employees should be able to show they have improved the organization by enhancing productivity through their specific improvements.

MAINTAIN OR ENHANCE QUALITY DURING TIMES OF SIGNIFICANT CHANGE

Significant change requires an enormous amount of resources. As a result, it is easy to let the quality of the core business deteriorate. Employees need to create a balanced focus on the transition and maintenance/enhancement of core business quality. Employees frequently ask how they can find the time and energy to focus both on transition and maintenance of the core business. This can be done where employees focus on the right things to do. Too often, the workday includes tasks or projects that do not add value to the organization. Employees need to reexamine what is important and what takes priority in the maintenance of business and the transition.

A regional restaurant chain concentrated its efforts on growth while allowing customer service to suffer. Whitney had taken over her father's bakery. She found a need for specialty breads and bakery goods in a sizable metropolitan market. Early efforts were concentrated on quality products and customer service. As the popularity of the restaurant grew, Whitney began to open up other stores. Employees at the original store were involved in all of the new store openings because the main store served as the main supplier of product. Over time, employees concentrated efforts on increasing the volume of product to ship to the other sites.

Whitney began to notice a decline in sales at the original site and less vibrant sales at the new stores. From customer surveys, she noticed that people were not grading the quality of the product as highly as before. She spent more time working with the staff in the original store and observing activities. Whitney discovered that employees were so concerned about meeting the higher volumes to support the other stores they were no longer providing service to the customer as was previously done. Product quality also suffered due to the narrow focus on higher productivity.

Recognizing this negative trend, Whitney placed expansion plans on hold and got back to the basics. She spent time with employees at the main store emphasizing customer service. Also, the staff was engaged in discussions about the difficulties of expanding while maintaining product quality. Ideas were provided during these sessions that could be used to improve service levels and product quality.

A year later, Whitney found the customer surveys were exceeding previous highs and product quality was at its peak. Employees were better able to deal with expansion and maintenance because they had discussed and identified what was important. Employees gained a better balance.

HELP THE LEADER GROW

Leaders need help, too. They are normally ill prepared for this dramatic change in focus, role, and skills.

Employees in an empowered environment are expected to provide constructive feedback to leaders. This runs contrary to the traditional command and control management approach that was based on the premise that leaders had all the answers. Leaders need to know the right questions, but they shouldn't be expected to have all of the answers.

A leader needs help through constructive feedback, both positive and negative. Leaders cannot maximize their skills without constructive feedback from employees. The bottom line for each employee is to help his or her leader grow.

A health and life insurance company was undergoing a cultural change following the hiring of a new president, Rod. The previous president had been with the company for most of his career while the new recruit was brought into the company from a larger competitor. His style and approach was less bureaucratic and more open.

During the first meeting of senior leaders, Rod asked each leader to take out a clean sheet of paper. He asked them to write down five headings in a vertical column: who we are, what is expected, where we are headed, how we will reach our goals, and how we are doing. Rod asked each of them to keep that list and grade his efforts based on his first ninety days. At each monthly meeting, Rod reminded the group that he wanted them to keep a scorecard regarding his performance on the five items.

At the end of the first quarter, Rod walked into the senior staff meeting, took off his coat and tie, and sat down with a notepad. He asked them to provide constructive criticism about how well he was doing on the five categories.

Rod had asked one of the senior leaders prior to the meeting to offer some comments. The senior leader shared a situation that had arisen during a meeting held earlier in the day. He emphasized the importance Rod placed on feedback.

Rod thanked the senior leader for his comments and asked others to pinpoint areas for improvement.

Several leaders said that Rod's style in a meeting was much different than the style used in the past. They didn't know what was expected of them in meetings. Rod thanked them and admitted that he could sense leaders were not comfortable but wasn't sure of the reasons. He said that he was going to discuss expectations at the start of each meeting.

At the end of the meeting, Rod realized that he had attained two goals. He had gotten the leaders to critically examine a situation and offer open and honest feedback. Second, he had received information that helped him improve his meeting style. The company continued to improve because Rod had created a clear expectation that employees would help him grow.

SO, WHAT'S THE POINT?

Achievement of organization success is a team effort. A Leader-Coach-Manager alone is necessary but not sufficient because employees must understand and fulfill expectations of them. The fulfillment of these expectations is significantly increased where leaders explain the case for change, model good character, build relationships, and teach.

Role 6   ## INTERVENE

The Only Place Where Agreement Comes Before Conflict Is in the Dictionary

FOR MOST LEADERS, the intervention role is like a new puzzle of a familiar scene or object. The puzzle scene is familiar, but the cut and size of the puzzle pieces are different and confusing. The intervention role requires a major paradigm shift—new skills and new responsibilities for both leaders and employees. Rather than create a new term to replace the word "intervention," leaders need to recognize the new definition and change their paradigms. This role addresses a new way of thinking about intervention and how it benefits both leaders and employees.

INTERVENTION IS LIKE A RIFLE TARGET

In the past, leaders hovered over the shoulders of employees telling them how to do the job. This was the traditional intervention role and employees disliked it because it did not provide freedom to create and make their own decisions. It became the antithesis of empowerment. Leaders, on the other hand, are comfortable with the term intervention because they misperceive it as the traditional command and control approach (tell employees what to do and how to do it) used for the last one hundred years.

The new intervention role is where leaders either correct inappropriate behavior or reinforce appropriate behavior of employees. "Punish" is the last resort in the new intervention definition. Intervention is a tool to help improve employee focus upon organizational objectives. In fact, a phrase

131

that best describes the intent of the intervention role of a leader is "learning interaction."

A learning interaction is a two-way, proactive approach. It is used in both positive and negative intervention situations to help others grow. Leaders help employees develop appropriate behaviors to handle matters. Learning interaction does not mean leaders are telling employees what to do and specifically how to do it. Instead, a learning interaction is focused on the behavior or how things are approached. Leaders offer help or suggestions without taking responsibility for a task or project.

Intervention is also a balancing act. Intervention balances employee freedom and organization boundaries. Some employees desire absolute freedom; however, organizations need to provide boundaries in order to properly predict outcomes. This is shown in the Balancing Freedom and Boundaries diagram where intervention is the fulcrum balancing both ends of the beam.

Contrary to what employees may feel, intervention is a friend of the organization and employees because it is an alignment tool. In other words, intervention reinforces behavior where employees are working on the right things and committed to implementation. Intervention also provides open and honest communication where employees are using inappropriate behavior or working on the wrong things. Intervention adjusts behavior to better align actions.

Balancing Freedom and Boundaries

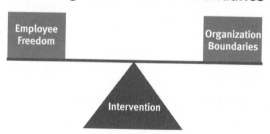

A helpful analogy is a rifle range. A rifle, when fired, will strike a target in a random fashion as shown in Intervention-Alignment A. If a leader fails to intervene and help employees, the situation will continue to appear as Intervention-Alignment A. Intervention-Alignment B shows what happens where rifle shots are adjusted to hit the bull's eye. The bullets strike closer to the bull's eye in B than in A. A similar analogy can be applied to employee behaviors. Behaviors vary on a daily basis. Intervention, used in an effective manner, will diminish the amount of variation in performance while providing freedom to employees to exercise their creativity while maintaining organizational boundaries.

Intervention-Alignment

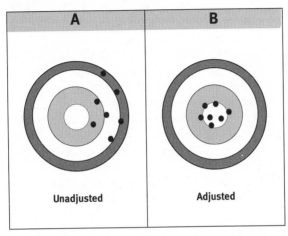

A	B
Unadjusted	Adjusted

In a large manufacturing organization, leaders on each management level agreed to attend workshops twice a month for a year to improve their skills, knowledge, and commitment related to new leader roles. New leader roles were considered by senior management to be the missing ingredient to attain an empowered environment. Therefore, they believed it was important to learn and apply the information shared at the workshops.

Following several workshop sessions with the top two management levels, some of the leaders were not really making a good faith effort to learn the material. Most leaders did not participate. Few leaders had taken the time to read the materials prior to the sessions. Instructors were offering too many of the answers to questions asked of the group while most leaders sat emotionless in their chairs. The need for intervention was apparent.

At the next workshop session, leaders were asked to individually complete a written test regarding material covered and hand in the answers with or without their name attached. Despite liberal grading of the test papers, most of the group scored far less than seventy of one hundred possible points. The results were shared with the group and they were asked whether these were acceptable scores. The first reaction was silence and astonishment. However, the group agreed this level of underachievement was unacceptable.

The group was asked what action should be taken to ensure effective use of resources and to maximize learning. Did the approach to these sessions need to be changed? Are the sessions necessary? Once again, the room was silent. Then, one-by-one, leaders shared their thoughts on how to improve. Interestingly enough, the suggestions provided by the group were focused on a change in their own behaviors. They stated emphatically that the workshop sessions should continue. However, they recognized they must be held personally accountable. They agreed to read the materials, interact in the sessions, and be tested periodically to provide a progress point for them.

Leaders' behaviors changed following the session. Most leaders interacted during the remaining workshop sessions and they read the materials before the workshop sessions. Because of intervention, the group understood their shortcomings, discussed the options to solve problems, recognized how their behavior needed to change, and dramatically increased their level of ownership.

The above story illustrates the purpose of intervention. The group was neither punished nor told how to deal with the problem. Learning interaction was created which encouraged group members to identify and correct problem behaviors. Patience was a prerequisite. While some group members may have considered the test as punishment, no individual was threatened, no self-esteem diminished, and no leader demoted. In sharp contrast, if a command and control approach had been used, group members would have been told what the problem was and how to solve it. The outcome from such a command and control approach would have likely been minimal commitment from the leaders. Instead, a collaborative approach was used with leaders to see the light and take appropriate action. Because intervention was used instead of command and control, the leaders took responsibility for the problem and decided how they would specifically "fix" the problem.

SO, WHAT'S THE POINT?
Intervention is a learning interaction. Leaders use intervention to correct inappropriate behaviors or recognize appropriate behaviors. Intervention is a fulcrum which balances the employee's creative freedom and the need for organization boundaries.

IS INTERVENTION JUST ANOTHER WORD FOR INTERFERENCE?

Intervention is not a synonym for interference. Interference is defined in most dictionaries as *to come into collision or conflict*. Intervention, on the other hand, is commonly defined as *to come between or to modify some action*. Intervention is focused on achieving proper behavior by lending a helping hand.

In contrast, interference is focused on helping employees develop the methods and actions to arrive at a desired end point. Interference is a word commonly associated with the traditional command and control management style.

Jennifer was a regional leader for a children's clothing and furniture retail chain. The company made a major commitment to develop management to increase the productivity levels of employees and enhance customer satisfaction. During the development process, Jennifer was personally involved participating in all sessions. One of Jennifer's leaders, Sally, took the same training as part of the first group. Following the first group session, Jennifer was interested in seeing how Sally fared in comparison with leaders who had yet to take the training.

Jennifer observed the quarterly outcomes from Linda and Sally's areas following Sally's training session. Jennifer used employee survey results, observations on the job, and customer satisfaction responses. The employee survey results showed that Linda's employees did not have ownership of their job and were not motivated. Sally's employees, on the other hand, were much improved when compared to previous surveys. Sally's employees exhibited high motivation, took their jobs seriously, and had a strong allegiance to the company. Sally had shown dramatic improvement over previous reviews.

At first, Jennifer was puzzled by the results because she did not expect such a major difference between the two leaders. On the surface, both Linda and Sally had similar skill levels and past management experience. Jennifer decided to use observation and feedback to gain a better understanding of the differences between the two leaders. She visited the stores operated by the leaders and spoke informally with employees about their jobs and how they were working with others. She also spent time watching the two leaders working with employees.

Sally was using the intervention role taught during the development sessions. When she encountered an inappropriate behavior, she would create an opportunity for an employee to "discover" and "acknowledge" the problem. This seemed to work best because an employee was not defensive and was more open to exploring the situation. Sally helped an employee "discover" the problem behavior by using customer survey results, employee survey results, and questioning techniques. Once an employee acknowledged an inappropriate behavior, Sally would use questions to help identify the preferred behaviors. Sally concentrated on changing inappropriate behaviors. However, she was careful not to take responsibility for an employee's task and how he or she performed those tasks.

When Sally used intervention for appropriate behaviors, she would reinforce an employee's behavior. Most often, Sally used an informal setting because she needed to provide the recognition immediately following the behavior in order to maximize reinforcement. When intervening with an employee, Sally would provide a description of the specific behavior, praise for using the behavior, and reasons why the behavior was appropriate. Every intervention for appropriate behaviors included feedback. Sally would listen to the employee to answer two questions: did the employee understand what Sally was saying and was the praise received positively?

In contrast, Linda approached inappropriate behaviors in the traditional manner. Once she discovered an employee acting inappropriately, she would meet with the employee and identify the problem behavior. An employee had no opportunity to "discover" the inappropriate behavior. An employee would become defensive and would not take ownership of the situation. Then, Linda would tell the employee what was expected from him/her in the future. Linda specifically outlined how the employee would perform a task in the future. Linda only used feedback from an employee to affirm that Linda's solution and prescribed approach was being used.

Sally and Linda exhibited the differences between intervention and interference. Sally intervened to help modify an employee's behavior, not how they pursued a task. Linda interfered to identify how a task would be completed. Interference robbed employees of any creativity while substituting micromanagement. Linda's approach created "inter-fearance." Employees became fearful and defensive. Employees were not motivated to take ownership of their job and to be innovative. Intervention provided more opportunity for employees to use creativity on the job because changes were behavior focused, not task oriented. Also, intervention allowed an employee to "discover" inappropriate behaviors. Interference did not allow employees to think on their own about behaviors. Instead, it immediately placed employees on the defensive.

SO, WHAT'S THE POINT?
Intervention is not "inter-fearance." Intervention focuses on employee responsibility, discovery, and development while interference is focused on leader responsibility, discovery, and direction.

THE FIFTH DIMENSIONS

Intervention is a key leader's role designed to maximize each employee's contribution to business success. It directly impacts the quality of work. The Dimensions of Intervention diagram provides the basic model for understanding the intervention role. The diagram is comprised of five major dimensions: what, how, when, who, and where. Leaders must understand each of the five dimensions to be effective interventionists.

Dimensions of Intervention

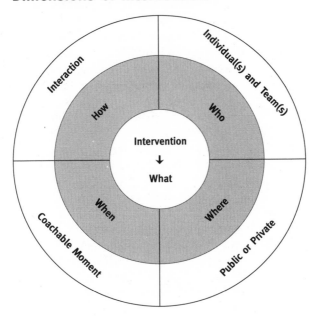

The "what" component of the diagram represents the situations where intervention is considered. This is where inappropriate employee behaviors must be corrected or appropriate employee behaviors must be rewarded.

One of the most critical components of the Dimensions of Intervention is "how." The mainstay of this component is interaction. Interaction includes eight basic points which a leader should consider.

When should a leader intervene? The answer is the Coachable Moment which indicates the appropriate time for intervention. A model of the same name is provided to answer "when."

Is intervention used only with individuals or only with teams? Intervention focuses on both individuals and teams. The "who" component of the wheel addresses this issue.

The "where" component of the Dimensions of Intervention addresses the proper location for use of intervention skills. This component addresses such issues as—is intervention a public or private interaction, should the interaction take place on the employee's own turf, and does intervention require a formal or informal meeting with employees.

Each component of the Dimensions of Intervention is defined, examples provided, and tips offered in the remainder of this role.

IF YOU DON'T WANT A FLAT TIRE, USE THE INTERVENTION WHEEL

Consider the challenge of raising children. Some days they can be like Dr. Jekyll and Mr. Hyde—sweet and angelic one minute, and devious the next. On these days, we recognized that intervention could be used almost every minute. However, intervention for inappropriate behaviors would not be effective if used too often and not balanced with freedom.

If used too often, intervention can become interference. It's like the referee in a football game. Both players and fans do not appreciate football games where referees are interrupting the flow of the game every other play. Fans can usually be heard in these games yelling in chorus, "Let them play ball, ref!"

Intervention can become interference if a leader "over-referees" a situation. Constant interruptions by a leader to address inappropriate behaviors will be interpreted by employees as manipulation and micromanagement, despite the type of management behavior used to intervene. Employees will likely equate the constant interruptions to traditional command and control management which was founded on interference. Therefore, interventions related to inappropriate behaviors must be carefully selected.

Interventions for appropriate behaviors are rarely used too often. Complaints from employees because leaders have reinforced behaviors or praised them too often are uncommon. The key to interventions for appropriate behaviors is to intervene at the right time, in the right place, and in the right way.

INTERVENE OR WHAT?

If leaders should not intervene in all situations where inappropriate or appropriate behaviors arise, how do leaders decide whether to intervene or not? The Intervention Wheel Focus Areas was created for leaders to use as a tool in deciding whether intervention is appropriate. This is one of the most important tools for a leader because intervention is a defining moment for successful leaders. Because traditional command and control management was strongly based on leader interruptions and intense involvement, inappropriate interventions by a leader are likely to be interpreted as the continuation of traditional management. Leaders can be ineffective at the outset because of poor intervention skills.

There are eight major situations where intervention is strongly advised:

1. Self-esteem
2. Legal issues

3. Safety
4. Customer/supplier relationships
5. Financial cost
6. Employee focus
7. Employee capability and ownership to perform
8. Other good works

Self-Esteem

Have you ever seen employees who no longer believe in themselves? They are unable to make decisions, show confidence, or be positive about their work. They are the walking wounded who decrease the ability of an organization to respond to problems and grasp opportunities. Employee self-esteem is another important component of organizational success.

Intervention is an important skill because, if done correctly, it safeguards and enhances the self-esteem of employees. If a task or project has been successful, intervention, when timed appropriately, can reinforce employees' use of similar behavior in the future. If a major task or project appears destined to fail, intervention is essential. If an employee is steadily losing confidence as a project deteriorates, intervention is needed. If a task or project places an employee in conflict with others and drains that employee of any remaining self-esteem, intervention must be called upon to strengthen their confidence. Otherwise, both the employee and organization suffer.

Eric and his team were star performers at a prefabricated home construction company. They were given an assignment to implement a new fastening device for the exterior walls of prefabricated homes. Because of his new product knowledge, vast experience in exterior wall construction, and desire to take on more responsibility, Eric was a clear choice for the leader position. However, despite Eric's experience, knowledge, and owner-ship of the project, the project was not proceeding as expected. Other employees were not responding to Eric's efforts because the new fastening device meant they had to change the final production step which they had been using for several years. In addition, the fastening materials arrived late from the supplier and harsh winter weather decreased productivity.

Altogether, Eric's spirited way of working disappeared and he was becoming less and less confident. He told his supervisor, Terry, that he had let the company down.

Terry responded that a job is not just what an employee has inside. A successful job depends on a number of things outside of the company that cannot be controlled. He added that good employees placed in an impossible situation will appear to be failures and become convinced they are failures. Terry reassured Eric that he was given a tougher assignment than expected but he was the right choice. In addition to his comments, Terry made a special effort to observe Eric using appropriate behaviors and to recognize his efforts. It was important for Terry to recognize Eric only for legitimate reasons. Otherwise, Eric's self-esteem could be further diminished believing management felt he was a failure and they were only trying to shore up any remaining ounce of self-esteem.

Should Terry remain at a distance from the project and allow Eric to learn from the situation or should Terry intervene to a greater extent and get the project on the right track? The situation continued to deteriorate and Terry decided to intervene because there was a high likelihood that the external problems were not going to improve sufficiently to allow Eric to succeed. Since this was the first major assignment for Eric, Terry thought that Eric needed some assistance to accomplish the project and avoid failure which would surely diminish his already sagging confidence level.

The decision Terry made was very subjective, not objective. He had to read the feelings of Eric and decide whether Eric would rebound without any intervention. What weighed heavily in Terry's decision was the uncharacteristic, steady decline in Eric's confidence level and the fact this was Eric's first major assignment.

How should Terry approach the conversation with Eric? What follows is a suggested approach that protects Eric's self-esteem.

"Good morning, Eric. As usual, I see you are on top of it, hitting it hard," said Terry as he entered Eric's office.

"Morning, Terry. I'm not sure I'm on top of it or on the bottom of it," responded Eric with a waning smile.

"I have been noticing your handling of the team regarding the new fastening device. You have done a good job being very clear and up front with the team about the importance of the project. It is good that you have been forthright. I think we all realize that this has been a tougher change for the team to make than what we thought. One thing that may be of help is to involve senior management in some of your meetings. This will allow you to emphasize the importance of this project and that the organization must make this change in order to survive," offered Terry.

"I sure can use all the help I can get. I've made a mess."

"You have not made a mess. You've inherited a situation that requires different behavior on your part. You need to find what connects best with this team. You've tried to use the approach where you are at the point on this issue and the team hasn't budged. That is no reflection on your skills or abilities. It just means that for some reason, the team is unwilling to respond. Also, you want to preserve your credibility with the team in order to be effective on the remaining steps of your project. Senior management is here to take some of that heat and help you to remove those tougher barriers. You need to consider whether you need to ask the president to join a meeting with the team or some other individual in senior management. What do you think?" Terry paused waiting for some signs from Eric.

"Well, you're right about the team being stuck in the mud. No matter what I do at this point, we don't seem to be going anywhere. I guess you're encouraging me to shake things up a bit. Right?" Eric was noticeably more comfortable with the conversation.

"That's a really good way to look at it," Terry responded. "However, I don't want you to do something that you're not comfortable with, because it will show and the team will pick up on it. So, where are we?"

"I like the idea of using someone from senior management for one meeting because I'm out of ideas. After that meeting, I can reassess whether we are moving ahead. Then, I can decide whether it is necessary to have senior management in other meetings. I guess I was starting to take this barrier too personally," said Eric.

"It sounds like we're in agreement, right? You'll consider the best timing and who from senior management should be used in a team meeting to shake things up a bit. Does that sound reasonable?" Terry inquired following a review of their agreement.

"Sounds good. Now I do feel like I'm on top of it," offered Eric.

"Great. You'll get there, Eric. I have no doubts," said Terry as he shook Eric's hand.

Following the meeting, Terry observed the situation. As they discussed, Eric set up a team meeting including a senior leader. All feedback from the meeting indicated that the team was moving ahead and Eric's credibility was firmly in place. Several days later, Terry made sure he stopped by Eric's office to find out how the project was proceeding. The feedback he received from Eric was very positive, indicating that the barriers had been removed and the team was moving forward. More importantly, Eric's self-esteem was intact and growing. Terry used the opportunity to praise Eric for his willingness to consider a change in strategy and to remain committed to the project despite all of the barriers.

Intervention related to self-esteem problems are the most difficult situations to diagnose because leaders may need to interpret feelings and estimate how the situation may positively or negatively affect an employee in the long run. In some situations, leaders must be futurists, guessing whether the situation may improve sufficiently to maintain or restore lost self-esteem. These decisions are especially difficult because concern normally is associated with the self-esteem of leaders and other employees. In other words, the failure of a fellow employee may lower the confidence level of a group of employees ("If Eric can't succeed, no one from our team can").

Legal Issues

Oftentimes, employees working on projects or tasks will encounter an unexpected legal issue. Where they have effectively dealt with a legal problem, intervention is appropriate to recognize their successful handling of the problem. Legal issues can also increase risk or force leaders to intervene in a given situation. Some examples of legal situations may include a new law affecting a project, threat of a legal action, or operational issues which may become legally entangled.

Let's suppose in our previous story about Eric and the construction company that Eric's fellow employees were concerned about their job futures because of downsizing in their industry. Once Eric started talking about a change in the final manufacturing step, employees began to seriously consider unionization. They interpreted Eric's actions as orchestrated by management to cut jobs. Once employees began to discuss unionization, rumors quickly spread to Eric's supervisor, Terry.

During the fifteen years that Terry had been with the company, they never had a union shop. Terry saw a union as a major threat because it would increase the cost of doing business and decrease the company's flexibility in scheduling and work assignments. Despite Terry's confidence in Eric, he recognized that Eric could not handle the union matter because of his lack of knowledge in this area and his relationship to the team.

First, Terry met with Eric. Eric stated that he was hearing some of the union rumors and that these rumors should be taken seriously. Terry used the opportunity to specifically explain why Eric's behaviors could lead to potential legal problems. Eric admitted that he did not have the background to deal with this issue and needed to obtain assistance.

Terry suggested that human resources get involved in order to keep Eric focused on the fastening device project while legally interacting with his team. If Eric was approached by an employee or asked to comment on union related matters, he was advised of legal *do*s and *don't*s. Terry also offered to meet with the group to reemphasize the purpose of the project and place proper focus on the project.

Eric was relieved to hear that he would not be the point person to deal with the union issue. Terry met with the employees to discuss the reasons for the new fastener device and a change in the construction process. He noted that he was hearing a number of concerns about the new fastener devices and the changes made in the construction process. He offered why Eric was not the right one to address these issues.

The employees slowly began to ask questions about the changes. By the end of the meeting, they were more comfortable with the new approach. Because Terry intervened as soon as rumors began, he was able to put to rest any concerns employees had about the changes. Also, Eric's credibility with the team remained intact and unblemished.

When compared to self-esteem, legal issues are easier to diagnose and less subjective. However, employees may not realize that intervention is necessary because they may not appreciate the legal issues affecting the matter. In the union example, legal counsel may not want a leader to communicate the unionization situation as the reason for intervention. In these situations, what do you do? It is important to be as up front as possible. Otherwise, employees may interpret an intervention as a crackdown by management. In the example above, it seemed appropriate to communicate that it was unfair to put Eric in the middle on such an issue because he was not involved in the initial decision. The best advice is to seek legal counsel, develop a business solution that maintains the confidence of employees in management, and approach the matter in the best legal manner. It is during these tense times that credibility can be effective to keep issues, not emotions, in clear focus for all employees.

Safety

Situations may arise that could affect the health and safety of the community, customers, or employees. Oftentimes, a safety issue has legal consequences. Examples of safety issues which may require intervention include successful resolution or handling of a safety issue, newly discovered product safety problems, potential disasters which may affect the company, employees at risk because of actions of other employees, or the discovery of new information which indicates that employees and/or community have been injured or may face possible injury.

Let's suppose in the story about Eric and the construction company that Eric received a preliminary report from a product safety governmental agency that the new fastening device to be used may be unsafe. Some recent accidents in similar companies indicated that the fastening devices were malfunctioning and caused a number of injuries. When Eric received the information, he called the governmental agency to discuss the matter. They indicated that the information was preliminary but the investigations seemed to heavily point in this direction. Following this, Eric contacted the internal legal counsel for his company to discuss the issues, share the information, and gain input regarding the risks associated with continued use of the fastening devices and alternatives open to the organization. With this information, Eric outlined on paper the issue, potential state resolution, alternatives that the company could use, and recommendations for handling the matter.

Armed with information from the state agency and legal counsel, Eric presented the information to Terry to make sure he was aware of the ongoing investigations and potential liability. Terry was both impressed with Eric's handling of the matter and with the substantial risks involved.

Terry began his intervention by recognizing Eric's excellent procedure used in addressing the problem. Quickly, Terry assessed whether this issue was of such magnitude that additional intervention on his part was necessary. Terry stated that when Eric was asked to head up the project, no information indicated that there were any safety issues related to the new fastening devices. Because Eric was put in the position of leading this project, Terry recognized the need to intervene, explain the matter to employees, and reiterate that Eric was asked to lead this project before any information became available on this safety issue. Terry recognized that Eric was put in a difficult position and the company should take the questions and any employee anger, not Eric.

In this situation, it was important for Terry to assure Eric that he was not asked to lead a flawed project from the start. This was a trust issue. It was also important that Eric clearly understood why Terry would need to intervene and that Eric had appropriately handled the project.

Terry discussed the matter thoroughly with Eric. As promised, Terry and Eric worked with the team to discontinue use of the new fastening device and switch to another product that was safer. Terry praised Eric for his effective handling of the matter.

Intervention related to safety issues usually requires immediate response by management. Because of the gravity of the safety issue, intervention is normally not questioned especially where sufficient information is provided to employees. Intervention in these situations is seen as management protecting employees, the organization, and the community from possible danger.

Customer/Supplier Relationships

Strong relationships with customers/suppliers may save an organization from disaster or failure. Long-standing relationships between organizations and customers can help an organization to weather a competitive storm or business crisis. Organizations will not survive without the interest and support of customers to purchase a product or service. Therefore, intervention is appropriate where customer/supplier relationships are at risk. Intervention is also appropriate where employees have successfully developed or strengthened customer/supplier relationships.

Let's suppose that the story about the prefabricated homes included another factor. Fred, the primary supplier of structural supplies for Eric's company, was upset. He had always dealt with the president of the company or Terry when negotiating supply contracts. Because of Eric's new leader role, he was negotiating with Fred instead of Terry or the company president. Terry was told by reliable sources that Fred was considering steering more of his product toward another construction firm because Fred felt that the company president or Terry should have been dealing with him. If this happened, Terry's company could possibly lose capacity to fill at least thirty percent of its orders. There were no other suppliers that could meet the quality and delivery specifications required by the company.

There was no doubt in Terry's mind that he had to intervene to mend fences. However, Terry needed to consider how Eric would feel and how others would view the situation.

Following careful consideration of all alternatives, Terry approached Eric in regard to Fred. Terry explained that Eric was doing an excellent job but Fred was a proud man who wanted to be wined and dined by the president of the company. Before Eric's emotions started to work on him, Terry asked him to accompany the president to the dinner with Fred. He also explained how devastating the loss of this supplier could be to the company, decreasing the number of jobs by 10 percent. Once Eric thought about the situation, he understood that the politics of this relationship had nothing to do with the way he was handling the situation.

Terry and Eric overcame a potentially destructive situation for the company. Fred felt better about the working relationship following the dinner meeting with Eric and the company president. Because of the intervention technique used by Terry, he was able to intervene while maintaining the self-esteem of Eric. Terry had saved an important supplier relationship and maintained the self-esteem of a valuable employee.

Financial Cost

Employees grow when they encounter and work on problems. However, the financial price of a mistake, in certain situations, may be too great for an organization. In these situations, a leader must intervene. Some examples of financial cost situations that require intervention include employee decisions that are too costly for the company, an unexpected financial crisis for the organization which requires a scaleback in plans, unexpected costs which require management expertise to control/lead, and employee mistakes that would be too costly for the company to risk.

Intervention is also appropriate where an employee has successfully dealt with a difficult financial issue. These situations can prove to be good examples for other employees to deal with financial issues.

Continuing with our story involving Eric and the prefabricated homes, Eric decided to add four more employees in order to handle the new production process. When Terry heard the news, he was concerned because there were two other alternatives available to the group that would be less expensive and not require the addition of four new employees. Terry figured that Eric's decision would cost the company an extra $200,000 a year versus the other two alternatives which would cost less than $10,000 each. The basic question Terry had to answer for himself was whether it was worth the extra $190,000 to allow Eric to make a mistake and learn from it. Terry decided that the error would be too expensive for the company when compared to a tight budget and decreased bottom line from previous years.

Terry met with Eric for their regular scheduled meeting. Terry began by praising Eric for a number of important decisions made. It was important that the praise was legitimate, not a smoke screen. Otherwise, Eric would see through the praise and feel that Terry was being less than honest with him.

The conversation shifted toward the minutes of the last team meeting that Terry just reviewed. Terry asked Eric to explain in more detail how he had arrived at the recommendation to hire four new employees. As Eric explained the situation, Terry listened intently. When Eric was finished, Terry restated the major points made by Eric. He then asked Eric what other alternatives were considered. Eric shared with Terry his frustration at not being able to identify other alternatives.

Terry suggested that Eric could consider a couple of options that may be much less expensive. Several cost models could be provided for Eric and the team members to discuss and consider. Terry underscored how this might help the outcome and save money for Eric's team. Eric quickly recognized that the cost savings was important and help from Terry was needed even in an empowered situation. He reached this conclusion because Terry had taken the time to offer suggestions instead of using command and control efforts.

Eric and the team took the latter approach to solve the problem and adopted a less expensive alternative. Terry closely monitored the situation and found that Eric and the team were comfortable with the final outcome. In fact, the group asked for a member of management engineering to be assigned to their team to assist with process development.

Intervention proved successful because Terry was willing to consider a number of ways to intervene and offered strong reasons why another approach to the problem should be considered. Eric and the other team members felt good about the decision because no one micromanaged the decision. Instead, they were asked to adopt a stronger cost saving alternative and involve more resources if needed.

Employee Focus—Working on the Right Thing

On a blustery, March day, an unexpected snowfall blanketed Tennessee. The next day, the snow melted leaving spring pools of water. Looking down at the water, one could see an almost perfect reflection of a blue sky overhead and surrounding budding trees. But, just as quickly as these pools appeared, trees and bushes soaked up the water creating dark foliage which blocked out the blue sky.

A famous poet, Robert Frost, recognized in his poetry that life is like spring pools. Both leaders and employees have, for just a fleeting moment, a near-perfect vision of the environment. But, all too quickly, their visions are clouded. They end up working on the wrong things because these are the tasks they are most comfortable performing. During these times, leaders must intervene because valuable time and resources are wasted.

Eric and his team members were misguided. As they planned for the new fastening devices, they decided that they needed to revise the entire pay incentive system for their area. Unbeknownst to Eric and his team, the human resources department had taken on this project for several areas that were being reengineered and the project was almost completed. When Terry discovered, by accident, that Eric and the team were working on the pay incentive program which was being addressed by human resources, he immediately knew that he must intervene. Otherwise, the team would waste at least twenty hours in needless meetings.

Terry stopped by Eric's area at the end of a Friday just as he did other weeks. During the conversation, Terry casually mentioned that he was aware the team was looking at the pay incentive program. Terry asked if Eric was working with human resources on this because they were well ahead of others in examining this area. When Eric realized that they were about to recreate the work of another area, he thanked Terry for suggesting this. In response, Terry praised Eric for recognizing when it was appropriate to leverage on the knowledge and expertise of others.

Intervention saved the organization at least twenty hours of employee time. It also saved Eric and the team from potential embarrassment. Eric learned the lesson of the spring pools.

Employee Capability and Ownership

As discussed previously in this book, empowerment is only effective where employees have the capability to perform a project and take ownership of it. Without capability, employees are likely to fail. Without ownership, employees will not take responsibility for a project and show the necessary level of commitment. In either of these situations, leaders must intervene to avoid failure, which can harm the organization and employees.

Where employees grow and perform a project and take ownership of a project that was once beyond their grasp, leaders should intervene and recognize the employees' progress. This is a time to reassure employees that they have increased their capabilities. It is also time to thank them for making the commitment.

Eric was asked to take on responsibility for the fastening device project which included financial performance. In the past, Eric had little, if any, experience with financial statements. Financial statements looked like a foreign language. In a nutshell, he was intimidated by finance and accounting. Recognizing this shortfall, Eric and Terry agreed that Eric would pursue training in this area.

After Eric completed his training, his first opportunity to apply the newfound knowledge was for the creation of an annual budget for his team. Without any hesitation, Eric worked diligently on the budget, shaving 10 percent off the expenses as compared to the three-year budget initially developed for the project. Eric and his team were able to live within the budget and added another 5 percent expense savings on top by substituting less expensive labor for certain stages of the project. From the outset, Eric had taken ownership of the budget, exclaiming to Terry that he would live by the budget and show that the team could succeed.

Six months into the fiscal year, Terry recognized Eric's efforts before a group of project leaders. "Eric rarely asks for much. However, we asked Eric to make a major commitment to grow in the financial area. Without intervention from the finance department, Eric and his team members developed a budget that many felt couldn't be done. They said they could shave another 10 percent of expenses off the three-year budget for this project. Eric and his team have definitely succeeded. And we are extremely proud. We're proud for two reasons. They took ownership of that budget and they showed everyone they could handle budgeting and find greater savings than we could imagine. We owe them a round of applause. What a success!" crowed Terry.

As expected, Eric was gratified because he was recognized for achievement in an area that he felt the weakest in and struggled to improve. The recognition created such a groundswell of emotion for Eric that his ownership of the project was increased tenfold. The other leaders in the meeting also saw that growth and ownership were valued and recognized.

Other Good Works

Work culture in the United States takes success for granted. However, when anyone fails, that is news. The trouble is, this is backwards. Look at any charts which show the success-failure rate of new businesses. Many more new businesses fail than succeed. Examine the track records today of the top one hundred United States companies from the 1960s. If they still exist, few of these companies are still on the top one hundred list. Success is hard work. In fact, it is downright difficult. Despite this, American culture has a misplaced expectation when it comes to success—success is the norm, while failure is the exception.

Our collective hang-up with and misperception about success in the United States affects how we work. Criticism on the job is quick to come while praise is too often a rarity. To better understand this, try keeping a log for one workday. Every time a compliment is heard, note it. When criticism is heard, record it as well. At the end of the day, add up the "at-a-boys" versus the "aw shucks." Criticism will greatly outweigh praise. Does that mean work performance in the United States is that bad or are we missing opportunities for praise? Most studies show that many opportunities for reinforcing behavior are missed. In fact, compliments should be used three to four more times than criticism. Leaders should seek out other good works and praise employees. It is amazing how productivity levels will soar with the proper amount of recognition. Recognition for good works builds strength.

Eric and his team faced another important deadline for the fastening device project. Despite major obstacles, they completed the new work staging area in time to start on their test phase of the new system. To many in the company, Eric and his team were expected to achieve this level. Anything else would have been unacceptable.

Terry saw this in a different light. No matter how good a worker is, success is difficult to come by. He also recognized that success came in small increments, not in major steps. Because of this, Terry made a point of finding different ways to recognize the small steps of success. If he didn't vary his recognition methods, his praise would no longer have its reenergizing effect.

This time, Terry decided to use an unusual way to recognize their achievement and those areas that supported the fastening device project team. At this point, they were more than three-fourths of the way through the project. They were tired and stressed from over two years of constant challenges and nagging doubts whether they would succeed. They were close to reaching the peak of the mountain but their energy was waning.

It just so happened that Terry was a good friend of the high school marching band teacher. Terry asked his friend if the school marching band might be interested in visiting the plant and sharing some pizza for lunch. And, by the way, would they mind an impromptu march through the fastening area to lift the spirits of employees? This was a most unusual request, but free pizza was the clincher. Unbeknownst to Eric and his team, the marching band burst into the fastening staging area with horns blazing and drums rolling. At the end of the final chorus, Terry jumped onto a work-table and addressed the crowd. "Too often, we think that brass bands are the rewards of sports heroes. We fail to realize that success is difficult, painstaking, and comes in small increments. The other day I looked at my calendar and realized that this team has been working diligently on this project for over two years. We are more than three-fourths complete on a project that literally means many jobs are going to remain here at this plant, in this town. Because we have been so challenged by this project, we may not have recognized some of the incremental successes along the way. We felt it important to let you know how we felt. And what better way to show it than an excellent marching band. They keep the spirits of heroes high. And you, you are our heroes. We have come a long way because of your tireless efforts. We are also honored to have the high school marching band with us today to share in our pizza banquet. They are fantastic, aren't they?" Terry's words echoed throughout the long building as the employees applauded. "Enough of all of this talk, how about that food?" the words trailed off as Terry jumped down from the worktable.

Later that day, Eric brought a large broken down pizza box into Terry's office. Crudely written on the box was "thanks for caring" along with signatures from each person on the team. Eric and the team were reinvigorated and ready to climb over the mountain peak. And Terry was reinforced in his understanding that other good works demand praise and recognition. In most cases, a brief word of praise will do. In unique cases, leaders need to recognize the heroes at work in unusual ways.

SO, WHAT'S THE POINT?
Intervention is the fulcrum to the personal freedom and organization control balancing act. Effective leaders use intervention, not as interference, but as a way to influence behavior and increase business success.

HOW DOES A LEADER INTERVENE?

The situations that require intervention can be simple when compared to how to intervene. The "how" of intervention is important and very difficult for two reasons:

1. Employees are sensitive to any management interaction because of past command and control management. Employees are looking for cues or signals that leaders have slid back into the darkness of command and control management
2. Intervention is a building process. If a bad foundation is laid, a building will sway and collapse. If intervention is handled poorly from the beginning, a leader's credibility will suffer. Later attempts at intervention will likely fail

The "how" of intervention can be divided into the following eight steps. These steps are described below and utilized in an example.

- Greeting
- Past Appropriate Behavior
- Identification of Current Inappropriate Behavior and Preferred Appropriate Behavior
- Provision of Reasons
- Discussion
- Agreement
- Practice
- Feedback

The following Intervention Wheel diagram reflects the eight step process and the focus areas. This interrelationship is critical to successful interventions.

Greeting—Creating Comfort in the Discomfort Zone
The intervention process begins with a greeting. On the surface, this may appear to be a simple step. However, a greeting is more than a brief "hello" or "how are you." In fact, this step sets the tone for the entire intervention. If a

Intervention Wheel

Intervention Steps

Greeting
Appropriate Behavior
Inappropriate Behavior
Reasons
Discussion
Agreement
Practice
Feedback

Self-Esteem

Legal

Safety

Customer-Supplier Relations

Cost $

Employee Focus

Capability & Ownership

Other Good Works

leader is noticeably agitated or insensitive, employee anxiety will increase and a defensive wall will develop. This step also sends a clear message to an employee about whether a leader respects him/her as a human being. If a leader does not establish good eye contact during the greeting step, employees will be less trusting. If a leader fails to establish a concerned, discussion level with an employee, employees will be less open. Some leaders may look upon this as "small talk." However, individuals are more receptive when they feel others care about how they are doing, whether on or off the job. Some initial discussions about how an employee's work day has gone will help to overcome potential barriers. The feedback received from employees during this discussion will also send cues to leaders about the state of mind and stress level of employees. These cues will help to set the stage for continuing intervention. If an employee, for example, is agitated due to an unrelated work crisis, a leader will know that it is important to get the person focused on the reasons for intervention. If an employee is emotionally charged because of a bad situation, a leader must carefully proceed, borrowing from his or her conflict resolution skills. It may be appropriate to postpone the intervention.

Past Appropriate Behavior—What is on the Right Path

Following the greeting, past or current appropriate behaviors of an employee should be sincerely and specifically recognized, if possible. This is effective leader behavior no matter whether a leader is intervening to change inappropriate employee behavior or reinforcing appropriate employee behavior. Most leaders fail to provide a sufficient amount of recognition for appropriate behavior. Because of this, employees tend to be defensive whenever they discuss behavior on the job with leaders. In addition, employees are always more receptive to discuss inappropriate behavior if leaders sincerely recognize that employees do have redeeming qualities as well.

Some leaders may be hesitant to use this approach. They may think that if they praise employees they will encounter more problems when correcting inappropriate behaviors. This is part of the command and control management baggage or paradigm that needs to be left behind. Leaders must recognize that all employees have both appropriate and inappropriate behaviors and need intervention in both situations.

If praise is going to be provided to employees, it is especially important that appropriate behaviors are clearly understood and recognition is sincere. Too often, leaders assume they are reinforcing behaviors when, in fact, they are not having any effect because employees do not understand what behavior is being discussed. Finally, recognition of appropriate behaviors by leaders must be sincere. Employees can tell if leaders are not sincere, increasing their level of distrust.

It is also important for leaders to clearly understand job descriptions and job expectations of employees. Without this information, leaders are merely offering uninformed opinions about employees.

Identification of Current Inappropriate Behavior and Preferred Appropriate Behavior—Where Has One Strayed From the Path

Inappropriate behavior is a deviation from expected behavior. Leaders must clearly define current inappropriate behaviors. If leaders expect employees to change their behaviors, leaders must clearly define preferred behaviors to replace the inappropriate behaviors. If this is done effectively, employees should understand and agree that problems exist. Leaders can gauge whether employees understand by using questions about inappropriate and preferred behaviors. This is a time to discuss, not to lecture employees.

Provision of Reasons—It's Not My Way or the Highway

One of the most important intervention steps is to provide reasons or rationale why a behavior is appropriate or inappropriate. Too many times, employees are asked to change behavior without understanding why their current behavior is unacceptable. The provision of reasons is the single most important step to obtain ownership by an employee. If an employee understands why certain behavior is appropriate or inappropriate, they are more likely to buy into the desired behavior. Discussion of the reasons for a change in behavior or continued use of appropriate behavior also focuses the conversation on what is best for the organization, not the leader's way. The reasons provided should focus on the impact on both business and employees.

Discussion—Let's Don't Run and Hide

Especially when dealing with inappropriate behavior, intervention can increase stress levels because of real or perceived conflict. Once the inappropriate behaviors have been clearly laid on the table, it is time for a leader to sit and listen empathetically, not to run and hide. A leader must understand why an employee is behaving in a certain manner. What is the employee's perception? What are the employee's feelings? What makes the employee use that behavior? An employee may have determined an improved way to perform a job and a leader may fail to recognize it. This step also encourages an employee to participate in solving the problem or improving the processes.

Agreement—Own the Issue

The discussion phase will move into the mutual agreement step where both the leader and employee agree upon current performance and desired performance. At this step, it is important that both the leader and employee are committed to the agreement and take ownership. Otherwise, an employee will be unwilling to perform beyond the compliance level. An employee will only do what is needed because the leader wants it, not because the employee believes it's the right thing to do. The leader must also take ownership of the agreement. This means a leader must be willing to support an employee to reach the desired behavior. Resources must be provided and barriers removed.

Practice—Perfect Practice Makes Perfect

If appropriate, an employee should be given the opportunity to practice. Both leaders and employees can learn a lesson from the sports world. Athletes spend a much greater amount of time practicing to achieve perfection than leaders in the business world. In business, too little time is spent on practice. Then leaders wonder why perfection has not been achieved.

Remember, practice does not make perfect. Practice makes permanent. Perfect practice makes perfect.

Feedback—Feed Me, Don't Leave Me

The final step in intervention is feedback. Feedback is information about past performance that helps with future performance. Without feedback, improvement is unlikely or impossible. If behavior is appropriate or at least headed in the right direction, desirable reinforcement is needed. If behavior remains inappropriate, a decision must be made to train, transfer, or terminate an employee.

For feedback to be successful, it must be helpful, not destructive. This is illustrated in the Feedback diagram. The primary reason for giving feedback is to help with blind spots. Most people do the right thing, if they know the right thing to do. If employees exhibit behaviors which are harmful to themselves or others, they probably have blind spots.

Feedback

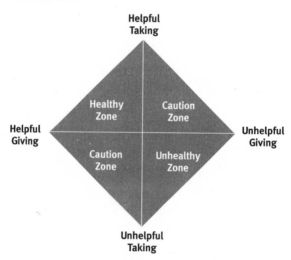

Feedback is on a continuum that runs from Helpful to Unhelpful Giving and Helpful to Unhelpful Taking. Helpful Giving is where a leader provides desirable information to an employee that will improve a situation while protecting the employee's self-esteem. Unhelpful Giving is where information is provided in an undesirable manner and harms an employee's self-esteem. Helpful Taking is where an employee receives the information from a leader in a constructive fashion. On the other hand, Unhelpful Taking results where an employee will not take constructive criticism from a leader.

Both leaders and employees should try to keep in the healthy zone of the feedback model during a feedback situation. In the healthy zone, Helpful Giving is characterized by sincerity, specific comments, timely response, and issues as opposed to individuals. Helpful Taking is characterized by listening, asking questions for understanding, being appreciative, and positive body language.

The unhealthy zone in the feedback model is characterized by giving and taking that is destructive to the relationship between leaders and employees. The caution zone includes a combination of helpful and destructive giving and taking. Because it is destructive to relationships, the caution zone should also be avoided.

Borrowing from the earlier story about Eric and Terry and the fastening device project, the eight steps of intervention are demonstrated. Depending on the situation, certain steps in the model may require little or no attention by a leader, while some steps may be used several times during the intervention.

Greeting

"Good morning, Eric," said Terry as he dropped by Eric's office unannounced. "How was your weekend? If you're like me, you spent most of the time cleaning out the gutters on your house and mowing the lawn. It seems like all of my time on the weekends is spent just keeping up."

As they were talking, they shook hands and settled back in chairs scattered about the round worktable in Eric's office. "I lucked out, Terry. I had some help from my brother-in-law. He brought over his new riding lawnmower. He cut off half the time required for mowing my lawn," Eric responded.

"Next time your brother-in-law stops by your house with his riding lawnmower, you need to send him my way," chuckled Terry.

Identify Appropriate Behavior

"I wanted to give you a call this weekend to let you know that we were very impressed with your presentation made at the management meeting on Friday. You were well prepared, well-focused on progress points and outstanding issues, and handled the questions with ease," offered Terry.

"I appreciate your comments. I was a bit concerned going into the meeting because we still had a number of issues that weren't resolved and really should have been by now," Eric responded.

"Despite those issues, I thought you did a commendable job. In fact, the other leaders were commenting about how excellent your presentation was," said Terry as he gestured toward the charts Eric used at the meeting which were hanging on the wall.

Identify Current Inappropriate Behavior and
Preferred Appropriate Behavior

"I needed to stop by your office this morning to spend a few minutes with you and discuss the handling of the matter regarding Rhonda. I happened to be in the area when the issue arose with Rhonda on Friday. What's going on?" asked Terry.

"Well, I don't know what you heard, Terry, but that was a situation that could have easily gotten out of control," said Eric in a defensive tone.

"As you know, my job is to support you. A good place for me to start is to hear the story about Rhonda. I probably saw the latter half of the discussions with her and may have drawn some conclusions that are not accurate," said Terry.

"I think it would help to share the whole situation with you. Rhonda has not been keeping up with the progress charts that we turn in on a weekly basis. We end up trying to recall what took place earlier in the week and record the data. Needless to say, our data is less than accurate. In the past, I've met with Rhonda and discussed with her the importance of the charts and their use. After our meetings, I thought she understood why the project was important and what we needed to do. I'll be darned if she didn't just keep up the same old habit. By the end of the week, I was frustrated. So, I sat down with her and told her that I didn't much appreciate her lack of responsiveness," Eric carefully recalled the matter.

"I see," said Terry. "This is helpful. Is there anything else?"

"I think you came in just after Rhonda said that she couldn't remember our previous conversation and when I emphasized the importance of the project charts. At that point, I just lost it. I just can't stand people who lie. It's a character issue with me," said Eric as he shook his head. "So, I told Rhonda that I didn't appreciate her jerking me around that way. I guess I kind of lost my composure."

"This is helpful to hear about the prior discussions with Rhonda, your thoughts on the matter, and your feelings. It's tough to keep your cool when you have a situation like that. However, I don't think the behavior shown was the best in such a situation," Terry patiently explained. "When you raised your voice, stood in Rhonda's face, and shook your finger in her face, that was not effective behavior. It would have been appropriate to terminate the conversation until later, when emotions were not as close to the surface."

"I know, Terry, but she was lying to me," Eric quickly offered to Terry.

"I think you hear what behavior I'm concerned about, right?" asked Terry.

"Sure!" answered Eric.

"I think it will help if I explain why that type of behavior was inappropriate," said Terry.

Provision of Reasons

"Have you considered how this was received by Rhonda and the others who were standing around? Based on what I thought I saw, you should have avoided sharing anger. I couldn't help but notice how the other employees reacted. They seemed to stare at you and recoil. In the future when they run into problems, this incidence may very well place them on the defensive," Terry explained calmly and patiently. "They don't understand all of the private discussions you have had with Rhonda in the past. Instead, they are thinking how they would feel if you did that to them. I can remember conversations with people like Rhonda in my past. It's tough to remain cool when you're trying to keep things moving and you see someone who appears to be less than honest with you."

"I guess I see where you're coming from," responded Eric.

"Rhonda, instead of taking ownership for being less than straightforward with you, will focus on the anger. She may even use the reactions of others as a way to paint you as the bad guy in this situation," Terry carefully recounted as he sat watching Eric's body language. "It may have been helpful for you to calmly recount the fact that there had been previous discussions and agreement about this. What do you think?"

Discussion

"Well, I guess you're right. But, I still don't think it's right for her to stand there and be less than frank about the problem," said Eric.

"No one said she was right. I am also disappointed when people fail to be straightforward. But I've learned that if I show anger they will use that as an excuse every time to gain support from their peers. It builds walls between you and your employees."

"You're right."

"How about if we agree on how to handle similar situations in the future? If you find that you are getting upset, either find a way to end the conversation and revisit it after you've cooled down or calmly turn the issue of responsibility directly back to the employee. Ask them to explain what they think, feel, and what the facts are," outlined Terry.

"I agree. It's just tough to do," said Eric.

Agreement

"Let me see if I can summarize what we've agreed to. When you encounter a tense situation like this, you will remain calm by either terminating the conversation until it can be handled more appropriately or proceeding with the proper behavior. When you do discuss the matter, you will ask the person to recount the facts—what did he/she understand. Then, you will ask that person to provide his/her thoughts and feelings. With this information, you should have a clear view of the other person's perception and offer your own. Finally, you can clearly underscore what is expected and what is not being completed. Does that sound reasonable?" prodded Terry.

"I think so," answered Eric.

Practice and Feedback

Following their discussion, periodically Terry would drop in to see how Eric was interacting with others. In addition, Terry watched the employee satisfaction results to see if the issue was surfacing and causing problems.

Since Terry observed Eric using appropriate feedback, Terry provided positive reinforcement to Eric to continue his behavior.

SO, WHAT'S THE POINT?
Intervention is like food to a newborn. In order to grow, an employee needs intervention.

WHEN SHOULD INTERVENTION OCCUR?
DOES ANYBODY CARE WHAT TIME IT IS?

Leaders interact with both teams and individuals. However, management is, generally speaking, a personal, daily, and one-on-one relationship building interaction. It is an eye-to-eye and toe-to-toe interaction. If the appropriate or inappropriate behavior is clearly a team behavior, then intervention should be at the team level. Otherwise, intervention should be on a personal level, one-on-one, and not before group members. This is a significant issue because most people do not deal well with intervention where it is provided before a group of people. Most people are embarrassed to have such a discussion in front of others. More information on this issue will be provided later in this role.

An issue related to this is whether employees can only grow if they are allowed to make mistakes. In fact, some leaders would argue that employees learn and become empowered through mistakes.

People learn through mistakes. However, it is foolish to deliberately allow employees to make mistakes that damage self-esteem, harm customer/supplier relationships, injure self or others, or add significant cost to the organization. It is best to intervene and help employees to understand why other behavior is more appropriate for a given situation.

Intervention is well used close in time to the appropriate or inappropriate behavior. In fact, intervening during the behavior is ideal. Where the behavior being discussed took place long ago, intervention has less of an effect. With the passage of time, employees forget the situation involved and are unable to relate as well to the desirable reinforcement or correction made. Therefore, leaders should use best efforts to provide timely intervention.

SO, WHAT'S THE POINT?
Intervention is directly related to time. With the passage of time, intervention has less effect upon employee behaviors. "Intervention in time" should be the catchphrase.

WHO DOES A LEADER INTERVENE WITH?
MANAGEMENT IS NOT MAGIC AND NOT BY NUMBERS!

Most leaders would like to see a set number of employees or teams that a leader should be responsible for. Sorry to disappoint those leaders, but it is impossible to provide a magic number for all occasions because it depends on at least seven considerations: technical knowledge, new areas of responsibility, maturity level of employees, pace of change, training processes, nature of the work, and culture.

First, how much technical knowledge is needed for a leader to help others grow? Some leaders argue that no technical knowledge is needed because only good people skills are needed for effective management. Experience has shown that this is wrong. Exceptional technical knowledge is a definite asset if a leader has good Leader-Coach-Manager knowledge and skills. Exceptional technical knowledge, however, is a disadvantage if a leader does not have good Leader-Coach-Manager skills and knowledge. The tendency in this situation is for a leader to be too "hands on" with employees.

Some leaders have asked if you can only choose one or the other, would you take a leader with good technical knowledge or a leader with strong people skills. It is best to take a leader with good people skills, assuming that leader has reasonable prerequisites for the job. The reason for this is that a large part of a leader's job is increasing the capability and ownership of employees, and this requires strong people knowledge and skills.

Second, does a leader have several new areas of responsibility? If a leader has a number of new areas of responsibility, he or she will need to spend a substantial amount of time understanding the key processes for those areas. In such a situation, it is best to provide sufficient time for a leader to understand the new areas. This will decrease the number of employees that a leader would otherwise be able to grow and time available for growth efforts.

Some leaders argue that it is good to put a leader in an area where they have little knowledge because it will force them to use their new leader roles. That may be true in one sense. But, if the deeper meaning is to help employees grow in all areas of empowerment, this is best accomplished through use of both people and technical knowledge.

Third, what is the level of employee maturity? The higher the maturity level of employees, the less time and effort required to grow employees. Where employees are mature, they are able to add responsibilities and assume shared leadership. Shared leadership includes such areas as employees developing and using team standards, increasing business knowledge, using team feedback, establishing and using measures to manage their part of the business, and serving as coordinators to handle parts of the job previously done by leaders. Employees that are willing and able to broaden their circle of influence in these areas will require less development time. As noted in the Develop Employees role relative to the Change Behaviors diagram (p. 103), employee maturity will affect the leader behaviors and involvement.

Fourth, what is the pace of change in an organization? If your organization is involved in such areas as work redesign, total quality management, new facility development, new product development, or globalization, leaders are most likely going to spend their time putting out "fires" while implementing change. Because of this, emphasis on new leader roles deteriorates significantly. The number of leaders may need to be increased during such major change or the timeline for the transition plan from command and control management to the new environment may need to be increased. It is generally best to focus on development after a greenfield site is up and running.

Fifth, what kind of training process does an organization have? Some organizations have an informal training process or buddy system. The quality of training will be significantly less where an informal training approach is used, instead of a formal approach. Organizations that have formal training processes, such as development, design, delivery, evaluation, and on-the-job evaluation, will have a well-developed employee who will require less development time on the part of a leader.

Sixth, what is the nature of the work? High-tech? Labor intensive? High labor intensity organizations will generally require greater time commitment from a leader than high technology organizations. High labor intensity organizations will generally have simpler work processes than high tech organizations. Therefore, the span of responsibility for a leader in a high labor intensity organization will be greater. However, high tech organizations are reluctant to significantly increase the span of responsibility when safety or major cost considerations are important factors.

Seventh, what is the culture of an organization? There has been a growing amount of conversation with respect to how many people can effectively be developed in an empowering organization versus a traditional organization. Traditional organizations expect leaders to be looking over the shoulder of employees, creating a more limited span of responsibility than in empowering organizations. Ironically, employees in traditional organizations are less developed because employees make fewer decisions and have less experience to apply to problem-solving situations.

Changing cultures is like watching a snail race up a hill or grass grow in Fargo, North Dakota in August. It takes a long time. Be very skeptical of leaders who claim to be successful in changing cultures in less than five years. For some organizations, it may take a generation to change the culture.

SO, WHAT'S THE POINT?
Increasing the span of responsibility requires consideration of several factors. It is not a linear journey, but more of a roller coaster ride with peaks and valleys. Given a mature leader and empowered employees, the average number of employees per leader should increase significantly, ultimately resulting in fewer leaders at all levels of the organization. This creates cost savings and leads to well-developed employees.

WHERE SHOULD INTERVENTION OCCUR?
TOTO, ARE WE IN KANSAS?

Intervention is usually an emotional event. Where intervention is used to correct behavior, most employees will be defensive and, possibly, embarrassed. Where desirable reinforcement is used, employees are often embarrassed as well.

Because of the emotional nature of intervention, it should initially take place in private. It should be a one-on-one interaction between employee and leader in an area where no other individuals can hear or see the discussions. In many situations, interventions are best held in neutral and casual areas such as a warehouse, lunchroom, or such places where employees are going to feel more comfortable.

In general, it is best to obtain agreement from an employee before a leader uses public desirable recognition. Careful consideration is also required to weigh the affects of the public recognition upon those who are not recognized but in attendance.

Two employees were recognized during a monthly meeting because of their efforts in establishing a local home for less fortunate families by using mental health services provided by the organization. Only one of the employees was aware beforehand of the recognition to be provided at the meeting. Although both employees appreciated the recognition, other leaders attending the meeting became more negative. They began to talk negatively about the two and were less supportive of the house for the less fortunate. When the CEO addressed the issue with one of the negative leaders, the CEO found that several people had wanted to participate in the planning and development stages of the house but they were not included. They felt slighted and became negative. The two that were recognized ended up regretting the recognition received.

SO, WHAT'S THE POINT?
The focus of all intervention is to work with people in a way to help them grow. Punishment or praise is not an end to itself. It is part of a growing, learning, and nurturing process.

Role 7

AVOID LEADER PITFALLS

It's the Grand Canyon, Not a Ditch

MANAGEMENT IS A tough job. It's a roller coaster ride with no final destination. Throughout the ride, there are arcane twists and turns. Around each curve, leaders flirt with failure, whether they know it or not.

There are a number of major factors that greatly increase the likelihood of failure for an organization that adopts new leader roles. Organizations will fail unless leaders are aware of and deal with these key failure factors. For this reason, one of the key leader roles in this book is the avoidance of pitfalls.

There are several key failure factors. In this role, these factors are defined, stories are included that show how others have dealt with a failure factor, and helpful hints are provided on how to overcome the failure factor.

LACK OF EARLY INVOLVEMENT BY ALL LEVELS OF MANAGEMENT

Failure is likely where all management levels are not involved in vision formation and new leader roles. Leaders who are not involved early in the process will likely not buy into the vision and they will not "walk the talk" because they truly may not understand the "talk."

John Daniel was the CEO and owner of a national food brokerage company. He was a pioneer of sorts who liked to find new ideas that could be used in his company. He became aware of new leader roles from attendance at a conference, and later visited a company that expected leaders to use new roles. He was excited about its potential for his company because it was based on the same philosophy as his company's employee stock ownership plan. He appreciated how much more productive staff could be and how much more rewarding work could be for employees. He was so excited that he decided to move quickly ahead and share it with all home office employees. Following the initial meeting with all of the home office employees, he was surprised to find less than enthusiastic response from senior management. Several senior leaders continued to question how effective such a program would be in their organization. Others were verbally supportive but failed to visibly support the new roles.

John Daniel's enthusiasm remained intact; however, he began to wonder if his approach had been faulty. Convinced that the new leader roles were critical to long term success, he telephoned the company he had visited to find out what may have gone wrong. They offered two pieces of advice: (1) From the beginning, the new leader roles must be embraced by senior management; failure at the top means guaranteed failure throughout. All levels of management must understand and be committed. (2) A plan must be used to build understanding and support for these new roles. John Daniel suddenly realized that he would fail because he did not build the involvement, awareness, and support of his senior team and other leaders. He had used a knee-jerk approach. John Daniel started over using a senior management retreat to lay the proper groundwork. The end result was acceptance and support from senior management and all other leaders because they better understood the plan and were less threatened by change.

HELPFUL HINT. The first phase for any organization interested in new leader roles should be to educate senior management. Effective educational methods are conferences, educational sessions that emphasize the purpose and benefits of the new roles to individual leaders, site visits to other organizations that have successfully implemented such programs, videos on the subject, and articles and books. Once senior management is committed, a plan of action must be created and shared with all other leaders to gain commitment. This is a long-term journey that requires a road map for leaders to understand where they are headed and why they are travelling down a certain pathway.

LACK OF FORMAL EDUCATION

If leaders do not receive formal education to help them embrace the new leader roles, failure is likely to be just around the corner. New leader roles require a major change in style and behavior for most leaders. Management metamorphous is normally attained only through continual education and on the job experience.

The healthcare industry was changing rapidly as managed care became more prevalent. Managed care plans decreased the demand for inpatient care and customer satisfaction became more important to health maintenance organizations. Because of growing managed care popularity, HMO competition began to heat up as more HMOs entered the market. As the president of a regional HMO, David appreciated the major changes required by his staff if they were to remain competitive and customer oriented in a crowded market. As part of their performance improvement efforts, David had implemented a new leader roles program for management following careful consideration of the merits.

The program began with senior management. As part of their implementation phase, David used twice monthly afternoon educational sessions to help senior management understand and adapt. Following three months of this education, this program was rolled out to all other leaders in the HMO.

Initially, the new roles seemed to take hold. Delegation of tasks increased while customer response times dipped dramatically. A few months later leaders were experiencing difficulty. Conflict among leaders had increased. Senior leaders were verbally supportive but did not seem to be involved in the transition. Because of growing concerns, David spent at least four afternoons per week in small groups listening to leaders regarding problems and issues related to their new program. After two weeks, it became quite clear that the issue was the lack of programmed training beyond the initial three months for senior leaders. Senior leaders needed additional education, as did others in management, to continue to adapt to the new leader roles.

It was apparent that senior leaders did not intuitively understand how their roles needed to change. They also did not feel comfortable enough with the new roles to actively train their leaders in the new skills and techniques. With this information, David created, with the help of a management team, a three-year plan for development. The plan included continual training for senior leaders in order for them to take greater involvement in training and education efforts. The plan was implemented and the outcome measures steadily climbed. Well-thought-out education and on-the-job practice is critical to success.

HELPFUL HINT. Before initiating any new leader roles education or program implementation, a development plan must be designed to fit the unique needs of an organization. The plan should include the use of feedback to measure whether the plan is on target and leaders are making the transition. The development plan must cover a number of years before leaders can be expected to make the transition. If an organization has a high employee turnover rate or high percentage of blue-collar workers, it may require more time for the transition.

The education intensity of successful programs is shown in the Leader Curve diagram. In the beginning, a concentrated dose of education is required for leaders because training must encompass the reasons for change, new roles and skills, and intensive implementation to master the newfound skills. The second phase of education is a bit less intensive than the first phase because leaders are focused on repeated use of roles and skills, not new paradigms or skill sets. In the third phase, education intensity is increased because leaders are more mature and skilled, allowing them to increase their education of employees. New leader roles require a greater amount of education and training than traditional management. However, the increased costs of education should be offset by increased organization effectiveness.

Leader Curve

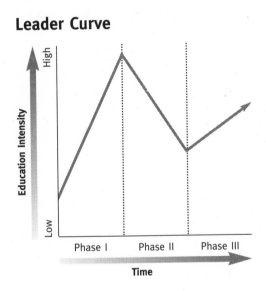

SPAN OF RESPONSIBILITY IS TOO BROAD FOR LEADERS

A leader may be asked to increase the number of employees or teams that report to him or her (span of responsibility) before building the employee or team purpose, capability, ownership, and authority. In such a situation, a leader will spend time on matters other than the new roles because employees will not understand how to deal with the day-to-day problems.

A toy manufacturer experienced sluggish productivity while competitors seemed to steadily improve their productivity through the addition of new technology. This toy company already had the newest technology but could not increase production. The CEO became aware of successes in some other industry where management adopted new leader roles. The CEO was attracted to these new roles because they increased the turn-around time on jobs and ultimately decreased the number of full-time equivalents required in management.

Following intensive education of management, the toy manufacturer implemented new leader roles. Soon thereafter, the manufacturer decreased the number of middle leaders in order to decrease expenses. At first, productivity seemed to increase. Then, productivity plummeted and morale dipped. A consultant was called in to review the operations and recommend what could be done to eliminate the problems. Following inter-views with employees in manufacturing and all other divisions, the consultant found that the span of responsibility for leaders had dramatically increased because of management downsizing. This came at a critical time when leaders were expected to increase their development of employees.

Instead of spending time growing employees, leaders were spending most of their time trying to keep up with the administrative demands associated with more employees. The new program suffered because many leaders saw the new roles as only a program intended to decrease the number of leaders in the company. The company failed to understand that a decrease in the number of leaders was not the goal but was a natural outcome over time.

HELPFUL HINT. Empowerment of employees should be attained prior to increasing the span of responsibility for leaders. During the initial phases, many organizations find more leaders are required to provide sufficient opportunities for leaders to grow their employees. If the new leader roles are appropriately pursued, increased span of responsibility will be a natural outcome.

DAILY LEADER PRESENCE IS MISSING

Employees and leaders need to grow on a daily basis. Too often, leaders fail to provide sufficient support. They are distracted or are more comfort-able working on technical processes or traditional management tasks. Because new leader roles are a major paradigm shift, leaders must walk the talk on a daily basis.

Elaine was the regional manager of a nursing home and assisted living company. She had five leaders who were responsible for combined nursing home and assisted living facilities. Elaine was a progressive leader who prided herself on being the trendsetter instead of trend follower. Once she had become familiar with new leader roles and the positive outcomes, she knew she needed to implement it within her areas of responsibility.

Elaine slowly began the program making sure leaders were appropriately educated and trained. However, once the new roles were initiated, Elaine started concentrating on some other critical projects. Soon, she found her leaders were not growing their employees. Elaine spent time with each leader to find out why the new program was not successful. She also carefully listened to leaders and employees as they discussed what was positive and negative about the new roles. A common theme seemed to run through the conversations—the new leader roles didn't seem natural at first and they required repetition to become a habit.

It suddenly occurred to Elaine that she had to pursue these new roles with her leaders on a daily basis. The new leader roles were not a once a week or once a month activity. It required a day in and day out commitment to help others grow in their roles. Otherwise, leaders would not gain sufficient practice to be more effective and Elaine would not become adept either. Once Elaine recognized the problem, she created a plan to focus on continued development of her leaders. Following a slow start, the efforts caught on and expected outcomes were surpassed. Elaine surveyed her leaders and their employees and found that the new leader roles were gaining in acceptance and were becoming a more natural part of their work.

HELPFUL HINT. A visible leader presence is needed to insure on-the-job application of the new leader roles. It is part of "walking the talk" and role modeling. The new roles, like sports, require repetition before they become second nature and are effectively used on a daily basis. The biggest challenge is for leaders to remember to seek out opportunities on a daily basis. Some leaders use simple reminders such as goals written on daily schedules, diaries recording activities, and boards hung on the back of a door that show a check mark for every new leader role activity pursued that day and week.

Other leaders find they are more effective if they create a new leader roles plan. This plan includes tactics that should be used by leaders to improve the understanding, skills, and abilities of others. Each day a leader has goals associated with certain teams and/or individual employees. These goals can also be related to a personal development plan that an individual leader or employee may have created. For example, if a leader has in her personal development plan the goal to increase her conflict resolution skills, the goal can be to find opportunities for her supervisor to work with her in a conflict situation and increase her applied skills.

NEW LEADER ROLES ARE NOT DEFINED OR UNDERSTOOD

Because new leader roles are frequently misunderstood, role definitions are important. New leader roles basically create the expectations for leaders. Some organizations tell leaders to manage without providing a definition of these new roles. These leaders are usually lost and send mixed messages to employees. In these situations, leaders, employees, and the organization suffer.

New leader roles, on the surface, seem straightforward. However, they are very complex and require practice and experience to fully appreciate. Few organizations provide too much training and education when it comes to the development of new management roles. The end result where roles are not understood is mental exhaustion for leaders, employees, and the organization.

"We learned the hard way. I mean, we had employee morale past zero. It was in the sub-basement," offered Shelley. Shelley was the CEO of a transcription agency that transcribed medical reports for physicians and hospitals. She started the agency with only two assistants and developed the business to eighty-five employees. "When I started the business, I could easily supervise the staff while I sold accounts and provided some transcription services myself. Once we began our rapid growth, I had to create several management positions. In the past, we were successful because of the service provided and our management style. People craved to work for us. When I hired more leaders, I expected them to be coaches. I even developed the new leader roles for everyone to memorize," added Shelley as she pointed to a poster hanging on the wall that outlined their first roles.

"So, that is your secret to success?" we asked.

"Absolutely not," chuckled Shelley. "We almost fell flat on our face. I thought the roles were so obvious that I failed to find out if leaders understood them. After I created the roles, I thought I had it made. In fact, I was in for the lesson of my life. Before I knew it, I had lost one quarter of my employees and the second largest account I had," she said shaking her head.

"New leader roles were not the key, then?" we wondered aloud.

"It was only part of the key. Without well-defined new roles, leaders wouldn't have been able to get to first base. My fault was in thinking that this was so straightforward. In fact, it's anything but simple. It's complex. And I failed to develop my leaders to make sure they understood the roles and actually used the roles."

"What did you do once you realized the problem?"

"I practiced what I preached. I started from scratch. I talked with each and every leader about the roles. Why were the roles important, why were they important to them, why were they important to employees, and why were they important to our customers? But, I didn't stop there. I kept on explaining what each role required and how to develop in that role. Very important! I also walked the talk. I used the roles. And after I did, I used that as a way to help them understand the roles."

"What was the result?"

"Things began to turn around. Customers started telling us how much they appreciated our work. Employees started bragging again about how much they loved their jobs. We even had leaders telling how the new roles had turned around their home life. It was powerful," Shelley explained.

HELPFUL HINT. Be creative with new leader roles. Ask leaders and employers to help define the roles. Discuss how the roles fit with the mission, vision, and values of the organization. Ask leaders to list the ways each of the roles can be used to help others grow on the job. Develop a survey to assess, on a periodic basis, if roles are being used properly.

LEADER ROTATION

Some organizations periodically rotate leaders in order to increase their overall understanding of the organization and their skills. Some organizations bring in new leaders from outside the organization to participate in this process. Depending on a new leader's understanding of the organization's vision and new leader roles, rotations can be distracting.

Jerry started his career with a food manufacturer that believed in rotating leaders to increase their knowledge of the entire organization and to provide an infusion of new ideas from the new leaders. Following an 18-month tenure in the baking mixes manufacturing center, Jerry was asked to take responsibility for the cracker manufacturing area.

Six months prior to Jerry's arrival in the cracker manufacturing area, they began their training for teams and new leader roles. Upon his arrival, they were well into the new leader roles and formed their teams. Jerry had previously completed the new roles training course. He felt confident and well prepared for the job.

Within two weeks of his arrival, Jerry found the teams were not productive because they failed to follow through with their team responsibilities. At first, Jerry wondered whether he was the problem. He later found that what he was experiencing was quite common in the organization. In fact, his area had four different leaders in the past three years because of the management rotation program. When Jerry inquired about the problem, several team members complained that frequent leader rotation kept everyone in tailspin. Because of these distractions, it was easier for employees to remain in the traditional management structure—i.e., "just tell me what to do."

Fearing that the new leader roles would fail due to a lack of continuity, Jerry raised the issue with his vice president. He was asked to prepare a presentation for consideration by the senior management team. Following the presentation, the company changed its leader rotation policy to assure that leaders stayed at least two years in a management position. Senior management agreed to compare employee survey results prior to the policy change to survey results following the policy change.

The survey results showed that employees agreed with the policy change. In addition, productivity rose while employee job satisfaction increased. In Jerry's area, teams were more receptive to the new leader roles than before and employees were more motivated than before.

HELPFUL HINT. Organizations must minimize the amount of leader rotation unless such changes will increase effectiveness. During the initial implementation stages, frequent management changes can have the greatest negative effect because the credibility of the role transition and understanding of it are at a delicate stage.

GOOD COMMUNICATION SKILLS ARE LACKING

Leaders with more formal education may feel that they do not need to learn communication skills because of their prior education. Many leaders fail to recognize that higher learning does not necessarily equate to higher communication skills. Unknown to leaders, their communications may be perceived as distant and cold. This leads to fewer ideas, lower self-esteem, and less risk taking by employees. Often, when conflicts do arise, leaders are not well prepared to handle adversity because they don't have the skills and tools related to conflict resolution.

Bob was the CEO of a small retail chain. He became CEO following ten years of experience within the company in sales and operations. Because of his experience and masters degree in management, he thought he was well prepared to deal with the types of issues that would arise. In the first two years of his tenure as CEO, he fared well as the company grew in sales revenue and market expansion. In his third year, the company encountered a number of problems. Sales languished apparently due to competition from superstores and employees became concerned about their jobs as rumors ran rampant that the company might be sold. Minor issues that had plagued the company over the past couple of years suddenly became major problems.

Leaders were asking for job severance packages in case the company was sold and their jobs were eliminated. Several suppliers of goods had been content to allow the company ninety days to pay their bills. With the declining financial performance, they now were asking for payment within thirty days. The retail clerks were asking for an improved benefits package competitive with some of the larger retailers.

Bob decided to handle the problem directly by interacting with the staff. He met with the leaders to address their issues. During the session, he became defensive about their comments and concerns. He was unable to focus the group on the problems and discuss them without emotion. This only further alienated the leaders. At the end of the meeting, they had not resolved any of the issues. Bob felt the leaders did not care about the long-term financial viability of the company. The leaders felt that Bob was defensive, unapproachable, and cold when faced with adversity.

When Bob met with the retail clerks, he became upset because they were making financial demands at a time when the company could not afford added costs. With the suppliers, Bob was unable to regain the desired payment terms. Bob felt dejected and alone.

Recognizing that the issues were growing, Bob met with a friend who had experience in the area of conflict resolution. Bob quickly recognized that he had made most of the mistakes that were critical to conflict resolution. Determined to turn the situation around, Bob asked for help in developing his conflict resolution skills. He also asked his friend to attend some meetings with leaders and employees to create an environment for them to discuss and resolve the problems. Following his training, Bob and his friend met with the leaders and employees. They used conflict resolution skills that Bob had learned. At the end of both meetings, the problems were closer to resolution and relationships were on the mend. Bob learned the hard way that communication is not an innate skill.

HELPFUL HINT. A leader must be a good listener, work actively with all employees to understand their points of view, and identify and resolve issues in an appropriate manner. Communication skills and, in particular, conflict resolution skills are critical to any leader's success. The implementation of new leader roles will create more conflict initially because it basically changes the environment and relationships. Leaders must receive proper training and support from their supervisor in order to be effective at conflict resolution. Communication skills can be improved through self-study of books on the subject. Seminars on communication and conflict resolution skills are excellent ways to fill the gap. Interpersonal Communication Programs, Inc., Denver, Colorado, offers an excellent program on this subject.

ASSUMING ALL LEADERS CAN MASTER THE NEW ROLES

Some leaders cannot master the new roles. Some leaders have excellent technical skills but have a real deficit in people capabilities that cannot be overcome through training or further experience. The bottom line is they are not going to adopt the Leader-Coach-Manager paradigm. Despite this fact, countless numbers of leaders will continue to try and mold traditional leaders into something they cannot attain. The outcome is ill feelings and frustration for the leader attempting to make the transition.

Bill, a vice president for a large teaching hospital in a southeast metropolitan area, was assigned to lead a wellness program as part of his responsibilities. The director for the wellness program, Kris, was a very efficient leader. She had an excellent track record in financial performance and program development that she took personal pride in. Bill thought that she would make an excellent leader because of her past success.

Kris trained in the new leader roles and skills. Despite Kris' efforts, employees were very negative. They said that Kris was abrupt and didn't listen to their advice. At first, Bill thought Kris was an entrepreneur who was misunderstood by employees.

The problems continued and the gap between Kris and her employees grew. Because of the continued problem, Bill spent more time in the wellness area casually observing Kris interacting with employees. He noticed that Kris seemed to avoid interaction with employees when given an opportunity. However, she seemed attracted to special projects that required solitary focus. Bill asked human resources to help diagnose the problem and identify how to address the growing problem. Human resources found similar behaviors. They found that Kris was not a good fit for a job that required interpersonal focus. Bill was trying to fit a square peg in a round hole. In fact, past employee surveys indicated that Kris was a very efficient person but lacked good interpersonal skills.

By her admission, Kris felt more comfortable working alone on a new program than interacting with employees. With the input and support of human resources, Bill recommended that Kris be transferred to the program planning area of the hospital where they had a need for someone with good program development skills. Following the transition, Kris was pleased with the job because it focused on the areas where she was most interested and felt most comfortable. Bill was able to fill the wellness position with a leader that had good technical skills and ability to grow people.

HELPFUL HINT. Good skills are not necessarily synonymous with experienced and educated leaders. The new leader roles are possibly more of an art than a science. Because of their personal makeup, some leaders are not capable of excelling at these new roles. They may not possess a personality type that works well with people. An improved leader selection process is important where new leader roles are adopted. It takes courage to transfer or terminate leaders who cannot or will not make the transition.

SOME LEADERS DO NOT WALK THE TALK

Some leaders have a political belief in the capability of people, not a spiritual belief. They "talk it" but they don't "walk it." Their actions do not fit their words. It's similar to peeling an onion. On the outside, the onion may appear to be fresh and white with few blemishes. As the layers of the onion are peeled back, spots appear on the skin. In some cases, the onion may be spoiled. Further peeling of the onion may show bug infestation. Leaders are like an onion in this respect.

The restaurant business was changing rapidly and Lee recognized that her restaurant chain must adapt or face continual decline. The market had changed with the influx of many white-collar workers from the expanding metropolitan market in the neighboring county. The majority of customers no longer were interested in inexpensive food and mediocre service. They expected good value and excellent service.

Unlike a number of Lee's competitors, her employees had half the turnover of other restaurants. However, Lee's stores were anything but value oriented. They hadn't been renovated for a number of years. The menu was limited and customers were not allowed to customize. Employees had little or no training and were not expected to make many decisions on the job.

Lee decided to implement new leader roles followed by empowerment. She wanted her leaders to make decisions quickly to meet the needs and interests of the customer. She also wanted employees to know that they could address customer problems immediately and be supported by management. She began the program with the training of senior management. All of the senior leaders outwardly voiced support for the program. Unbeknownst to Lee, one of her leaders was secretly critical of the program. In meetings where Lee was not in attendance, the leader would offer criticism of the program. For a period of time, these comments were not shared with Lee for fear the leader in question would retaliate against the informer.

Over time, Lee noticed that most senior leaders were supportive of the new roles. A consultant shared with her some observed comments of the leader in question who was not supportive of the program. Lee was faced with a dilemma. Should she keep the leader in place because she was a good technician or should she be terminated or reassigned? Following several weeks of soul searching, Lee terminated the senior leader who had been silently undermining the program. When asked why the employee was terminated, Lee answered that senior management must walk the talk if a new program is going to have any credibility. Otherwise, the CEO could be seen as less than credible and not 100 percent supportive of the program.

HELPFUL HINT. If leaders do not develop a strong belief in the capability of people, they must be reassigned or terminated. A leader cannot empower employees with a foot on the brake pedal looking in the rearview mirror. New leader roles mean the foot is off the brake pedal and a leader is looking toward what may be, not what was.

LACK OF INTERDEPENDENT MANAGEMENT CULTURE

Where leaders do not share ideas, experiences, problems, and solutions with other leaders, the potential for failure is significantly increased. New leader roles require a free flow of information throughout the organization. Success is born from interdependent relationships. Cooperation and collaboration are the key elements of an interdependent culture.

"How do you create an interdependent culture?"

Ruth slowly considered the question. "My company didn't have an interdependent culture until the last couple of years. Before interdependence, our culture was held together by organization charts, a common name and logo, and a common history. We quickly learned that interdependence required more than this. We found that department budgets needed to be dependent on others. So, we placed marketing budgets for all products in marketing, we put financial people in multidisciplinary teams, and blurred all departmental lines wherever possible."

"You destroyed as many boxes as possible, then?" we asked.

"No, we looked upon it as creating more boxes, overlapping boxes. Everyone was dependent upon a number of people and areas for their survival. Look at a woven basket. Notice how one strip of material crosses all the other pieces making up the basket. It is based on engineering principles of strengthened structure. Organizations are like woven baskets. Computers have made it possible to intentionally blur the lines. Before the proliferation of low-cost computers, we had to put people, money, and equipment in neat little boxes in order to keep track of them. Since then, we have created baskets," Ruth gestured toward the large basket sitting on the bookshelf.

"You manufactured complexity to create a single focus. Is that what you're saying?"

"That's right. We created the opposite situation, complexity, to create that single focus. I guess it goes to show you that opposites do attract," Ruth chuckled as she finished the interview.

HELPFUL HINT. An organization should have a structured networking process to allow leaders to learn from each other and grow. Some organizations have created management councils that are focused on performance improvement. All leaders are expected to actively participate in the council to improve organization-wide processes. Create shared goals for groups of leaders. Financial goals can be established that will require cooperation and collaboration among leaders if they are to succeed. The key point is to create an opportunity for leaders to see that their success or failure is not solely dependent upon their own actions. Many leaders fail to see that their jobs are dependent upon the success of others because they have been working within a well-defined area with tightly defined responsibilities.

FEAR

Fear has always been a basic emotion of mankind ever since the dawn of civilization. In the beginning, fear focused on survival, such as food, shelter, and safety. In organizations, there are similar basic fears but they focus on safety. Fear within organizations normally is focused on safety—safety from reprisals, safety from embarrassment, and safety from termination. Fear of punishment from a leader for having made a mistake or speaking out leads to failure just as fear of embarrassment and termination. Fear is a deterrent to growth because, like the caveman, we tend to find refuge in some hidden quarters of an organization. Fear makes employees less likely to take a chance or try something new.

Fear comes in strange ways and strange packages. Employees expect punishment, reprisals, and terminations because they were used often or as threats in the traditionally managed organizations. An employee survey brought this to light in a large consulting firm. Ian, senior vice president of the firm, prided himself on being empowering and willing to vigorously argue a point with any employee. With one group of employees, he tried to increase conversation by using vigorous debate or openly challenging ideas raised during discussions. He failed to recognize that many employees were frightened by his lively debate. Instead of increasing discussion, he literally sealed the lips of many employees. They saw the lively debate as dangerous. At some point in time, the lively debate would likely end up in embarrassment or ridicule.

As the group of employees became quieter, he became more vocal and lively in his debate trying to draw them out. Instead, they receded into a cave. Later, he reviewed the employee surveys and found that the empowering style was a fear generating style. Following that experience, he never used lively debate to attempt to generate discussion.

HELPFUL HINT. Examine leader styles. If the new leader roles are successful, leaders must consistently empower employees. If employees are allowed to make reasonable mistakes in this environment, employees should see that failures and mistakes from reasonable risk taking are appropriately handled. Support systems, such as pay systems, must be consistent with the new leader roles and empowerment. Reward successes and educate failures. Discipline must be relegated to situations where leaders have exhausted the reasonable options. Actively drive out fear in the organization. Fear is not a good motivator because it rather quickly degenerates into terror or panic. When this happens, paralysis sets in or irrational actions take place. A certain amount of stress does help to sharpen senses and quicken the pace of change.

THIS IS A JOURNEY

If leaders are not careful, the potential failures outlined above could take an organization off course. A leader must make continual adjustments to make sure the organization attains business success and quality of work life.

Keep in mind, new leader roles are not a quick fix. It's a journey. It will take several years, even for the best leaders who are strongly committed, to make the transition and become effective.

SO, WHAT'S THE POINT?
It does not make any difference whether an organization is ahead, equal to, or behind its' competitor. Employees in an organization need to be running. Who is it that runs beside employees enabling them to run faster and longer than ever before? It's the leader!

Role 1
Role 2
Role 3
Role 4
Role 5
Role 6
Role 7
Role 8
Role 9
Role 10
Role 11

INTEGRATE TO ACHIEVE ALIGNMENT

There Are No I's In Synergy

IMAGINE, LAUREL WITHOUT Hardy, or the Lone Ranger without Tonto. Apart, they were less than whole. But together, they were powerful, unforgettable. In fact, they were greater than one plus one.

Organizations are like famous duos. When parts of an organization are well integrated, synergy erupts creating value greater than the sum of the parts.

Where does this increased value derive? Does it only come from the wisdom and leadership of a CEO? In part, but it is all too often overemphasized. Greater value is created where leaders aggressively work to link, in a meaningful way, their respective parts of an organization to the whole.

Integration is a special role for leaders that brings pieces together where they relate to an organization's mission, vision, and values. Another way to think of integration is alignment. Consider a dog sled team in Alaska. If half of a dog team pulls north while the other half pulls south, the dogs are unaligned and the dog team makes little or no progress. If a dog team pulls in the same direction, they are aligned or integrated and become a powerful force.

Despite the power of integration, it isn't a natural process for most leaders. This is especially true in the United States because of strong and diverse cultures. From kindergarten through high school, individualism and competition are emphasized in lessons and play more than interdependence and collaboration. Mass media also celebrates strong individuals who succeed against all odds. Let's face it, integration is about as natural as riding a bicycle backwards.

If integration is so alien and awkward, is it worth pursuing? The answer to this question is found in organizations that have learned to adapt and use integration to their benefit. The payback from integration is long-term success, not the relative short-term success related to individual efforts. To understand this point, try the following exercise. Find a one-inch rope that is at least twenty feet long. Position one strong individual on one end of the rope. On the other end, position three individuals. After a count of three, ask the three individuals to pull in three different directions while the one individual on the other end pulls in another direction. Usually, the one individual will win because the power of the three individuals is unaligned. Next, ask the three individuals to pull the rope in the same direction. Unless Hollywood Hogan is the lone individual positioned on one end of the rope, chances are very good that the three individuals will win the rope-pulling contest.

In the past, organizations were like the strong individual competing against the misdirected masses. However, a small but growing number of organizations have learned the value and power of integration defeating the strong individualistic organizations. Future organizations that master integration as one of the new leader roles will experience long term success.

LAYING THE FOUNDATION

Try the following exercise. Lay your hand open with your palm face down. The fingers of the open hand are pointing in different directions. Now, try hitting a hard object with your open hand. It doesn't take too much effort before your fingers begin to hurt and bend under the pressure. Your immediate reaction is to pull back your hand.

Next, tighten your hand into a fist. The first point you should notice is that the fingers are no longer focused in different directions. In fact, the fingers are focused toward the inner circle of the fist. Next, try hitting your fist against the same object that you struck with your open hand. You should notice that you are able to exert greater force than where you used an open hand. You don't feel like you need to remove your hand.

Integration is like a fist. An integrated organization is tightly bound together and focused with its energy. The individual pieces are focused on an inner core. It has greater power than the unaligned organization. What then provides the energy, motivation, or force for integrated organizations? The answer is quite simple: it takes focused efforts on an inner core. Long-term success through integration is associated with six components. These are outlined in the Integration Formation diagram shown below. Integration Formation (IF) consists of key organization documents, goal setting, decision making based on principles, shared leadership, team feedback, and role modeling. These six components lay the foundation for success

Integration Formation

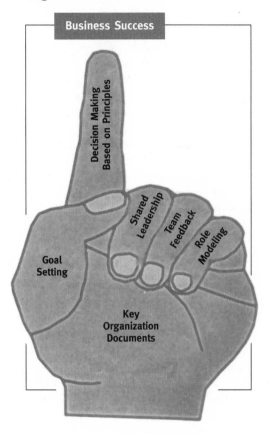

through integration. They are the fist—five fingers and the palm of the hand. In this role, we will cover key organization documents, goal setting, shared leadership, and team feedback.

WHAT'S IMPORTANT ABOUT KEY ORGANIZATION DOCUMENTS?

We were traveling on a commercial airplane to attend a conference. In the seat next to us was a young woman. We struck up a conversation with her and learned some interesting facts about her business. She talked enthusiastically about a major project her employer had started. The health maintenance organization she worked for was sponsoring a new childrens' immunization program in cooperation with a local school system.

She said that she was actually excited about the HMO she worked for because mission and vision were taken seriously. Every employee was expected to know and use the mission and vision in their work.

She definitely caught our attention with her exuberance and emphasis upon mission and vision statements. We asked her about the HMO's mission statement. Without hesitation, she was able to share the mission statement and provide examples of how the HMO lived it. She even described the vision and values and how well the HMO performed on key indicators such as number of patient days per thousand, member service response times, and member complaints compared to the industry average.

Because she knew so much about her employer, we thought she must be a senior leader or marketing representative who had been with the company for a number of years. We were surprised to find that she was a claims clerk who had joined the company only eighteen months ago. She shared in depth how new employees are expected to know about the company in detail. A partner is provided for the first four weeks to help each new employee learn, understand, and commit to the mission, vision, and values. Key documents are discussed during department meetings and new projects are related to these key directions. Once the key documents are mastered, employees are educated about and practice empowerment on the job.

After the flight, we researched this HMO and found its journey was truly remarkable. We were startled to find that everyone from the janitor to the president of this HMO understood where the organization was compared to competition and where it was going. For each employee, this HMO was an adventure, a way of life.

These employees knew that the key documents, such as mission, vision, and value statements, were more than words. They were guides to live by. This exuberance paid off because the HMO was succeeding in a highly competitive and tightening market.

This story highlights the importance of key organization documents. Without a strong knowledge of and commitment to the documents, an organization cannot truly empower employees. Key organization documents include—besides mission, vision, and values—strategic plan, quality plan, safety plan, and any other major documents that provide a strategic focus or direction for the organization.

Leaders cannot empower employees where there is no target or sense of direction. Without both, employees will be in chaos. Chaos is essentially a lack of direction, focus, or growth in an empowered environment. Some organizations have experienced this and decided that empowerment doesn't work. What they usually fail to understand is that empowerment only works where employees understand and commit to key organization documents that provide focus.

The relationship of empowerment and key documents can be easily shown in the following equation:

$$E = KD \times EL$$

E stands for empowerment while KD is key documents and EL is effective leader. Empowerment is a function of key documents and an effective Leader-Coach-Manager. A word to the wise: if your organization seems out of control consider whether empowerment is being pursued without a strong understanding of and/or commitment to key documents. This tends to be a major void where leaders have failed at empowerment.

Key organization documents (KDs) require mastery of processes and innovative implementation. The KD processes can be simplified into five steps.

1. Develop KDs utilizing at least mission/vision/values statements, strategic plan, and quality plan
2. Involve leaders and employees in the development of KDs wherever possible. This helps create ownership of the process increasing the commitment to KDs
3. Provide high visibility for KDs. Do not place KDs "on the shelf to draw dust." Create expectations when and where KDs must be used in the organization. Most important, the CEO must be the biggest cheerleader for KDs. The CEO sets the expectations and pace. KDs should not become the fad of the month club
4. Require use of KDs for certain processes or activities. KDs should be used for any new services or products being considered. Identify whether a potential new product or service fulfills the KD requirements or expectations. At the beginning of meetings, ask employees to outline the mission/vision/values and how the meeting advances these. Or, end a meeting with employees outlining how the meeting outcomes have strengthened mission/vision/values. Review the strategic and quality plans on a regular basis
5. Leaders at all levels should be involved in the review to understand advances made in the journey and distances remaining. Newly hired employees must be thoroughly educated to understand KDs and expectations to emulate and use KDs. Use this opportunity for veteran employees to teach the KDs. Senior leaders should know KDs. Ask all leaders to teach the KDs. Teaching a subject can be one of the best ways to understand and demonstrate the value of KDs

A sound process for KD development and implementation will not be successful without innovative ways to reinforce KDs. Humans learn by repetition. The principles contained within each of the KDs must be taught or used at least four or five times by employees before the principle and KD become part of everyday behavior. Some creative ways to use KDs and avoid boredom or burnout are outlined below:

- Keep it simple! Mission, vision, values, strategic goals, and quality goals are used where they are simple and easy to recall. If employees are going to remember and use these principles and goals, keep statements to a few words.
- In organization newsletters, use a game or quiz with prizes to reinforce awareness of KDs. Prizes could include such things as a free lunch or a baseball cap.
- Place mission, vision, and value statements on the reverse side of employee badges/passes.
- Place mission, vision, and values statements on important meeting minutes.
- Provide employee strategy sessions at least several times a year to reinforce strategic goals and quality goals. Use the time to explain why these goals are important to the organization and to each employee.
- Periodically show how the KDs contribute to the community. Employees are more excited with organizations that contribute to the community. It creates pride.
- Celebrate achievement of goals. Impromptu free meals go a long way.
- Don't use slogans to kick off KDs. Employees have come to equate fancy slogans with management fads.
- Ask employees for suggestions. Ask customers for suggestions on how to focus on KDs.
- Investigate how other organizations grow and improve through use of KDs.
- CEO talks with employees go a long way toward support for and commitment to KDs where the CEO talks about what the mission, vision, values, and other KDs personally mean to them.
- In an organization newsletter, encourage employees to write about key moments where KDs made a difference or were personally meaningful.
- Celebrate mission, vision, and values with an employee fair showcasing achievements that reinforced or supported the principles.
- Ask employees from other organizations to speak to employees about extraordinary KD accomplishments and stories from their organizations.
- Encourage leaders and employees to share the mission, vision, and values with other organizations through community speeches to clubs and other organizations. This builds pride and expectations.
- For new hires or potential new hires, use innovative processes to gauge their commitment to mission, vision, and, especially, values. An ice cream retail chain asked candidates to create a structure out of a paper bag that related to their organization and its mission, vision, and values. A fitness club asked candidates to suit up and exercise with an

interviewer to test their commitment to customer service principles.
- Create an incentive system for new ideas that support KDs.
- Ask leaders in a group setting to identify appropriate and inappropriate behaviors associated with each of the values. Encourage leaders to use these lists to become role models for employees. Individually, ask leaders to use these lists of appropriate and inappropriate behaviors to identify how appropriate their behaviors are relative to the organization's values.

SO, WHAT'S THE POINT?
Empowerment starts with key documents because they provide a focus, boundaries, and sense of direction needed by employees before taking on additional responsibilities.

GOAL SETTING: THE BIG O AND LITTLE O!

Key organization documents provide an organization's big picture. The **Big O** is the strategic direction the organization pursues. Goal setting provides the proper picture for an area within the organization because it's tied to the Big O through its relationship to a key organization document. For a department or division within an organization, its' strategic direction is referred to as the **little o**. The Big O affects the little o and vice versa.

Despite the existence of key organization documents and the use of goal setting, many organizations are unaligned. Some areas of the organization are not supportive of the Big O. Other areas of an organization treat the Big O as a "windshield experience." Like driving through a national park in an automobile and never stopping to step outside and experience the outdoors, some leaders view the Big O from inside their area never really experiencing or supporting the Big O.

An organization's strategic and business plans encompass the strategies for the entire organization. Goal setting is a tool to link the strategies of an entire organization to the goals and objectives of a department, service line, or division. Leaders use goal setting to establish a clear path that a specific important area of an organization can follow. Leaders identify where that part of the organization is presently located and where it needs to be in the future.

There are six steps to the goal-setting process and are outlined in the Goal Setting diagram. Each of the steps in this diagram are examined and examples provided.

Clarify Strategies
Strategies identify where major improvement opportunities exist for an organization. Strategies are clearly linked to quality improvement

Goal Setting

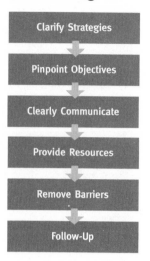

opportunities because strategies are about making improvements to reach business success. Strategies are also linked to and consistent with the mission, vision, and values. Examples of strategies are: increase market share or grow people in order to increase customer satisfaction.

Strategies for an organization are identified by several methods. Strategies may be identified based on the perceived weaknesses that require improvement if an organization is to succeed. An organization may not have certain services that are needed, lack sufficient talent, need additional technology, or require greater access to customers. Another way to identify strategies is through benchmarks. Benchmarks are the best or leading key practices of an industry. Examples of benchmarks may include the best market share growth rate, leader to employee ratios as a surrogate measure of empowerment penetration, and customer satisfaction. Threats to an organization from the external environment can help to identify strategies. Where organizations have been deregulated, they have found it necessary to focus on a strategy of being customer focused.

Strategies should be created with input from stakeholders, employees, and other key sources. Goal setting provides an important opportunity for leaders to increase the level of employee knowledge and support. goal-setting sessions can be held where employees are provided information regarding the strengths, weaknesses, opportunities, and threats related to an organization. With this information, employees are asked to comment on these and potential strategies.

Pinpoint Objectives Through FOCUS

The lack of alignment among key organization documents and goal setting is a problem many organizations face. Too often, a part of an organization creates objectives that are not aligned with the overall strategic plan or mission, vision, and values. The little o strategies are not aligned with the Big O objectives. In some situations, the objectives may be aligned but implementation fails to follow the path as intended. In still other situations, the objectives are aligned with the organization's strategies; however, some leaders fail to support the strategies. They are neutral players within an organization. It's unacceptable for leaders to oppose or fail to support adopted organization strategies. Yet, how can organizations avoid these problems? How can an organization avoid failure caused by asymmetrical thinking? How does an organization align the interests of all parts of an organization?

FOCUS!

FOCUS helps to avoid asymmetrical thinking and similar problems and align the entire organization. FOCUS stands for—Fewer Objectives Cause Us Success. In other words, the likelihood of success is greater where leaders and employees are focused on a few important objectives that align with the strategies of the Big O. FOCUS is based on a very simple notion—organizations are aligned where all areas concentrate on improving key factors.

An organization implements FOCUS by identifying the key factors that will be consistently and visibly supported by all departments and divisions. Each area of the organization is expected to show how they support a key factor and measure how they improved this key factor. FOCUS requires use of Critical Success Factors, Measures, and Improvements/Projects.

Critical success factors (CSFs) are components that are important to the survival and success of an organization and are directly related to the organization's strategies. These can also be thought of as the objectives. For example, the new leader roles and empowerment could have been identified under a people CSF. Other examples of CSFs may be cost efficiency, accessible information, increased sales, or quality. A CSF should be defined in a few words and easily understood by all employees because they need to know and understand the importance of a CSF

The people CSF will be used as an example. The organization could have defined the people CSF as "people growth and delegation." This CSF aligns with the organization's strategy of empowerment. People growth will allow employees to better respond to customer needs and address problems. It is important that all employees share a common definition of the CSF because they must align their efforts to improve the organization. Senior leaders usually develop the CSFs with input from other stakeholders.

Once a CSF is defined, **measures** are created. Leaders know whether they have improved a critical area by measuring progress. Otherwise, how can you tell if the organization is successful? Some examples of measures for people could have been the percentage of people trained in empowerment or other specific skills or the percentage of specific processes that were delegated to employees within a specified time. The percentage of people trained would have indicated whether everyone had participated in the training/development work. If the percentage were low, the likelihood of success would be minimal. A low percentage would also indicate that additional emphasis upon training is necessary. The second measure, percentage of specific processes that were delegated to employees within a specified time, would have indicated to senior management the extent to which delegation had taken place. If the percentage were low, senior management would determine why delegation had not developed as planned.

The final component of FOCUS is **improvements/projects**. Each division, department, or area team will concentrate on a process to improve the CSF. Data will be collected to measure progress. If a division, department, or area team has a different measure than the one identified by senior management, that measure should be tied to one of the organization wide measures. The measure and success in attaining the measure will be provided to senior management to show how an area has improved a CSF. Senior management may find from the data that minimal improvement was attained. In this case, leaders may be asked to pursue additional efforts to improve a CSF.

Performance improvement projects within departments are pursued using teams. Teams select a project that is focused on a CSF based on data that shows the need for improvement. Data is collected to show how the measure associated with the CSF is improved. Where several CSFs are pursued by an organization, departments may create a project team for each CSF. This will increase the involvement and support of employees for the performance improvement efforts. A number of organizations have used storyboards to collect information on how a process was improved. A storyboard is a word picture of the improvement process. It includes the process concentrated on, problem pursued that is related to the CSF, and the plan of action. Storyboards are useful to leaders and employees because they outline the performance improvement project, provide visible reminders of improvement efforts, and record the improvement methods used.

Denver was the clinical leader of a medical air transport team provided by a renowned regional health care system. In support of the health care system's Childrens' Hospital, the medical air transport team (MATT) provided air support for neonatal babies that were born in outlying, rural hospitals and required specialized medical support. In neonatal flights, MATT added a pulmonary team member to the flight crew because neonatal cases normally included severe pulmonary problems. Denver had recently taken over responsibility for MATT. In the past, MATT had personnel problems and lack of team unity.

The health care system had recently instituted the FOCUS program concentrating on best clinical practices as one of the critical success factors. Using data to identify problem areas, MATT selected its flight response time as an area for improvement. In the past, neonatal flights had taken as long as fifteen to twenty minutes before a takeoff. The best average response time in the United States was under five minutes.

Denver gave the challenge to his team sharing with them their average response time and the best time recorded in the United States. The helicopter pilots, nurses, and pulmonary staff were not about to be outdone by any other flight team. They were determined to meet or beat the U.S. benchmark. Since Denver's team was less than twelve members, all MATT staff participated in the performance improvement project. The team first looked at the causes for the response time. They used a cause and effect diagram (also known as a fishbone) to identify the root problems. Once the diagram was complete, they listed the main causes of the long response time. They found several items led to the longer than acceptable response time. Equipment needed to be located closer to the assembly area, pulmonary staff should be physically closer to the medical air transport service, and pilots needed faster access to weather condition reports. During these meetings, a sense of team spirit and commitment developed as they worked toward a solution. The team created a storyboard and placed it in their team area to daily remind themselves of the team goal.

MATT developed solutions for the problem areas and implemented these. Data was collected to identify response times. Within thirty days, the average response time decreased by one-half of the historical time. Continued efforts were made to improve as average response times continued to decline. Another added benefit from the FOCUS program was MATT increased its commitment to continuous performance improvement and teamwork.

FOCUS is a powerful tool because it aligns the entire organization to improve critical factors. It is a dynamic tool because it concentrates on improving organizations by improving processes. Another important point is FOCUS is a continuous process. Leaders can use FOCUS on an ongoing basis to improve a CSF for several years. FOCUS can send a very quick message to employees that performance improvement efforts are not a management fad.

Clearly Communicate

Goals and objectives must be simple and easy to understand. Leaders should use desirable reinforcement to encourage progress, expected results, and appropriate behavior. A good way for leaders to know if communications are clear is to ask employees for feedback. What was communicated? What is expected of employees? If the response is similar to the leader's communication, employees are probably on the right track.

Communication is important at every step of the goal-setting process. Leaders should use questions to gauge whether employees understand and support the process and the outcomes. If employees do not understand or do not support the general direction, it is important for leaders to fill the knowledge gap or assess why support is not forthcoming. Normally, senior leaders pass along information rather than being personally involved throughout the organization. As a result, gaps in communication exist. In other words, leaders with the most information and intense communication levels are least involved. This practice is a mistake for organizations.

Provide Resources

It is unfair to ask employees to pursue a project and not provide necessary resources. Resources that leaders may be called upon to provide are tools such as quality tools (i.e., cause-effect diagram or brainstorming), training, time to implement the program, capital to develop the program, and Leader-Coach-Manager support to help employees grow in their capabilities. It is common in empowered environments for leaders to ask employees what resources are required to help them successfully complete the assigned project.

Resource planning and implementation are important factors to any successful goal-setting process. Resources must be provided at the right time and place. Sufficient education needs to be provided to ensure that employees know how to use the resources in the most efficient and effective manner. Too often, resources are provided but leaders fail to educate employees how to appropriately use the resources.

Remove Barriers

In many projects, employees will encounter barriers. Barriers are the things that get in the way of leaders and employees as they pursue goals and objectives and when they take their eyes off the goals and objectives. Barriers take such forms as outdated organization policies and procedures, uncooperative employees or leaders, insufficient capital, or lack of equipment or technology. Barriers are commonly viewed as a part of boundary management, which is covered as a separate role later in this book.

Leaders must remove barriers where they interfere with the goals and objectives that are being pursued. This may require assistance from other leaders because a barrier may be under the control of others or require certain talents that other leaders possess.

If a barrier includes uncooperative employees, the basic choices are the Three T's: train, transfer, or terminate. If an employee is uncooperative despite training to the contrary, a leader has two remaining choices—transfer or terminate. In general, problem employees should not be transferred to another area of an organization because they will believe they can continue to create barriers without any major consequences. Therefore, the focus should be termination. If an employee cannot be turned around in a reasonable period of time, termination is the proper course for the organization and the employee.

Follow-up

The final step in the goal-setting process is follow-up. The goal-setting process requires feedback on the process and implementation status. Feedback can be gained through formal or informal methods. One of the best feedback methods is to ask employees whether the process was effective and whether implementation is going well. Be specific when asking for feedback (What is your progress? What are you learning? How can I help?).

Employees also need feedback from leaders regarding goal setting. Leaders need to periodically report on the implementation status. Are the goals being attained? If not, why not? How might employees help make the goals and objectives more attainable?

SO, WHAT'S THE POINT?
Integration—Key Organization Documents + Goal Setting.

SHARED LEADERSHIP

One Saturday afternoon, we took a break from writing this book and went for a walk. We ended up sitting on a park bench watching the world pass us by. Across from our bench, four small boys were playing "king of the mountain" on a mound of sand. They couldn't have been more than five or six years old. As we sat watching their game, we realized that the boys were sharing the role of king regardless whether the king was dethroned. In our youth, the king of the mountain was always the king until someone could throw him off the mountain. For them, the king was a role that was shared.

For many generations in business, leaders have played "king of the mountain." One person was allowed to exercise his or her will and faculties while other leaders and employees were cast in roles that used limited skills. Somewhere along the way, some leaders began to realize that "king of the mountain" was just that—king of a mountain, but not of the people.

Shared leadership is about being "king of the people." It's about power with, not power over. Shared leadership recognizes leaders and employees grow and contribute more when they are challenged. Shared leadership means specific areas, functions, or tasks that were previously under a leader's control are delegated to capable employees who demonstrate ownership. The supreme way to challenge leaders and employees is to share leadership with them. In fact, shared leadership increases the power of a leader who shares control. How is that, you ask?

Consider the story about Alice who was president of a catering business. She started the business out of her own kitchen and developed it by emphasizing service and quality. The business grew to thirty employees. Some of the employees manufactured a line of specialty foods that she offered in her catering business and in specialty retail shops.

From the beginning, Alice was a jack of all trades. She could work the food manufacturing line and coordinate a catered party for two hundred attendees in the same day. As the business grew, Alice became more and more concerned that she was unable to oversee the manufacturing and catering businesses because of increasing demands on her time. She decided to find out how other business owners had coped with growth. She found many owner-leaders that prescribed a tight hold on the business and a keep-it-small attitude. However, a small minority of leaders preached shared leadership as a way to deal with a growing business. They found that employees rise to the challenge when challenged. The problem in many small businesses was that too few leaders were willing to let go long enough to challenge employees. For those who shared, they were able to grow and prosper while maintaining their focus upon service and quality.

Alice was intrigued by the concept of shared leadership. This meant the business could continue to grow without Alice sacrificing all her time to the business. But, she wasn't quite convinced that shared leadership would work. Because of this, she started out by turning over a few tasks to several people in the food manufacturing division. These employees were asked to lead teams and make decisions regarding work assignments, time off, and training.

Several weeks after the experiment began, Alice noticed that employees seemed to be taking a greater interest in their jobs in the food manufacturing division. Since they seemed to respond well to shared leadership, Alice used shared leadership in the catering division. She assigned work selection and quality improvement activities to two different teams. Once again, she found that employees were more responsive and took greater ownership of the job.

The power of shared leadership became clear during an employee annual evaluation. An employee offered that he had never been so excited by work than when asked to take responsibility and make decisions previously made by Alice. The employee finished by saying that employees were more impressed by Alice as a leader because she had the vision and courage to share the load. Alice gained power by sharing power. Alice suddenly realized that $1+1=3$. Shared leadership equals greater power. Shared leadership is not about losing power in a zero sum game. Alice learned the day-to-day, practical point of sharing.

Shared leadership that Alice practiced was not about letting go with reckless abandon. A good example of a shared leadership system was provided above in the section on FOCUS.

The FOCUS process creates stewards or leaders of teams working on Critical Success Factors. These stewards are actually sharing leadership that was once thought to reside wholly and only with senior leaders. The stewards of CSFs help to define the goals and objectives while improving performance in an organization. A steward in one part of an organization integrates leadership with that of other stewards, linking together an organization.

Shared leadership requires the right skills, the right commitment, and the right work. Shared leadership consists of the five following components:

- Employees must have the right skills. If work requires adept skills in conflict resolution, leadership should not be shared until employees possess the skill level required for success. Shared leadership failure teaches one thing to employees—failure.
- Shared leadership works best where employees are challenged and take responsibility for the work. Shared leadership is more successful where employees are personally motivated to succeed. Leaders cannot motivate employees to succeed at shared leadership. Only employees can motivate themselves. This is the very essence of ownership.
- Communication before, during, and following work is a must. Before the work is begun, expectations must be clearly outlined because shared leadership is perceived as foreign to most employees. During the work, leaders should provide feedback to employees to reinforce desired behavior. Following the work, communication is important to reinforce the desired outcomes. Where work has undesirable outcomes, leaders should use the opportunity as a learning experience.
- Support systems should be used to improve employee skills, overcome barriers, and reinforce employees. In the story about Alice and her catering business, she needed clear work assignments for employees to use as they took over responsibilities in this area. In work areas where there are few support mechanisms, leaders should reconsider whether shared leadership is appropriate. Support systems include having measures which are indicators of success or lack of it.
- Leaders must have the "right stuff." The "right stuff" means that a leader needs to let go and allow employees to make decisions and pursue work in their own way. Shared leadership requires finesse in "touching base." This is a slang term meaning someone keeps in contact with another to make sure everything is going well. In organizations using shared leadership, "touching base" means informal contacts to find out how work is progressing without interfering with the flow of work and decision making. "Touching base" is more difficult to master than it may first appear. The first time leaders use shared leadership there is a tendency for them to feel awkward and act awkward as they attempt to interact with employees. Interactions during shared leadership are more on an equal level than in the traditional leadership roles and tend to create discomfort for most leaders. The only way to overcome this is through repetition and support from the leader's leader.

A last point on shared leadership is don't confuse it with shared authority. Shared authority is where a leader and employees share a decision regarding a certain subject. Contrast that with shared leadership where employees are empowered to handle a task, function, or area. A good example of shared authority is where a leader holds a group meeting for the purpose of discussing and making a decision on a specific issue while involving employees in the decision. This is commonly referred to as a shared decision. It is important to note that shared leadership is broader in scope while shared authority is narrowly focused. Shared authority does not include shared leadership. In fact, shared authority only means that leaders and employees have shared decision making on an issue or set of issues. Employees are not provided any leadership role where shared authority is utilized.

Why is it important to recognize the difference between shared leadership and shared authority? Some leaders practice shared authority thinking they are sharing leadership. They're surprised when employees complain about the lack of empowerment. Shared authority is a minor step toward empowerment while shared leadership is a major step in the direction of empowerment. Shared authority creates a small amount of integration; however, shared leadership provides a vast amount of integration because of the increased involvement and commitment. In fact, some organizations use shared authority as a development step toward shared leadership. Shared authority is used as a way to educate and train employees to make decisions. Once this has been mastered, shared leadership is pursued for a small number of tasks or functions.

SO, WHAT'S THE POINT?
Shared leadership is a major step toward integration and requires special skills and commitment from both leaders and employees. Shared leadership is power with instead of power over employees. Shared authority does not equal shared leadership.

TEAM FEEDBACK

One of the most fearful encounters for a leader is team feedback. Leaders are used to providing feedback but less prepared to receive it. Team feedback is where employees provide constructive communication to leaders (and to each other) on the performance, projects, or concerns in the workplace and vice versa. Some organizations use employee surveys as a tool to promote team feedback in the workplace. The problem with team feedback is too often organizations use this method before both leaders and employees have the necessary skills for this type of interaction. In situations where skill levels are not properly developed, employees may use the forum to "get even" with a leader. Team members may even use this situation to try and intimidate or ridicule each other.

Where leaders have not received sufficient training beforehand, leaders may fall back on command and control techniques to deal with criticism from employees. This will only reinforce employee perceptions that management doesn't really care what employees think and team feedback is just another management fad of the month.

Too many organizations fail to recognize that few leaders have had sufficient training to deal with team feedback sessions. Most management courses in college provide minimal experience in this area. The team feedback exercise is less effective than would otherwise be the case because leaders are not prepared to create the proper environment for a positive interaction.

For constructive use of team feedback, training is required in a number of areas:

- Key company documents
- Personal character
- Leadership styles
- Feedback principles
- Conflict resolution
- Problem solving
- Decision making based on principles

Team feedback becomes a very powerful part of integration where employees hear their peers using principles and team standards to address difficult issues. The place for team feedback to start is at the top. If senior management doesn't walk the talk, the rest of an organization will not adopt team feedback.

Team feedback is usually best started with some ground rules:

- Everyone should agree that a team feedback session must be focused on issues and behaviors, not people.
- Maintain self-esteem.
- Remind everyone that team feedback requires a commitment from employees and leaders to work on the problem or issues. It is a shared issue with shared solutions.
- Constructive criticism should be used when emphasizing areas for improvement.
- All team members should take responsibility for issues and behaviors. Issues and behaviors exist because more than one person has allowed a situation to develop. Therefore, it requires a team commitment to resolve the problem.
- Try to separate the facts from fiction from feelings. Too often, issues are clouded by feelings but brightened by facts.

- Solutions to the issue or problem should be focused on what is good for the organization, team, and individual.
- Listen to understand.
- At the end of the discussion, clearly communicate and record what has been resolved. Get commitment from the team to pursue the solution as agreed upon.
- Set periodic meetings to check on progress made.
- If tempers erupt, try to steer the meeting toward constructive discussion or take a time out.

SO, WHAT'S THE POINT?
True organizational empowerment cannot be achieved without effective team feedback. Effective team feedback is one of the most difficult skill sets to achieve.

COMMUNICATE EFFECTIVELY

Where Light Flips the Switch

COMMUNICATION IS RELATIVE, or so we learned one Sunday morning in Chicago. There we were—two southern boys at a conference in the Windy City. We decided to attend a church that neither of us was familiar with. After glancing through the telephone book, we decided to attend a church located in a nearby suburb.

We arrived early for the religious services at a Russian Orthodox Church. There was one lone worshipper seated in the front row. We sat directly behind the gentleman and agreed to follow his every move. Soon the church was packed with worshippers, and the services began with great pomp and circumstance. Much to our amazement, the services were spoken in Russian leaving us even more dependent on the gentleman in front of us. Whenever the gentleman in front of us stood up, we stood up. Whenever he kneeled, we kneeled. When he sat, we sat. This approach worked well and we grew confident by the minute.

We were quite proud of ourselves until the end of the service. The priest made a number of comments as we all sat in silence. Suddenly, the gentleman in front of us rose proudly to his feet and looked around the church. Instinctively, we copied him. The congregation broke into laughter.

After the service, we walked out of the church. The priest was still shaking hands, kissing babies, and exchanging prayers with the elderly. We slowly approached the priest.

"You gentlemen, you are not from here?" he asked in his strong accent.

"That's right!" we answered in chorus. We finally gathered enough strength as we stood in silence. "What was all of that laughing toward the end about?"

The priest shook his head confidently. "I had just shared with the congregation that we had a new addition to God's family, and I asked if the proud father would please stand up so we could congratulate him. Our church is not accustomed to having more than one father for a child."

Somewhere in Chicago there is a child with three fathers because we couldn't communicate effectively. Business is oftentimes like the communication challenge we faced in Chicago. Leaders may not understand what has been communicated because of a deficit in listening skills. Also, leaders may have to deal with conflicts that complicate business transactions.

Leaders, however, can take one thing for granted—change will continue to play a dominant role in the future. Where there is change, there is bound to be conflict. Communication skills are extremely important for managing conflict.

WHAT IS COMMUNICATION?

Craig was given his first two-wheeler bicycle on his fifth birthday. He proudly strapped on his helmet and attacked the street, wobbling from side-to-side supported by the training wheels on the shiny new bicycle. Before either Craig or his father could react, the bicycle was careening down an incline. In a panic, Craig pedaled the bicycle faster and faster instead of putting on the breaks. He screamed at the top of his lungs for someone to rescue him. Several onlookers yelled for him to avoid hitting the parked car along the curb. He barely avoided the parked car and suddenly struck the curb, flying over the handlebars, and landing like a dodo bird in a neighbor's lawn. As luck would have it, he was unscathed except for his pride.

Without communication, Craig may not have noticed the parked car. Through the use of communication, he avoided broken bones.

Communication is a process of listening and talking to achieve understanding.

Communication is dynamic—requiring both listening and talking. Most people say listening is more important than talking. In fact, both are important. Listening should come first, but it is not the most important of the two.

Sometimes, there is minimal need for communication. This became clear when visiting the Mobile Vietnam Memorial in Battle Creek, Michigan. Carefully laid beneath one of the tablets listing the names of the deceased was a shriveled red rose taped to a plastic sandwich bag. Inside the plastic bag was a handwritten message—"Paul, what can I say?" No need, no room for further communication.

THE SOLUTION(S) MODEL

Despite a heavy emphasis upon enlightened management in the 1990s, leaders fail to reach the most effective solutions because they don't use the important stages of communication. Examples of failed communication are everywhere—employees feel alienated and don't trust management because management did not take the time to understand them, the solution failed because management didn't consider all of the alternatives, or management jumped to conclusions before they sorted out the facts from feelings. In the new millennium, conflict resolution or communication skills may be the most important skills to possess if leaders are going to succeed.

To overcome these past failures, leaders are provided a new tool—the Solution(s) Model. The Solution(s) Model is designed for easy use by leaders and employees as a process to reach agreement. The Solution(s) Model may be broken down into four basic components: Foundation, Understand You Cycle, Understand Me Cycle, and Solution. The foundation to effective communication includes problem(s) and caring. The Understand You Cycle is a simple method to enhance a leader's appreciation of the issue and the position of others. The Understand Me Cycle helps leaders share their perception of the facts, their feelings, and alternatives to arrive at the best solution and increase synergy among employees. The Solution(s) Model is the outcome of effective use of the Understand You Cycle and Understand Me Cycle. Both parties use synergy to arrive at the best solution to the problem.

Solution(s) Model

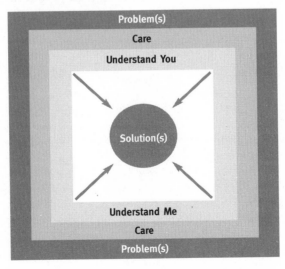

FOUNDATION

A foundation is the rock upon which a greater structure is created. A foundation must be broad and strong. Where leaders work on conflicts, they must have a strong foundation. It requires two basic components: a continual struggle to define the problem(s) and caring about both business and people.

Problem(s)

During the second day of a three-day seminar for senior and middle leaders of a health care system, conflict resolution skills became the focus. The leaders were divided into five separate teams and each team was given a set of facts and leader behaviors. Three teams spent little time on the definition of the problem. They quickly reached consensus regarding the solution. The other two teams carefully defined the problem and later redefined the problem after they had worked on the facts and feelings. At the end of the exercise, the two teams that carefully defined the problem were more successful in finding an effective, long-term solution.

Problems are questions or situations that are in need of solutions. Problems are not easily defined because they tend to be complex and subject to differing perceptions. Leaders may believe that problems are only defined at the start of the Solution(s) Model. In fact, problems are defined and redefined throughout the Foundation, Understand You Cycle, Understand Me Cycle, and Solution(s) components. As leaders progress through the Solution(s) Model the problem will become clearer and better defined. That being the case, leaders should begin with a brief draft statement of the problem. Throughout the process, the problem definition should be revisited and redefined where appropriate.

Care

The second stage of interpersonal effectiveness requires caring. Leaders will not be successful unless they care about their business. This is a lesson learned by most leaders. Moreover, leaders will not be effective communicators unless they care about the employees they are trying to communicate with. This lesson has been learned by too few leaders. If employees perceive that a leader really doesn't care about them, they won't listen or participate as intently. Why is that? Employees connect with leaders when they know they really count. They form a trust connection with leaders. Leaders who "care" are as concerned about the welfare of employees and the organization as their own welfare. Employees know that makes a difference. Leaders who don't care can't understand employees' feelings or thoughts.

Sally was a clinical leader responsible for the pulmonary department of a large teaching hospital. Sally's predecessor was a recognized leader in pulmonary medicine. Despite this fact, the department employees had been less than willing to follow the previous leader. Ultimately, her predecessor left the organization because he was frustrated with the lack of support.

When Sally arrived, she spent time with each pulmonary employee to understand his or her concerns, problems, and perceptions. Sally was determined to develop a strong department that supported the needs and focus of the hospital. To that end, Sally met with leaders and supervisors in other areas to understand their needs and how the pulmonary department could help them. Some indicated that there was an attitude problem. Pulmonary employees seemed to feel and act like they were unimportant. Other areas indicated that the pulmonary department was unresponsive or lacked motivation to respond quickly to crises. The pulmonary employees thought that the answer was to hire more staff.

Sally recognized that the department had not made changes that could have improved productivity and minimized stress. This was baffling because all of the employees stated they were overworked and wanted relief. Sally asked the senior technician why this was the case.

He said that the previous leader never cared about them. The previous leader was more interested in looking good and using new technology. The senior technician carefully selected each word because he was fearful what the new leader may think of his candor.

Sally asked if even though that may have been the case, didn't the previous leader show employees how they could improve productivity and help deal with their stress? The senior technician admitted past leadership had, but that everyone knew he didn't care about the employees. Since he was just looking out for himself, the employees decided they wouldn't listen to him.

Sally sat back in disbelief. Despite the suggestions that could have improved their plight, the staff felt their leader did not care about them. Because of this, they were unwilling to increase their knowledge and reach an understanding with their leader. Instead, they continued to face the same challenges with the same mediocre level of performance. It all came down to caring. At first, Sally was frightened. What if she was unable to convince them that she cared about them?

Little did she know, the employees in the pulmonary department had agreed that Sally cared about them. Because she spent time individually with each of them to understand their problems, she showed that she cared about them. Because she spent time with other leaders within the hospital to understand their problems, they felt a connection to Sally because she cared about the organization as well as her department.

Sally was then able to make the necessary changes to the pulmonary department. Because her employees knew she cared, she was able to share new ideas with them and increase their understanding by providing examples of other successful pulmonary departments. The employees agreed with Sally that the department should change systems and processes instead of hiring more staff. Because other hospital leaders knew Sally cared, they were more willing to accept and support the pulmonary department changes.

Why is "caring" so powerful? Where a leader "cares" about employees, other leaders, and the organization, they know that their concerns and interests will be strongly considered when issues and options are reviewed. As a result, employees feel more comfortable about understanding new ways of approaching problems, expanding their knowledge, and finding a solution with management.

What this story underscores is the important question—what should a leader care about? An initial listing might include the following:

- Employees, both personally and professionally
- Business results
- Customers
- Suppliers
- Community
- Environment
- Government
- Family

In other words, leaders should care about stakeholders and those aspects which affect or are affected by business.

THE UNDERSTAND YOU CYCLE

In the 1980s, David Feldman authored a number of books that explored curiosities in life. These books sold like wildfire. From "Why is there no Betty Rubble in Flintstones vitamins?" to "What does the Q in Q-Tips mean?" Feldman tickled our interest in understanding the world around us. Our society isn't content unless we understand what is going on around us. In other words, we need to understand others, grasping or comprehending the issues and related facts. Without understanding others, a situation is like a play without a stage or a jigsaw puzzle without a picture. Understanding provides the context. Understanding You is the outcome of intense listening. It is impossible to understand a problem if a leader does not understand the perceptions and problems of others. The key to this communication component is the use of the Understand You Cycle diagram. This simple cycle can help leaders increase their level of understanding employees and their problems.

A good example of the importance of understanding problems can be found in dentistry. Early in dental history, dentists knew that teeth were attacked by cavities necessitating extrication at later stages. Despite this

The Understand You Cycle

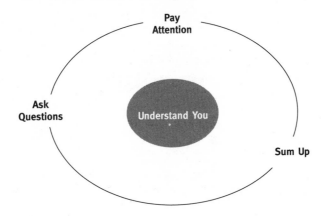

knowledge, dentists didn't really understand cavities. At one time, some dentists believed in "tooth worms" as the cause of cavities. They actually believed in human versions of earthworms that burrowed their way through the enamel corridor. Some prescribed leeches while others used urine mouthwashes to ward off these slithering beasts or whatever else was thought to create cavities. Because dentists couldn't understand cavities, they couldn't reach agreement on the proper way to fight tooth decay. They really didn't understand cavities, their cause, and the best way to fight cavities.

Communication is like the dental story. Leaders will not find a solution with employees unless they understand the problems, concerns, and issues held by employees. Likewise, before employees can reach a solution, they must understand their leader.

Many leaders do not understand this simple lesson. Oftentimes, leaders attempt to leapfrog from the recognition of a problem to the solutions phase of the communication continuum. The end result is no agreement—only confusion, disinterest, or anger.

A jet was positioned to take off down the bleached runway of a small Caribbean island. The captain and his crew were forced earlier to land on this island while fog blanketed their European destination. The Caribbean airport looked like a used jetliner lot for international airlines as many waited out the cursed European weather.

The air traffic controller finally released the crew for takeoff much to the relief of the captain.

The jet was ready, quickly picking up speed as it accelerated. Several hundred feet later, a lieutenant noted that another jet appeared to be moving toward their airstrip, possibly in their pathway. In his typical style, the captain barked orders to continue because they had been cleared by traffic control.

Seconds later, the lieutenant warned that his scope showed an obstruction entering the runway. The captain was furious, telling the lieutenant to remain silent. The lieutenant did just that, carrying the silence to his grave, as the jet sheered off the top half of an international airliner and exploded in a red ball of fire. Hundreds died in tribute to the lack of listening skills of a single leader.

Unlike this true story, few leaders place the lives of employees in actual peril where they fail to understand others. However, the reason for increased work conflict is, in part, because of leaders' meager efforts toward the development and use of understanding skills. Some authors refer to this as listening skills. We prefer to use understanding skills instead because this focuses on the intended outcome.

The dawn of the new management age is dependent upon finely tuned understanding skills that are readily used by leaders. These skills are imperative because leaders must understand empowered employees. Leaders must understand the comments offered by their customers to employees.

Understanding begins with recognition of the importance of first hearing and understanding the needs, concerns, and interests of employees or customers. Understanding is about connecting with employees.

Like so many things in life, understanding is associated with a cycle. The Understand You Cycle essentially consists of three components outlined in the diagram shown earlier: Pay attention, Sum up, and Ask questions.

Understand, as used in the name for the cycle, is a verb and an active role, not an inactive role. Each of the components of this cycle also begin with a verb. It is hard work if done correctly because leaders must sort out facts and feelings. This is no small chore in this age of stress and change.

Pay Attention

Understand You requires observation and intense listening. Leaders must closely watch how employees are positioned as they speak. Are they in a defensive posture with arms folded? Are they mad, gesturing wildly into the air? Are they stressed out as evidenced by nervous gestures? Do they fear you, moving away from you as you move closer? By observation, it is possible to enhance your understanding of employee feelings. Too often, leaders are so taken up with their own talking and message that they fail to recognize certain signs from others involved in the communication. From observation, leaders can gain additional tips or cues that will help them understand what employees are thinking and feeling.

Intense listening is one of the most difficult things for leaders to master. While leaders' minds are whirring away over 150 miles per hour, oftentimes employees seem to be talking thirty miles per hour. Because of this perception, leaders tend to listen to only part of the comments offered by employees. They miss the message. How does a leader intensely listen?

Use focused listening. Leaders must stop whatever they're doing and thinking to concentrate on the conversation and establish eye contact. If an employee catches a leader midstream in a task, it is appropriate to ask an employee to wait a few seconds until a good stopping point is reached and concentration can be focused on their important issue. Once the stopping point is reached, ask the employee to resumé. Sounds simple, doesn't it? But, how often have you continued to write as employees are trying to explain problems that are the most important thing to them at that time? This becomes more and more difficult for leaders because of the work pace. However, it is important for leaders to realize that more time will be consumed if an issue isn't clearly understood and dealt with as expeditiously the first time around. Stop, gain eye contact, and say "go ahead—I am listening."

Sum Up

How do you know if you understand what an employee is telling you? Leaders may think they know what has been said. It is their perception of the conversation.

An important part of the Understand You Cycle is to sum up what has been said. After an employee has finished or there is a break in conversation, this is the time for a leader to summarize what has been said. It is merely a rephrasing of statements made by employees. The summary is important for several reasons.

Where a leader is able to summarize the conversation, employees know the leader understands them. Their issues do count.

The summary allows those in the conversation to reach agreement regarding the content of the communication and the steps to be taken to resolve the matter. It is a way to bring closure to the communication and clearly set the course for action steps. A leader can be sure that an employee is understood.

Summing it up can be done as simply as saying, "For purposes of making sure I understand the issue, I understood you to say that . . . " Then, outline the important points of the conversation and any action steps that were agreed upon. Following this, employees should either agree that the summary accurately portrayed the issue or revise the summary statement. If employees fail to respond following the summary, just ask for confirmation. "Did my summary accurately state what the problem is and any action steps we've agreed to?" It may be necessary to remind employees that confirmation of the summary guarantees that you have a clear understanding of the issue.

The sum up stage of the Understand You Cycle is also an excellent tool to be used at the end of a meeting. Summarize what the group has discussed and action steps. It is a good way to assure that all agree upon the meeting and outcome. It also sets the stage for future activity. This is a way to formalize any agreement reached during the meeting.

Ask Questions

In traditional management, leaders thought they needed to be in control and had all of the answers. They told employees what was important and how to deal with the issues. New leader roles run counter to this ancient approach. Modern leaders must master questioning skills. Since leaders aren't expected to have all of the answers, they should know the right questions to ask.

The use of questions serves several purposes. It allows leaders to ascertain whether employees understand an issue. Questioning skills also allow leaders to understand the issue without monopolizing the discussion. Questions can also be used to help focus discussions where employees may need help in keeping on the right track. Last but not least, questions provide a barometer for employees. Based on the type of questions being asked, an employee can judge whether they are being understood and what issues may need further clarification.

Questions should not be used to steer the conversation. Lawyers oftentimes use questions like knives or signposts in a courtroom battle. They may use questions to "nail a witness," showing the judge or jury that the witness is not to be trusted. Lawyers also may use questions to force discussion in their direction, driving the witness from their train of thought. Questions are also used to startle or stop a witness in his/her tracks, like the question "Mr. Smith, when did you stop beating your wife?" All of these approaches are inappropriate uses of questioning skills for leaders in normal business situations. The business field is not a courtroom for Perry Mason wannabe's. Questions should be used to improve a leader's understanding of the issue and to help employees think through situations. Therefore, it is important for leaders to use questions at the right time and in the right way.

Questions should be used sparingly—if at all—at the beginning of an employee's discussion of the issue. Otherwise, a question may stop an employee from sharing important information about an issue. Questions may push the discussion in a direction that was unintended by an employee. If too many questions are used, leaders will start to direct the conversation. The pace of questions is also important. Leaders should look for breaks in the conversation before they ask questions. For example, at the end of one part of the conversation, it may be appropriate to ask questions to make sure the issue is clearly understood before moving on to the next part of the discussion. Some leaders will ask employees if they would prefer questions at this point or later in the discussion. This keeps an employee in control of the discussion. This is exactly what is needed if a leader is to hear all that employees want to share.

Questions are used to enhance a leader's understanding of an employee's perception of a problem. Questions can fall into several categories and can be used for various purposes. The major types of questions are outlined below with examples of each.

1. *Feedback*—This question type asks for information about the past. Example: What was the reaction of employees to this new policy?
2. *Feedforward*—This question type is similar to feedback except it is a request for information about the future. Example: What would be the reaction of employees if we created a new policy regarding vacations?
3. *Overhead*—The question is thrown out and any employee can answer it. Example: Can anyone tell me why the sales staff is less than enthusiastic about the new marketing campaign?
4. *Ricochet*—This is where a question is answered with a question. Example: In answer to your question about our new product line, why is this important to our delivery staff members?
5. *Direct*—This is a rifle question because it is focused specifically on an employee or group of employees. Example: Rob, why do you question whether we need to expand our production capability?
6. *Open*—These questions are broad and open-ended. They require more than a yes or no answer. Example: What is the response of employees to our announcement to close our plant in the state of Texas?
7. *Closed*—Opposite to an open question, closed questions require short and direct answers, such as yes or no. Example: Will you support the new policy on hiring managers only from internal staff?
8. *Bayonet*—This is known as the loaded or biased question. Example: When did you stop loafing on the job?
9. *Rhetorical*—This type of question does not require an answer or an answer is not intended. Example: Do you think you are better than the rest of your employees?

The first six types of questions are appropriate for communications with employees because they increase the amount of information shared. For purposes of communication with employees, questions should be used to increase the level of understanding. The first six types of questions also are not intended to be offensive and should not be used to control, steer, manipulate, or punish employees.

A book publisher created a new line of books designed for young children using computer discs (CD's) for on-screen interaction. The books provided the story line or problem and the CD's provided an interactive environment for them to problem solve. This was a revolutionary product for this book publisher because this was his first computer interactive product. Sales staff was concerned whether they could appropriately support the product in the bookstores. The president of the publishing company met with the sales staff periodically during the year to address important issues. Originally, the president ended up talking during most of these sessions. Following training in understanding skills, the president was able to generate discussion among the group and allow him to listen to concerns.

He asked them to present issues for discussion during the session.

During a joint meeting with the president, the sales employees said they were interested in discussing the new computer related product. They started out by providing information to the president regarding how they intended to support the product. The president sat quietly, carefully watching and listening to their comments. At one point, one sales leader raised an issue as to whether their merchandising materials would address the interests of the targeted buyer of the product. In the past, the president would have jumped into the fray and tried to steer the conversation as they struggled with this issue. Instead, he watched body language and listened to their discussion. The issue was apparently resolved as several talked about their experiences in bookstores using the new merchandising package. When there was a slight pause in conversation, the president asked a question, "I seem to be hearing from several of you that the package is working. Is that the experience of everyone at this point or do we need to rework the merchandising package? If so, we just need to understand this point, don't we?"

Each person agreed that the merchandising package was effective and was well received by the targeted market. With the obvious pause in discussion, the president asked if he might summarize the discussion.

As employees shook their heads in agreement, the president offered, "The computerized book offering has changed the way we look at our product and our merchandising. An issue we need to understand is whether we are properly positioned with the new merchandising materials. Based on the in-store research of the sales team, the target market is being reached by this material. However, we appear to agree that the issue requires some further research by all sales team members who visit the stores. At a future meeting, we have agreed to discuss the research and see if any revisions are needed. Does that pretty much frame our discussion?" The group agreed and the president asked the group to proceed with issues they wanted to discuss.

One employee raised concerns of a new benefit package. Previously, the company offered an all expenses paid group health package. Last year, the company adopted a managed care plan. Under the new plan, employees had minimal expenses so long as they used health care providers listed in their network. However, if they used a doctor or hospital that wasn't in their network, they would have to pay at least 20 percent more out of pocket. The employee talked about the financial consequences of this program.

In the past, the president would have felt compelled to interrupt the employee and explain why this was a better plan than the previous plan. Instead, he remembered the understanding training and the importance of understanding the issue. He continued to listen and observe as an employee described her physician visit and the added cost in health care she faced. He noticed that a few employees were monopolizing the conversation while the others failed to provide any signals whether they agreed there was a problem.

During a pause in the discussion, the president offered some comments: "This is helpful for me to understand how the new plan has affected your situation. Let me ask, what is the experience of others here and your understanding as to why we changed our program?" The president wanted to understand if this was an issue of a few employees or whether it was widespread. He also asked whether they understood the reason for the change. This would help him to understand the level of their appreciation for the change. Additionally, he once again explained the cost saving need for the plan.

Several employees offered situations where they used the new health plan. They said they understood how much health care costs had increased for the company and why a change was needed. However, they felt the system didn't seem to work.

Once again, the president asked a question. "What is really the nature of the problem here. I'm paying more for more health care like all of you. We don't like it, but I think I'm hearing that we understand we need to take some greater responsibility for the cost. Unless we do, it is a free commodity that we will use without considering the cost. By solving one problem, what new problems have we created? I would like to get a real handle on this because this problem is important."

As the president listened, the group discussed what the major problems were with the new program. Several ideas were shared with the group. As they discussed each, the group finally settled on one problem that appeared to be pervasive. The new plan worked well except for the fact that it failed to include a broad enough panel of physicians in the obstetrics/gynecology areas. Many female employees or spouses were going outside of the participating network to see their Ob/Gyn physician. They stated that the list of such physicians was very limited for the total number of employees, and it failed to include one of the more popular groups of Ob/Gyn physicians. As the discussion dwindled, the president was pleased to hear one of the sales staff summarize the discussion and identify the root cause of the problem.

"This has been very helpful for me to hear your discussion about this issue. Without me being here, I wouldn't have as strong of an understanding. Thank you for answering my questions. I now see that we have some work to do on the new plan to address this issue. I will report back to this group in thirty days on how we have done in increasing the Ob/Gyn physician panel." The president learned more from that one meeting than he had learned from the voluminous stacks of reports on his desk.

The president was pleased with the meeting for several reasons. He had paid attention by observing body movements and participants in the discussion. In the past, he would have jumped in and monopolized the conversation. At the end of the discussions, a summary of agreed upon issues and action steps were outlined. This provided consensus and the agenda for future discussion. Finally, the president felt good that he had not directed the discussion. In the past he had consistently focused discussions on matters that were important to him. However, he missed the issues that were most important to employees. The use of well-timed questions helped the president to clarify important points and provide cues to employees about issues in need of additional definition. The president was pleased with the meeting and his actions. In the future, they were able to dramatically increase computer interactive products and the group health plan was improved with the addition of the popular Ob/Gyn physicians.

SO, WHAT'S THE POINT?
To understand is to walk in someone else's shoes. Try on a new pair!

THE UNDERSTAND ME CYCLE

If we were born in 1790, we could have used the knowledge we gained from our early schooling for the rest of our lives. Two hundred years ago, new knowledge came slowly, without surprise. Knowledge became outdated every one hundred years. The number of books we would have read could have been easily counted on both hands.

How things have changed. If you pick up a business book or magazine, you're likely to see an article or chapter about the importance of knowledge and the speed at which it changes. Knowledge has become important to business because it is one of the key predictors of success. As we discussed earlier in this book, knowledge is changing so rapidly it can become outdated in three to five years. In addition, access to knowledge has skyrocketed owing to paperback books, internet, books on audio tape, and multimedia sources. Any organization that captures and effectively manages knowledge will excel in a rapidly changing environment.

Because of the rapid pace of change, employees and leaders are stressed. What might otherwise have been a minor problem may turn into major conflict. Conflict is a good thing when employees know how to resolve it; otherwise, the organization experiences chaos. Where there is no conflict, oftentimes employees become complacent and satisfied with the status quo. The real challenge is to nurture the proper amount of conflict. Where conflict grows, leaders must know how to cope and help others to use it as a way to improve the organization.

Conflict, left unattended, can lead to chaos. Employees are pulled in various directions. There is a lack of knowledge about what other employees are thinking and why they perceive things the way they do. There is a lack of focus. Cooperation and collaboration are nonexistent. The organization flounders.

Where conflict is resolved, order appears. However, gaps still remain among employees because they still do not have a strong knowledge of the facts and perceptions of others. Employees haven't learned enough about others to allow them to be similarly focused. When a substantial amount of conflict is resolved, the gaps disappear and employees are aligned. They are focused in the same direction. Conflict resolution is intended to help employees and leaders reach a level of knowledge that allows them to agree upon a plan of action.

Knowledge is basically facts, data, thoughts, and information. Knowledge is important where it is understood and applied. Otherwise, knowledge is just interesting trivia that may come in handy at a social outing.

Knowledge is synonymous with change. In fact, it is like a cement mixer truck—so long as the cement truck keeps turning, the cement can be molded. However, once the cement mixer stops turning, the cement hardens. It becomes immovable. Just like this scenario, employees will excel where they keep moving and learning. Employees are stale where they are stationary and knowledge is no longer added. Employees are no longer able to adapt; they become hardened like cement.

When Bennett became the leader of the cellular telephone company, he was astounded to find hardened employees in a dynamic industry. The company had once been a leader in technology but had fallen behind the competition. The more he examined the culture, the more he understood the problem. Employees said that they received little or no education from the organization. Upon further inspection, Bennett found that leaders spent little or no time providing knowledge for employees. Several leaders stated that employees were expected to learn on their own. The once dynamic company was lethargic. Despite the efforts of a number of progressive leaders, employees would not change. They could not understand the need for change and would not agree to any new programs that several leaders rolled out to their departments.

Bennett recognized that communication failed to go beyond "caring." Bennett started the change efforts at the top of the organization. Leader roles were redefined. They were expected to increase the knowledge of those who reported to them. Financial incentives were added to their bonus program to reward those who focused on this. Knowledge enhancement skills were taught to and practiced by leaders. Once this was completed, leaders worked with employees to increase their knowledge. Financial incentives were also created for employees. Over a period of several months, the organization started to blossom. Employee satisfaction surveys showed an increase in support for the strategic direction of the company. Employees finally could appreciate why they needed to change because they were knowledgeable about strategic trends and challenges the organization faced. The bottom line to Bennett's story was the bottom line—sales increased, market share leaped, and net income steadily grew.

The Understand Me Cycle has three components that are interrelated: Obtain Facts, Explore Perceptions, and Determine Fix. The Understand Me Cycle diagram is designed for easy use by leaders and employees in order to resolve disagreements or conflicts. Each of the three components is further defined and examples provided.

Obtain Facts

Consider the last time a group of employees experienced a major conflict.

How many employees knew the facts surrounding the conflict? Most likely, they couldn't agree upon the facts versus their untested perceptions. If employees could not agree upon the facts, it would be difficult at best for them to understand the perceptions of others. At this point, employees are focused more on their own perceptions instead of the perceptions of others.

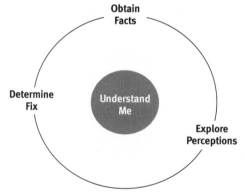

The Understand Me Cycle

Employees need to be able to discern the difference between perceptions and facts. Too often, employees respond to their perceptions without carefully considering what is fact or fiction. This is largely to blame for the lack of trust and rising level of conflict between employees and leaders. Especially in the heat of a battle or fast-paced action, employees may overlook the facts instead of their own perceptions. What is the solution? Employees need to sort it out. For an issue or crisis, carefully outline the assumptions. Examine whether the assumptions are based on hard cold facts or lukewarm perceptions. Where hard cold facts are not the assumption, management risk has increased.

The first step in the Understand Me Cycle is to obtain facts. What exactly happened? When did the event happen? Why did it happen? How could this have happened? Why did management respond in this manner? The best way for an employee to reach an understanding of the facts is to first agree that everyone has, at best, a perception of an event or situation. This is like the story of the three people who were blindfolded and allowed to wander in a room where a huge, stuffed elephant was standing. One person felt the leg of the elephant and thought they had found a tree trunk. Another person found the tail of the elephant and believed they had discovered a snake. Still another grasped hold of the tusk, certain she had found a long lost treasure.

Sometimes it is necessary for someone possessing facilitation skills to help a leader and an employee discuss the facts especially where they have minimal experience with the Understand Me Model. It is easier for an experienced facilitator to disengage from the conversation and focus on the facts than those who are emotional about the issue. Sometimes this person can be another leader. Other times, the issues are too volatile and related to a leader so that a third party is needed to help facilitate discussions.

A fact is things as they really are, not based on an individual's perceptions. Examples of facts are events, numerical results, cause and result relationships, and other objective results. As a leader and an employee struggle with the selection of the facts, it is helpful to list facts as agreed upon. One way to test whether a data point is a fact is to ask questions. Will the data point hold true in all similar situations if this test is rerun? Is the data point based upon some objective observation or measurable information? Is supporting evidence available to confirm that the data point is true? Have several objective parties observed a similar occurrence? If not, can the leader or employee agree upon this because others have observed the situation, overheard the conversation, or been involved in the situation.

Lynnis was a project leader assigned to coordinate a new real estate development project created by her firm. The project was a multi-million dollar development of prime real estate for a medical and technology office park. She was so interested in this project that she personally asked the owner of the firm to allow her to lead the project in the implementation phase.

Her supervisor, Jeff, was a bit nervous about Lynnis taking on this project because she lacked substantial implementation experience and any mistakes would reflect poorly on him. The implementation meetings would be high profile and include several prominent business leaders from the community who were going to make major commitments for their organizations. After several hours of discussions with Lynnis, Jeff supported Lynnis and asked the owner to assign her to the project. Although Lynnis had minimal experience in project implementation, she was given the responsibility.

Lynnis handled the first implementation meeting well. She prepared all materials in advance, designed a fast-paced agenda, outlined the key steps in the process, and effectively facilitated discussion.

At the second meeting, Lynnis provided a tight agenda. Although the project was off to a good start, the development timeline was confusing. Lynnis was not well informed and could not answer all of the questions posed by the business leaders. But she promised to provide the information prior to the next meeting. Jeff immediately jumped to the conclusion that Lynnis had not done her homework. Following the meeting, Jeff stopped Lynnis in the hall and shared his concerns about her lack of preparation. After listening to Jeff's remarks, Lynnis explained that the site work manager failed to provide a status report as requested prior to going on vacation. No one else could assemble the timelines that would be needed for the meeting. And, the meeting was not cancelled because other potential investors were closely following whether the project was being pursued in an aggressive manner. Since Jeff was out of town during that time period, he was unaware of the problem. Lynnis recounted the steps she had taken to try and work around the problem.

Jeff apologized for his inappropriate comments prior to understanding the situation. Despite the stress of the situation, Lynnis accepted Jeff's apology. He added that he should have worked on the facts before discussing his perceptions. Leader's perceptions are too often taken as fact.

Explore Perceptions

The second part of the Understand Me Cycle is explore perceptions. Leaders and employees are challenged to identify and share their perceptions associated with a problem or disagreement. Perceptions, as used here, are not facts. Perceptions are opinions, assumptions, and emotions.

Leaders can reveal their perceptions by asking themselves the following questions: How did I see this problem? How did I react to this problem? What are my assumptions? What conclusions have I drawn? As a leader and an employee share their perceptions, it is helpful to list them on a chart without attributing them to any individual. Once they have shared their perceptions, it is easy to identify the commonly held ones. This part of the cycle helps a leader and an employee understand how the problem has affected them individually and in their relationship.

Determine Fix

Once the facts and perceptions are outlined, a leader will begin to fix the situation. Based on the facts, alternatives will be outlined by a leader. The "fix" is a leader's perception of the needed solution to the problem. **This is different from the solution component of the Solution(s) Model where a leader and an employee agree upon a solution to pursue.**

The Understand Me Cycle requires the sharing of information by leaders to increase employee appreciation of the complexity of the issue and the leader's perception. It requires naked honesty on the part of management. This opens up management to the possibility of being ridiculed by employees. Over time, however, employees will start to focus on the problems and issues at hand.

The Understand Me Cycle is dependent upon the use of questions. In this case, the questioning expertise is required of both leaders and employees. Leaders must ask themselves critical questions to provide their perceptions to employees. Employees must become comfortable asking questions of leaders. They need to understand that the use of questions is intended to elicit sharing of information or ideas without injuring the self-esteem of others.

Solution(s)

The final component of the Solution(s) Model is the Solution(s). Once a leader understands an employee (Understanding You Cycle) and an employee understands a leader's point of view (Understanding Me Cycle), it is time for both a leader and an employee to work on the solution. A good starting point in the Solution(s) phase is for a leader and an employee to revisit the definition of the problem. They should also establish criteria to assess the impact on key stakeholders. Once they agree upon the problem statement, a list of potential solutions should be created through use of brainstorming. From this list of alternatives, both a leader and an employee can rank the alternatives that best address the facts as agreed upon. The top two or three alternatives will be identified and discussed. Discussion should focus on the alternatives that best tie to the facts as understood. Also, it is important to ask the following question: what alternative is best for stakeholders? Normally, the best alternative will be a win-win—the best alternative is best for all of those affected by or associated with the problem. However, some problems cannot be addressed by alternatives that will meet the interests of all of the parties. In these situations, it is best to follow the alternative that addresses the needs and interests of the organization. This point recognizes that a sacrifice by a few may be necessary to serve the needs and interests of a larger whole.

Once the solution is agreed upon, a leader and an employee will agree on responsibilities and deadlines. Who is responsible for implementing the desired alternative? When will this happen? How will this be measured or tracked? When will they convene to review the results of the implementation and consider whether any revision is needed?

The Understand You Cycle, Understand Me Cycle, and Solution phase are important tools not only for one-on-one sessions but also for group conflicts. A leader will need stronger facilitation skills where group conflict resolution is pursued. The following story provides an example of the Understand You Cycle, Understand Me Cycle and Solution phase applied in a group setting.

A small tool manufacturer in the rural Midwest received bad news. The railroad line that cut through their town was going to be shut down. For years the firm had used the railroad to economically ship their tools to market. They were now faced with the tough decision of whether they could continue to compete against the bigger tool suppliers if they had to depend on the higher priced and less than dependable trucking firm in their area. The president of the company was beside himself. His father had started the company well over fifty years ago. It was the largest employer in the town. It was not unusual to find third generation workers in the plant.

The president decided to share the dire news during a meeting with all employees. After he made the announcement about the railroad shutting down the line, the only thing that could be heard were sighs. Employees talked about the facts of the situation and their perception of the problem. The president used the opportunity to ask employees questions about their perceptions.

Once the president understood the employees, he outlined the facts, his perception of the problem, and the only fix he could envision which was closing the plant.

"Let it out, folks. Tell me how you feel," urged the president.

One by one, they shared their fears, anger, and surprise. After a period of silence, the president shook his head and said he had no solution. One employee in the back of the room asked why the group couldn't figure out the solution. Soon, others were echoing the statement.

"Okay. What do you think?" asked the president.

"What if we asked the railroad to reconsider?"

"We already had that conversation." The president paced back and forth in front of the group.

"Maybe we just need to move the company to a bigger city," another quipped.

Many employees angrily talked about their home and why they didn't want to leave the town. Others offered that the cost of moving would bankrupt the company and leave the workers stranded in a foreign town.

"What about switching our business to some other product that would use our skills?"

"Okay. What might that be?" the president responded.

"We don't need to do that." A lady near the front of the room rose to her feet. "Why not buy the school buses from the county that are no longer needed but too good to scrap? They've been a real sore spot with the taxpayers after the elementary school closed down. We can deliver our product to a shipment center where the transportation prices are more competitive and the service more reliable."

The room grew silent, but everyone was on the edge of their seats nodding their heads. They realized that the group had gotten beyond their perceptions and used the facts to find a solution that made sense to the company, employees, and customers. Discussion was rampant across the room as they discussed the pro's and con's of the last alternative. Before long, they agreed that they would approach the county regarding the unused school buses. In addition, they would approach the local trucking firm to discuss the potential for a buyout. The company later settled a deal with the county. The stripped down school buses were used to deliver the tools to large purchasers and a central shipping depot. The company was saved because the company reached the Solution(s) phase.

THE EMPOWERING STYLE AND SOLUTION(S) MODEL

The Solution(s) Model is best used with the empowering style. It provides the necessary ingredient of employee involvement and commitment.

The Solution(s) Model is a combination of five major components: Problem, Caring, Understand You Cycle, Understand Me Cycle, and the Solution(s). The Solution(s) Model is used where a problem is identified and pursued by leaders and employees within an organization. The Solution(s) Model may not be appropriate for reaching a solution with other organizations. After all, some competitive interfaces between organizations may require concealment of some information.

As part of the solutions process, leaders must be committed or care about the problem and be willing to spend time and energy to address the problem and reach a solution. Where a problem and caring exist, the Understand You Cycle is used to better understand the other person's point of view. The Understand Me Cycle is also used to insure that all parties working on the problem thoroughly understand a leader's point of view. Finally, the solution is arrived at by use of quality tools such as brainstorming, root cause analysis, and fishbone diagrams.

The Solution(s) Model is based on an empowering style, not telling or yo-yoing. Telling is where one side is victorious over another or what we refer to as a win-lose solution. The side that dominates wins; the other side loses. Yo-yoing is where each side gives up something to reach a peaceful solution. In yo-yoing, neither side gets exactly what they want. Therefore, both parties end up feeling like they have sacrificed their interests and reached a solution that is less than acceptable. Over time, yo-yoing may tend to fall apart because the parties are less than satisfied.

The empowering style is where both parties find a third solution that will include the interests of each party without sacrifice. It requires use of innovation on the part of leaders as shown in the following example.

Two departments in a hospital disagreed over which supply item should be included for use in the surgery suites. The director of materials management decided that Brand A should be used because it was cheaper. The surgery department director, on the other hand, strongly believed that Brand B should be used because it was easier to use. Instead of selecting Brand A or B, the two directors identified the key attributes desired by the two departments. Using the combined list of desired characteristics, a third brand was found that was cost competitive and met all of the surgery teams' needs. The third brand was purchased and stocked instead of the other two brands. Both directors were satisfied with the solution because they avoided an either/or decision and created a third way to address the problem.

Here are characteristics of the Solution(s) Model:

1. Ownership of the issue/organization increases where employees are intimately involved in decision making
2. The quality of an agreement is normally increased where the number of leaders and employees who provide input increases. In other words, two heads are better than one if skillful communication is used
3. Communication intensity (number of leaders/employees communicating and volume of communication) will increase overall where leaders use and encourage open communication (i.e. empowering style)
4. In times of crisis where there is minimal time for communication, survival of the organization is more important to management and employees than communication intensity. NASA learned that open communication is preferred except where astronauts have only a split second before disaster. In such a situation, the commander must solely make the decision
5. Routine decisions are made without a significant amount of input and a telling style is appropriate
6. The use of teams is generally overemphasized. Teams don't need to make all decisions. Use teams where synergy is desirable and the quality of the decision and acceptance of those impacted are needed

SO, WHAT'S THE POINT?
Working effectively with others to resolve issues is the responsibility of a leader. Reaching a solution requires an interdependent process based on understanding and synergy.

Role 1
Role 2
Role 3
Role 4
Role 5
Role 6
Role 7
Role 8
Role 9
Role 10
Role 11

Manage Boundaries

Role 10 A Mountain is Flatland With a Point

AN EAGLE SOARED overhead, tilting its golden wing toward Hawk Mountain as if in deep respect. To the Cherokee Indian tribe camped near the edge of the mountain, it was home to the spirits that lifted the souls of their ancestors toward everlasting life. Hawk Mountain was a monument to those ephemeral spirits. The Cherokee tribe was inextricably tied to that place.

Five miles from the mountain, down a rocky trail, lived a small settlement of Scottish immigrants who lived in distant harmony with the Cherokee tribe. To the settlers, Hawk Mountain was a formidable barrier. The harsh winter storms that tripped over its peak drove merciless winds down toward their homes. The settlers referred to the mountain as Raven Mountain because of its harsh nature.

The Cherokee Indians knew of the settlers' disdain for the mountain. The Indians, on the other hand, respectfully referred to the mountain as "a flatland with a point." They believed that the gods had created the mountain upon flatland for the grand purpose of transporting their ancestors' souls to heaven.

Like Hawk Mountain, organizational boundaries are perceived differently by different employees. Some see boundaries as barriers while others see them as bridges. Where employees are given specific geographic boundaries to pursue, they may see boundaries as walls where an opportunity that cuts across several territories cannot be pursued in a timely manner. Boundaries, in these situations, obstruct communication, increase stress, and encourage failure. On the other hand, employees may view a boundary as a bridge, such as where a new product organization is carved out as a subpart allowing their organization to gain a strong foothold in a new market. This new organization within an organization may open a new passageway or bridge to a more vibrant market.

Aside from the barriers and bridges analogy, boundary management can be defined as the skillful resolution of issues dealing with interfaces. More simply stated, boundary management is about making it easier for employees to do their jobs. Leaders work on interfaces, barriers, and bridges.

Why is boundary management important? Organizations run most effectively when employees are empowered to solve problems. Effective empowerment involves the right processes, which enable employees to deal with change and conflict. Boundaries may severely cripple processes, thus requiring management of these boundaries. If leaders do not practice boundary management, employees will get stuck. When employees get stuck, organizations become unproductive.

Boundary management philosophy is based on the belief that people are the solution, not the problem. Encountered boundaries are most often systems problems. Most employees want to "do the right thing" and do not want to create obstacles. Another basic belief is that boundary management is a choice. Leaders may choose to manage boundaries or to allow fate to take its course. Because boundaries may cripple empowerment, boundary management is a very important role for leaders because it enables employees to do their job and build success.

SO MANY BOUNDARIES . . . SO LITTLE TIME

At first glance, boundary management appears simple and straightforward. But, appearances aren't everything. Boundary management is complex. There are four types of boundaries:
1. Boundaries within an individual employee
2. Boundaries between/among employees
3. Boundaries between/among teams
4. Boundaries outside an organization

Boundaries within an individual employee are the self-imposed limitations that employees may place upon themselves. For example, an employee may incorrectly believe that he or she should not help any other employees in other departments because of the narrowly defined job description. In this situation, an employee may believe that all work efforts should remain within his or her department. Because of this, synergy is lost because there can be no shared efforts. Another example is where an employee believes he or she cannot expand knowledge or skills. This is a self-imposed boundary that threatens every organization striving to succeed.

Boundaries between/among employees consume vast amounts of time for most leaders, especially when the boundaries are barriers, not bridges. A good example of this is an employee that does not like or respect another employee and may decline to cooperate because there is no trust. A traditional example of such a boundary is where employees have narrowly defined job descriptions and expectations. Where work needs do not clearly fall within the defined work, an employee will decline to help because "it isn't my job."

Boundaries between/among teams are the classical problems faced by most traditional organizations. This situation develops when one team mistakenly believes that they have the sole authority to pursue a project. Any other team that attempts to work in a related area will not gain any cooperation or, worse yet, will face outright opposition. Another example of such a boundary is where a team charter is unclear who has responsibility for certain tasks or situations that may arise. We have all seen such situations where teams are caught in gridlock because the definition of responsibilities is unclear and no one will take action. Market opportunities are missed.

A final type of boundary is the most thought of boundary, namely, outside the organization. Most leaders tend to think of boundaries as the virtual walls surrounding an organization that set it apart from other organizations. An example of such a boundary is commonly found in police work. Where a crime is committed that involves federal and state infractions, the state and federal governments may fight each other for the right to control the investigation and pursuit of the court system. The United Nations is a prime example of an outside boundary created for the purpose of bridging differences among nations. Where a situation falls under the United Nations, nations will work together using recognized processes to solve a world problem.

Most of the examples provided for each of the four types of boundaries tend to focus on barriers. The majority of times, leaders will find that boundaries are barriers creating impediments to improved productivity. However, boundaries can serve positive purposes where they are bridges. New product divisions can be bridges to new found revenues and growth markets, and overlapping job descriptions or team charters can be bridges because they help to create synergy by prodding employees to work together.

PRINCIPLES OF BOUNDARY MANAGEMENT ARE OF VALUE

Leaders are most effective when they manage boundaries by principles. It is important to understand boundary management principles because they help to define the management skills required for success in boundary management.

The list of principles for this role could be exhaustive. However, there are five major principles that are the most critical to the successful practice of boundary management. The major principles are defined below.

Build Bridges To Achieve Effectiveness

Leaders must use barriers and bridges in a manner that will improve business success. Sometimes this may require the removal or building of barriers, or both. Or, situations may require the building of bridges to overcome boundaries. A good tool used to form bridges among employees is the creation of job descriptions that have overlapping responsibilities between departments. This requires employees to overcome what would otherwise be significant turf issues. These bridges are commonly known as a matrix organization—a more complex form of organization that requires greater skills. Despite that fact, matrix relationships can minimize turf and inward thinking.

Work in Partnership To Create Synergy

Boundary management is based on quality and the importance of serving the needs of the customer. If customers are not satisfied and boundaries are in the way, leaders must work to remove the boundaries and increase customer satisfaction. Customer surveys are good sources of information to identify where boundary management is needed.

Use Current Processes Until Better Ones Are Available

In other words, don't let go of a process until a better process is available. Employees tend to change a process or even remove it prior to the creation of an improved process.

The best way to understand this principle is to compare work processes with wing walkers. Following World War I, the United States was in love with airplanes. People were infatuated with heavier-than-air vehicles streaking across the sky. During that time, wing walkers took to the airplanes. These were people who walked on the wings of airplanes as they flew through the sky. At county fairs and expositions, people would watch in awe as daredevils would fearlessly walk along the wing as the plane heaved from side-to-side and rolled 360 degrees. Jim Franklin and his wing walkers recreated these long lost days at the 12th World Hot Air Balloon Championship Air Show held in Battle Creek, Michigan. Lee Oman, one of Jim Franklin's wing walkers, stood on the lower wing for takeoff of a biplane. Once airborne and traveling at speeds in excess of 180 miles per hour, Lee climbed to the upper wing and stood in the wing walker rack as Jim Franklin performed torque rolls, tail slides, and spins. One important rule that Lee exercised each time Jim flew the biplane was never let go of one strut before he had hold of the other. If Lee failed to follow this simple rule, death would be certain. For leaders who fail to hold onto a process until another is created, failure is likely. Just like the wing walkers, leaders must have the right balance and support when working with processes.

Be Proactive in Identifying Boundaries
Boundaries are usually not self-evident—leaders may not notice boundaries until they are already on them. Boundaries are easy to miss because they are camouflaged by problems and system failures. Leaders must proactively look for boundaries by asking questions of employees.

Look First for a Systems Solution
Most failures in business are systems failures. Many times it's a systems problem where people did not understand the system and how to work it. Too often, leaders presume employees have failed instead of looking to the systems issues. This leads employees to be defensive and less likely to provide feedback to leaders looking for the employee mistakes.

SKILLS AND BOUNDARIES . . .
LEADERS LIVE ON HAWK MOUNTAIN

A leader's purpose with respect to boundary management is to integrate processes which create outcomes that increase business success. To accomplish this, leaders need to be skilled in four competencies: destroy boundaries, build boundaries, reshape boundaries, and coexist. In this section, we will outline each of the four competencies and relate it to the Solution(s) Model.

Destroy Boundaries
Where boundaries are impediments, leaders must be willing and prepared to destroy them. A good example is when a department is unable to pursue its responsibilities because of a useless, conflicting policy.

The grounds department was expected to maintain all of the campuses for the computer manufacturer's three locations. The department was to maintain or decrease the maintenance costs over time. Despite these expectations, the company implemented a policy that required use of only internal staff several years ago. This policy was created in response to an internal audit that showed senior management was creating sweetheart deals with outside companies owned by suppliers and wholesale customers to the computer manufacturer. Because of this policy, it was impossible to bid out the maintenance business even when the company could gain best pricing. When the vice president found this barrier with the assistance of a department director, they immediately began to rectify the problem by following the internal audit department's required process to be excepted from this policy. This was the first situation where internal audit was asked to provide an exception. They finally gained an exception to the policy but only following extensive work and affidavits from the potential outside sources of maintenance services.

Boundary destruction can be exhausting work because leaders must overcome the status quo which is often well entrenched in an organization. Not only must a barrier be overcome but the company culture, in many cases, must be changed to effect the change.

Build Boundaries

Boundaries can be necessary evils. For example, when an organization is creating and launching a new service or product, it is often effective to create a protective environment where the traditional structure cannot impede progress relative to an innovative product. Boundaries can also be effective as structures to force organizational teamwork. For example, some organizations will create goals and objectives for leaders that explicitly include coordination of work with other departments and/or approval of other areas prior to implementing a program. In these situations, leaders can only move forward if they include others in the planning efforts or decision making.

A cereal company had a long, impressive record as a leader providing several major cereal brands. Despite their market position, the cereal company was experiencing difficulty in launching new cereals that would capture new growth markets. In the past, the company had always been able to create new cereals within the traditional structure of a research and development laboratory. This worked well for the company during three-fourths of the century; however, the last ten years were barren of any innovative products. The company had grown in size and the cereal market had become more complex and competitive. This dilemma wasn't a concern to the stockholders because sales and net income remained strong for the company. Senior management was concerned because the long term future looked dim without the ability to take advantage of new growth markets where profit margins were substantially higher than traditional cereal lines.

The company president decided it was time to break with tradition and create a new research and development plant where new cereal products could be freely explored and incubated away from the stifling traditional structure and culture. The cereal company was then able to create several new brands in growth areas previously unexplored.

Reshape Boundaries

Boundaries, like the latest clothing styles, can become outdated requiring reshaping or a facelift. In such situations, boundaries don't disappear. Instead, their process or structure will be revised to meet the current and future needs.

Several years ago, a healthcare system created a policy that required vice presidents to gain prior approval for any purchases exceeding five hundred dollars. The policy's purpose was to insure that expenditures were appropriate and necessary. This worked well in the days where healthcare providers did not have to worry about being competitive. As the healthcare environment changed to a customer driven environment complete with managed care and growing competitors, it was becoming almost impossible for vice presidents to react in a timely manner and meet the needs of patients. The health system's CEO recognized the policy still served a purpose but needed overhauling. The policy was changed to allow expenditures up to five thousand dollars by vice presidents. The number of related patient complaints dropped dramatically following the implementation of the revised policy.

Coexist

Sometimes, both leaders and boundaries must coexist. In these situations, leaders must be flexible and adaptive because boundaries must remain in place.

A manufacturing firm was strongly supportive of the American quality movement. Over a period of several years, management developed departments in the areas of quality, organization development, and reengineering. In the last year, there were continued conflicts arising where organization development complained of a lack of cooperation from the quality department. Because of this, organization development was being asked to provide educational programs where they were unaware of the quality department's efforts. The reengineering department complained that the efforts of both quality and organization development overlapped with their department. The CEO recognized the conflict. However, she also saw that it was a healthy tension that forced each department to be more productive and responsive to the needs of leaders in their organization. The CEO told the heads of the three departments that they needed to improve their communication levels and coexist. The departments were not going to be consolidated and the reasons noted above were offered as the rationale. Once this was communicated to the departments, relations improved.

No matter whether boundary management is focused upon boundary destruction or one of the other outcomes, leaders must master the Solution(s) Model that was outlined in the Communicate Effectively role. The Solution(s) Model is the key to effective boundary management for the following reasons:

- Boundaries are normally discovered early on by leaders who use effective listening skills.

- The revision of boundaries takes place once leaders understand the nature of the problem and the best alternatives. To arrive at this point, leaders must master listening, questioning, and talking skills.
- Boundaries are perceived limitations or needed safety valves that leaders can only understand where they appreciate the perceptions of other leaders and employees.
- Boundaries inherently create conflicts. Leaders must have skills to effectively manage conflict.
- Boundaries can only be overcome, reshaped, or created, as the case may be, if leaders can effectively communicate.

BOUNDARY-SMITHING . . . SOLUTION(S) MODEL

The best way to understand how to use boundary-smithing through the Solution(s) Model is by case method. The following case was taken from several similar situations where leaders and employees faced significant problems. As the story unfolds, the Solution(s) Model components will be parenthetically highlighted. At the end of this book, you will have an opportunity to use the Solution(s) Model to approach a boundary problem in your organization.

Jerrod was responsible for a new entertainment product line within a computer software development firm. This was the first company development following numerous years of success with business related planning and strategies software. Jerrod and his team were excited about the new product and its potential in the adult interactive entertainment area. Survey research showed that the software would be strongly received by the baby boomer target audience.

As they approached the second quarter, Jerrod was concerned that sales numbers were languishing instead of skyrocketing as expected. Because the sales plan was created to be a conservative picture, the weak sales picture relative to the budgeted figures raised grave concern **(Problem Defined)**. During his next meeting with his sales director, Jerrod asked why they were encountering the sales problem and what ideas she had to address the problem. When he voiced his concern, he recognized that sluggish sales over several quarters could place the organization and the many people who had made commitments to the product at great risk **(Caring for Organization and Employees)**. Since the company had been hesitant to pursue a new product line, Jerrod knew that senior management would be cautious and reactive.

The sales director, Beth, expected that Jerrod would raise this issue following the publication of the first quarter figures. She voiced her concern as well, stating that the initial sales projections were reasonable. However, she was unable to figure out why they were facing a soft market. Despite an intensive session with her sales team to thoroughly examine the problem, they were initially unable to offer an explanation.

Jerrod listened intently without interrupting Beth's response (**The Understand You Cycle—Pay Attention**). He appreciated the fact that Beth needed the opportunity to answer his question without interruption.

Beth recounted that the team found what they believed was the root cause. The marketing expenditures for the product were carefully examined. The revenue numbers jumped in response to the media campaign. When a promo ran, the sales figures increased for several days. The problem the team noted was that the marketing campaign did not continue. After the campaign kickoff, the marketing department did not provide any additional support. It appeared the marketing department was more focused on meeting the needs of the existing product line than the new product line.

Following this discovery, Beth had a serious discussion with the director of the marketing department. The first clue that supported the root cause finding was when marketing said they couldn't meet for at least two months. Marketing was busy with a new survey and campaign for an existing product line. Following continued efforts to schedule an earlier meeting, Beth talked with Sue who was the vice president responsible for marketing. Sue was strongly focused on the existing lines and didn't have too much to say beyond defending the marketing director.

Jerrod responded to Beth's problem by outlining the major points she had made (**Sum Up**). He heard that data showed sales figures were running way behind the budget. Beth and her team considered whether the sales projections were reasonable or some major assumptions had changed. Then, they examined the sales trends and found a relationship existed with the timing of the media campaign and sales. Finally, in the last part of the quarter the media campaign had not been supported by marketing despite the existence of substantial marketing funds for this product line. Jerrod also recognized that Beth tried to gain support for the media campaign but it appeared that marketing, for whatever reason, was very focused on a new survey and campaign for the existing lines. The bottom line appeared to be the product would die without stronger support from the marketing department.

Following his review of the issues, Jerrod asked several questions: What were the overall trends for software sales during the same time period? How did the entertainment software segment fare? (**Ask Questions**)

Beth responded that entertainment software sales for adults went up during the quarter in question. The strongest trends were in the interactive software products. Jerrod asked if they had any idea what the competition was experiencing.

From interviews with a person from the competition's call center, Beth had found their telephone calls picked up 20 percent. The candidate indicated that sales were supposedly rising at a similar pace.

Jerrod shook his head in agreement as he listened to Beth. He offered there were some issues causing him some concern. He recalled the competition came out at the same time with a media campaign that wasn't as vigorous of a campaign **(The Understand Me Cycle—Obtain Facts)**. However, the customer service department had gotten a number of calls from purchasers that complained of glitches in the software. In fact, they were unable to quickly address those issues and a colleague reported earlier in the day the problems were still being addressed. Jerrod said that he was as surprised by the report as Beth appeared.

Without additional market survey information, Jerrod offered his perception that software problems appeared to be the main culprit behind the lackluster sales. Jerrod reminded Beth that the competition showed stronger sales from a smaller media campaign. Beth continued to emphasize the lack of marketing support as the main problem because of the historical sales trend data she and her team reviewed **(Explore Perceptions)**. Jerrod suggested that the resolution to the problem was fixing the software and creating a new campaign to hype the improved software **(Determine Fix)**.

After prolonged discussions about their respective perceptions of the problem, both Beth and Jerrod agreed the real barrier was their perceptions about the cause of the soft product sales. They both agreed to focus on the software problems and how that compared to other new product rollouts. They finally agreed to compare the marketing campaign to other competitors using competition sales numbers in comparison to their campaign. They discussed several alternative solutions including increased marketing, revitalized software, outsourced distribution of the software, and sale of the product line to a competitor.

Oftentimes, we look toward others when a problem is encountered. Sometimes, the barriers are leader's perceptions. Jerrod left the above meeting to discuss the matter with his colleagues. He used the Solution(s) Model as a way to increase the level of understanding among leaders. In the end, they found that Beth's perception was more accurate. The software problems were not greater than any other new product introduction in the industry. The marketing campaign needed to be spread over a longer period of time especially in the early introduction stages **(Solution[s])**. They implemented a new marketing campaign using customer surveys and sales data. They resolved the lackluster sales problem and created a new product winner for the company. From Foundation to Understand You to Understand Me, Beth and Jerrod were able to develop a better understanding of the barrier.

Since the story was told from Jerrod's point of view, it is important to emphasize that Beth used the Solution(s) Model as well. For example, when Jerrod worked through the Understand Me Cycle, Beth used the Understand You Cycle to grasp Jerrod's understanding of the problem. In the end, they reached a solution because they used critical skills.

BOUNDARY MANAGEMENT OR THE ART OF HERDING BUTTERFLIES

When was the last time you saw someone herding butterflies? Of course, it is impossible to herd butterflies because they are quite independent. It is an impossible task. On even the best of days, boundary management is like this—herding butterflies. Boundary management is dynamic and very complex. Leave aside the skill levels required to effectively manage barriers and bridges, and there are major issues that sprout like mushrooms in manure.

Management has helped to create some of the daunting boundaries while trying to remove traditional boundaries. Many organizations have embraced the concept of the internal customer. Too often, the external customer is king while the internal supplier is a slave. The most likely resolution of this issue is to adopt different language. We like to use the term "partner" when addressing this issue. All leaders are partners that rely upon one another either for inputs or outputs.

Following the myth of the internal customer is the big boundary bugaboo. After management broke ancient paradigms, new paradigms were formed that created new barriers and bridges. One such barrier is team turf. Where leaders have created teams, they have taken ownership and pride of authorship to a new level—"this team is mine, don't touch it." Leaders have failed to recognize that there cannot be a sole decision maker in a complex environment of modern day organizations. That is because processes cut across organizations—they cut across teams.

Silos are only good for farmers. Despite all the modern management talk, leaders remain uncomfortable with matrix organizations. Matrix means we all step on each other's toes. Processes do not follow clean lines of authority or responsibility. The complexity of the world demands that leaders get comfortable with matrix organizations where they may share responsibility for an individual with other leaders. Matrix is here to stay. So, get rid of the farm and silo thinking.

SO, WHAT'S THE POINT?
Boundary-smithing is a required sport for leaders. Learn and use the key tool—Solution(s) Model.

Role 1
Role 2
Role 3
Role 4
Role 5
Role 6
Role 7
Role 8
Role 9
Role 10
Role 11

DEVELOP PERSONALLY

Without a Map, Destination Has No Direction

WE TOOK A vacation in Middle Tennessee just in time for the fall color season. The trees were brilliant, the weather crisp and clear. During our journey, a local farmer told us of a small orchard that we should visit to purchase some apples and pears. After traveling on a back road, we realized we were lost. So, we stopped at a country store. The owner was on the porch, resting with his feet propped on the handrail.

"Excuse me, maybe you can help me find the old Smith orchard?" we asked.

"What's the name of the town it's in?" the storeowner inquired.

We couldn't remember.

"In that case, you can go anywhere," he advised.

What a prophetic statement! Like this fall excursion, leaders must focus on a target if they are going to grow or get to a destination.

Change is all around us. It outdates our knowledge and information at least every three to five years. Without continuous learning, leaders have old skills to address new problems. It's like trying to repair a computer using radio repair tools from 1910. It just won't work because the tools are too antiquated to be effective.

INITIATE, VEGETATE, OR DETERIORATE: PRINCIPLES FOR PERSONAL DEVELOPMENT

Leaders set the pace for employees. If leaders are not aggressive, it is more likely than not that employees will fall behind the lead of their leaders.

Leaders have a choice—initiate, vegetate, or deteriorate. If leaders vegetate or deteriorate, failure is not far behind. It is that simple. If the commitment is to "initiate," leaders need to follow three principles for personal development: learn, understand the new roles, and seek meaning and pleasure in work and personal areas.

The first principle is **learning is fundamental to the development of all leaders, no matter what age.** Leaders must learn or deteriorate. Once leaders take a ride on the learning curve, they need to develop skills to address work demands. Moreover, leaders are almost always setting the learning pace. If leaders are not on an aggressive learning curve, employees will be close behind. Employees will only learn as fast as their leaders.

Ted was assigned a new department, Planning, to include in his division. The planning director was known for being overly cautious and hesitant to take risk. Some executives had voiced concerns about the effectiveness of planning because of these limitations.

In Ted's first meeting with the planning director, he discussed his management style and basic expectations of himself and the directors in his division. Ted also outlined the personal development plans used by directors to help them grow in their jobs. He noticed that the new director was especially interested in the personal development plan because he asked numerous questions about how the plan was to be used.

Ted explained that the personal development plan focused everyone on areas in need of improvement. The new director shared his own personal story how he had gotten into planning somewhat by luck. He didn't have a MBA or college training in the planning area. He was concerned that he may have some problem in the future if he had to compete in the job market.

Later that year, Ted and the director worked out a development plan with the help of a recruiter on staff. The plan was carefully monitored. After the first year, the planning director had increased his skills and gained certification in a planning related area. Because of the personal development plan outcomes, the director became more confident and took appropriate risks on projects. He was no longer scared about making mistakes and being out of a job without skills to fall back on. This was a win-win situation for the director and the organization.

Another important fact is the effect of continuous learning upon longevity. In a study of volunteers who sought volunteer roles in churches, hospitals, or other community agencies following retirement, researchers found that those who pursued volunteer roles experienced longer lives than those retirees who did not pursue volunteer work. The reason for this was their continued growth from the volunteer work. Learning is an elixir.

A second principle for personal development is **leaders must understand and practice the new leader roles.** Why? Leaders must model the new roles in order to affect the behavior of others. The Romans recognized this fact hundreds of years ago. They would use war and political heroes as role models in order to increase desired behaviors. Understanding and constant practice are needed for organizations to survive and thrive. Thriving organizations will offer the potential for pay increases and job security while those organizations in despair will not offer these perks.

The second principle is important to leaders because practice helps to reduce stress for self and others. Think about the last time you were asked to make a presentation and you had no time to prepare or practice. You were most likely nervous. If you had time to practice the presentation, you would have been less stressed.

Because the new roles are so different from traditional roles, a substantial amount of practice will be required. Consider the amount of time sports players spend in preparation for a game or contest. They use many hours of practice. Leaders tend to spend too little time on practice. Later in this role, this important subject will be explored.

Practice needs to be focused on the three functions—Lead, Coach, and Manage. Lead is the visionary part of the job while Coaching is people oriented. Manage is the technical part of the job. Successful leaders must master all three functions.

As the second principle suggests, understanding is necessary but insufficient alone. Both understanding and practice must be pursued if leaders are going to be successful. Would you be willing to ask a doctor to operate on you only after having read about it in a book without any practice? Of course not! Then, why should we do differently as leaders?

Bob joined the faculty of a growing college that prided itself on teaching and research. The college hired Bob because he brought a substantial amount of experience from the business world. Despite his lack of teaching experience, he was assigned the normal class load. His department leader called him two months before his new job started in order to ask that he join a small group of professors examining issues critical to the development of a positive business climate. Bob readily accepted the opportunity because he was interested in developing a good working relationship with other staff members. He was surprised to find that the group asked him to present his view of the critical business issues in industry. During each session, Bob received constructive feedback from his colleagues in regard to the effectiveness of his presentation. At first, Bob was defensive. Later, Bob found the comments helpful in preparation for his arguments at the next session. After several sessions, he polished his presentation skills and used different presentation approaches and more effective arguments.

One week before the fall semester, Bob met with his department leader to discuss his teaching assignments. He was excited about the class sessions, especially following his summer work group. He found that the sessions better prepared him for his new teaching role.

The department leader recognized that Bob's insight was extremely helpful to the group. However, the department leader recognized that a secondary goal of the work group was to provide a setting for Bob to practice his teaching skills prior to being thrust into a classroom setting. It was a win-win situation. The work group finalized plans for research and Bob sharpened his skills. The department leader likened the sessions to heart surgeons who continue to improve their knowledge and skills. Running wind sprints are important to work as in sports.

Practice was important in the academic setting because it prepared Bob and his colleagues to better serve the needs of their students. The results showed in the performance of students on graduate management entry tests.

Understanding and practice require leaders to incorporate new roles into a plan. Part 2 of this book is focused on this. An exercise is also provided for leaders to gauge where they are on the personal development curve.

The third principle of personal development is **leaders must seek meaning and pleasure in their work.** On Galapagos Island they have huge turtles that slowly traverse the sandy topography. These turtles live upwards of one hundred fifty to two hundred years. By this standard, humans live a relatively short period of time. If a leader is forty to fifty years old, it is likely that the leader has lived over half of his or her expected life span. Leaders should seek to maximize their meaning and pleasure gained from the many hours spent on the job. If not, life is too short to spend in such misery. Dissatisfied leaders should find other jobs that are more meaningful.

Positive interactions with people create meaning and pleasure in life. This is part of the foundation for the new roles—to use roles that lead to meaning and pleasure. People derive meaning in life from interactions with others and pleasure in life can increase longevity. A University of Texas Medical School study by Thomas Oxman focused on patients who were undergoing heart surgery. He asked the patients two basic questions:

1. Do you participate regularly in organized social groups like a club, bowling league, church, synagogue, or civic activities?
2. Do you draw strength and comfort from your religion or spiritual faith?

Six months following the surgery, Oxman found that those who answered "No" to both of the above questions were seven times more likely to have died. Growth in relationships creates meaning that is important to both leaders and employees.

DO YOU NEED TO RUN WIND SPRINTS
ON THE GROWTH CURVE?

The principles of personal development underscore the fact that leaders have an infinite opportunity to grow on the job. Leaders must spend countless hours practicing for future opportunities. Leading actors are like this. A good example is Harrison Ford, who debuted in "American Graffiti" but is most noted for his portrayal of Han Solo in George Lucas' "Star Wars." Harrison Ford practiced diligently and took bit roles hoping for an opportunity to make it big. Despite constant preparation, he only had a minor role in "American Graffiti" to list as notable accomplishments.

Job blight forced Harrison to take a full-time job as a carpenter while he continued to practice acting. By coincidence, Harrison was installing a door at the American Zeotrope Studios when actors were reading for the part of Han Solo. George Lucas spotted Harrison, recalled him from "American Graffiti," and asked him to read for "Star Wars." A few years later, he earned an Oscar nomination for Best Actor in "Witness." The rest is history.

If Harrison had stopped growing as an actor, he wouldn't have been ready for future opportunities. Leaders who fail to spend time and energy on continuous learning will likely fail. As the former coach of Notre Dame football, Lou Holtz reminded players and leaders alike—"when you're through improving, you're through." Being a leader is similar to a physician, lawyer, or professional athlete. A leader must continually practice in order to grow. However, most leaders tend to spend very little time on practice. Consider sports professionals. They spend a substantial amount of time on wind sprints in football, batting practice in baseball, and putting and driving in golf. Sports professionals spend as much or more time on practice as they do in the actual game. Leaders need to learn from sports professionals and drill or practice for the game. A leader's effectiveness is directly proportional to his or her time commitment to personal growth.

So, you want to be a successful leader in the new millennium? The best way to prepare for this is to understand where you are on the growth curve. What areas will require more emphasis and practice to succeed as a Leader-Coach-Manager?

PART 2

Making the Transition

Lesson 1

Lesson 2
Lesson 3
Lesson 4
Lesson 5

Lesson 1

Lesson 2
Lesson 3
Lesson 4
Lesson 5

How to Overcome Resistance

RESISTANCE TO CHANGE. Resistance to new leader roles. Everywhere leaders look, they seem to encounter resistance. Change will inevitably lead to resistance because individuals may want to maintain the status quo, they may fear what will happen if change occurs or they may disagree with or misunderstand the change efforts. What may start out as minimal resistance to change can become totally antagonistic. Resistance can also take on many forms. Resistance can be within a group or between groups. Individuals may resist change because of personal goals and agendas.

We accept the fact that not all change is improvement. Leaders have shot themselves in their proverbial feet by attempting changes that were not appropriate. The bankruptcy court files offer prime examples where leaders ventured into markets that were not well planned, well timed, or well chosen.

We also recognize that some leaders have abandoned change efforts too early. Oftentimes, leaders expect immediate results. Where an expected change does not materialize overnight, a standard approach has been to pull the plug. This can create fad management. If one cure-all doesn't work, get rid of it, and pursue another cure-all.

Overcoming resistance has become a full-time job for leaders because of the quickening pace of change during recent years. It is a Leader-Coach-Manager process—it has a starting point and an ending point traditionally driven by the stages of resistance. Basically, resistance comes in five stages: business as usual, threatened and angry, create a coalition against change, create obstacles, and destroy successes.

235

Business As Usual—Be Happy!

The earliest signs of resistance to any change efforts are quite subtle. Employees usually talk about keeping business as usual or remaining content with past actions. When employees are complacent, it is difficult to gain their attention, let alone adopt change efforts.

Buck was a leader of a manufacturing division of a multinational firm. When the organization's development department approached him to work on the creation of new leader roles and related skills, he said it was unnecessary. He had read many books, seen many management fads come and go and had well over twenty years of experience under his belt. From his point of view, it was best for the organization development department to use their time and efforts where they were really needed. Organization development's response to Buck's comments was to matter-of-factly contact his senior vice president to let him know that organization development would not pursue efforts in this area because of the lack of recognized need.

Organization development recognized that Buck was at the first stage of resistance. He didn't want to change. It was clear to the organization development department that without support from Buck, their efforts would be futile. A postscript on Buck. He is headed toward a different position where his resistance will not negatively affect the organization.

Threatened And Angry—What's Happening To Me?

Where changes start, the immediate response by employees and leaders is usually anger and fear. Change is a vast unknown. Few employees and leaders will see opportunity.

A rural hospital was acquired from a for-profit hospital chain by a local healthcare system. The purchase was part of the largest acquisition of for-profit hospitals by not-for-profit hospitals in U.S. history. The rural hospital had lost money and faced a shaky future. After the purchase, the buyer stated that the hospital would remain open and services would be strengthened. Despite these public statements and consistent actions, employees of the acquired hospital were threatened, awaiting bad news. The fear was grounded in concerns for their jobs. Their basic question was—"what's happening to me?" Management spent a significant amount of time and effort reassuring employees that the sun was rising and not setting.

As promised, the rural hospital was given a new lease on life. Services were strengthened because the hospital was able to provide more cost efficient care than larger medical centers with substantial overhead costs. Over time, the employees found out that fear and anger were unwarranted.

Create A Coalition Against Change—What's Happening To Us?

Given time for anger and fear to grow, shaken employees and leaders will gravitate to the third level of resistance and seek comfort in numbers.

Basically, employees will throw a "pity party." Those who are threatened will complain about change, "pitying" themselves and their dim future.

Senior leaders of a publishing company announced plans to bolster lackluster sales. Their message created fear among employees and management. Because the company had made few changes throughout its one hundred year history, any change created a negative ripple within the company. Following the first announcement, senior management said the company had acquired a firm that was well positioned in electronic media. A few employees and leaders were ecstatic while a substantial number of employees became even more fearful for their jobs. Soon, employees formed a small group meeting and some even discussed the option of unionization. The pity party had begun. Those who perceived they had the most to lose sought out those who faced a similar fate. Their perceptions increased the level of fear and anger.

Create Obstacles—They're Not Going To Get Away With This!

Security in numbers can quickly lead to expressed resistance. Talk is no longer sufficient. Some will intentionally create obstacles—purposely seeking to stop change. Others will unconsciously build barriers to thwart change. This could come in the form of less than enthusiastic support for such programs as critical new systems or education for employees. Whatever the driving force, the result is to complicate change efforts.

The publishing company from our third stage of resistance was trying to merge the electronic media operations into existing operations. Thorough education was pursued in order to acquaint all employees with the new product lines and how these would enhance existing products. The initial integration steps were not well received. Productivity dropped because employees felt that the company had abandoned them.

Destroy Success—If You're Going Down You Might As Well Take The Company With You!

The fifth stage of resistance can be the most destructive. In this situation, employees perceive they are in a death spiral. It's the kamikaze mentality—if you're going to get terminated, you might as well do as much damage as possible.

The publishing company in our above example began to see troubling signs. Decreased productivity soon turned into sabotaged machinery in the printing area. Threats regarding the new employees from the electronic media firm were written on the restroom walls. Once they reached the fifth and final stage of resistance, employees and leaders had placed their organization behind their competition because they focused on regression. They had succeeded at increasing risk to their job security and to the organization's risk of failure.

HOW SHOULD LEADERS DEAL WITH RESISTANCE (CREATING A SUCCESSFUL CHANGE EXPERIENCE)?

Like our example of the publishing company that faced escalating resistance to change, most leaders use a reactive approach. They try to deal with each stage of resistance responding to threats and actions. In many cases, leaders will give up and abandon change where resistance continues despite all of their efforts. The reactive approach to resistance is like pushing an automobile from destination to destination because it has run out of gas. It takes more effort and time to accomplish matters in a reactive mode than a proactive approach. Automobiles with gasoline can obviously go farther than automobiles without gasoline.

Leaders are not succeeding as expected in quality, reengineering, and other new approaches because of a missing link. Failure in change efforts is a failure to embrace new roles. Using old roles to address new approaches is

New Leader Roles

Roles	Relationship to Change
Create a new mindset	Exercise fundamental managerial beliefs daily while maintaining an open mind. Integrity and willingness to be open is essential during change.
Adopt the Lead-Coach-Manage paradigm	Effectiveness in all three functions is essential. Coaching is normally the missing link for successful change.
Develop your leader styles	The empowering style builds ownership.
Develop employees	Employees cannot develop capability in a vacuum. They need help from management.
Clarify employee expectations	Leaders must explain the case for change, model good character, build relationships, and teach.
Intervene	Shaping behavior is essential to arrive at the vision.
Avoid manager pitfalls	There are a number of common pitfalls that leaders/employees must avoid.
Integrate to achieve alignment	Expectations of departments, division, and areas must be integrated with the company's mission, vision, values, and strategies.
Communicate effectively	Leader must help employees resolve conflicts.
Manage boundaries	Boundaries are highly affected by change and vice versa.
Develop personally	Leaders must grow to succeed.

like the analogy of pushing an automobile without gasoline. Leaders do not have the right stuff!

New leader roles clearly address how to overcome resistance and succeed in a changing environment. As shown in the above table, each of the eleven roles outlined in part 1 of this book specifically address how to overcome resistance. The bottom line is if you want to continue to be stressed and experience failure in change efforts, continue to pursue the same leader roles as you've always done. However, if you want to be successful and quickly adapt, embrace the new leader roles.

Part 1 dealt with critical new leader roles. Part 2 is just as important because one must know how to develop management to effectively use these new roles. As shown in the Management Vision diagram, the change vision can be attained only where three strategies are aggressively pursued using the new leader roles. Management must select leaders with Lead-Coach-Manage capability, develop leaders emphasizing coaching, and provide support to leaders creating an expectation that all leaders will be HOGs—**H**elp **O**thers **G**row. The remaining lessons of this book will focus on these three important components.

As shown in the Management Vision diagram, the new leader roles require specific development steps where leaders are no longer content with "business as usual." New leader roles don't just happen. New leader roles require formal processes and dedicated resources such as time and organizational development to make the change. Part 2 will help you to make the breakthrough and implement the new leader roles.

Management Vision

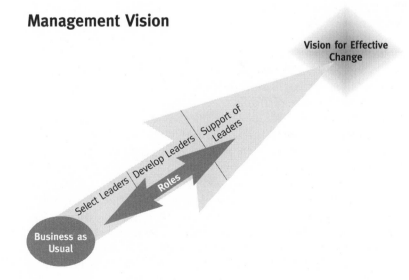

Lesson 2
Lesson 2

How to Be
A Leader's Leader

FRANK WAS THE newly appointed CEO of a publicly-traded software company. In the past, the company was heavily dependent upon Federal Defense Department contracts for its revenue source. With the demise of the Cold War, revenues dried up. Frank was brought in to transition the company from defense industry dependency to a cottage industry, namely health care.

When Frank took over the corporate reins, he acquired several small divisions that had well defined software products and services, reorganized the company by health care product lines, and implemented a new leader roles program. He strongly felt that the company needed to expand from traditional management that was reflective of the staid military environment to empowerment. Frank had closely followed how financially successful empowerment had been for some other companies with young cultures. With use of intensive training and employee surveys, the company implemented the new leader roles.

Frank saw his main role as supporting his vice presidents and department directors who made this transition. Having a Leader-Coach-Manager paradigm was very important. He recognized his duty to help other leaders in the organization grow. Frank knew the roles of leaders in the company and how they used Leader-Coach-Manager to make a difference.

On the surface, the company seemed right in line. However, Frank didn't know how he was going to support leaders in their growth journey.

Frank did not see how his role changed with respect to helping other leaders grow within the company. Leader-Coach-Manager was something that happened within the bowels of the company, not within the board room or executive suites. Frank's situation was not unlike many other executives who have been supportive of new leader roles.

For most senior and middle-level leaders, the new leader roles are a company strategy designed to help employees on the front line deal with the ever-changing environment. It's what other leaders do on a daily basis. Senior and middle leaders just need to be supportive. Yes, they need to be supportive. But, they also must change their roles if the organization's transition is to succeed.

New leader roles don't just happen—because leaders aren't just born, they're developed. A leader of other leaders within an organization, like Frank, must practice the roles identified in this book and use two other unique roles—Role Modeling and Piercing the Veil. These are two special roles that must be mastered in order to help other leaders grow.

Throughout this lesson, we will use the phrase "leader" in a different manner than we have previously used. Leader will be used to refer only to those who supervise other leaders within an organization. For example, a director may supervise a first line manager or a vice president may supervise several department directors. In these examples, a director and a vice president need additional skills to help grow their subordinates in their leadership positions. This lesson will concentrate on leaders who supervise others who need to adopt and grow as a Leader-Coach-Manager.

ROLE MODELING: LEADERWALK AND LEADERTALK

To borrow an old expression, a leader needs to talk the talk and walk the walk. However, there seems to be too much talking and not enough walking. The leader must model the new roles by using **LeaderWalk** and **LeaderTalk**!

LeaderWalk

What we see has a greater impact than what we hear. The following is a practical example frequently used in groups.

A group leader asks everyone in the audience to raise their right hand and form a circle by touching their thumb to their index finger. Next, the group leader asks the audience to follow instructions. The group leader asks the audience to place the circle on their chin, while he/she simultaneously places his/her circle on his/her cheek. Most members of the audience end up following what they see the group leader doing instead of what is said—they place their hand on their cheek instead of their chin. Most studies show that, a majority of the time, people will follow what is seen versus what is said. Especially with the advent of television and expanded use of visual communications, the power of the image has surpassed the power of the word.

The best learning experience is to see other leaders modeling the new roles. Employees need to see that leaders, senior to them, believe in the new roles. Employees also need to see how the new roles should be practiced. Walking the talk on a daily basis by senior leaders is also a continued reminder to others that new leader roles are a daily practice.

LeaderWalk should not be confused with the management practice of "management by walking around" (MBWA). MBWA is founded on the principle that leaders need to be visible, they need to be in the workplace to interact with employees to reinforce that management is available and what employees do is important for leaders to see. Some use MBWA as a way to keep an eye on employees in case they are working on the wrong tasks or not working hard enough.

LeaderWalk, on the other hand, is visibly practicing the new leader roles while in the presence of other employees. LeaderWalk is showing others how to interact and use the new leader roles on a daily basis. LeaderWalk does not mean that a leader only needs to walk through an area of the organization. LeaderWalk means a leader uses the eleven new roles in the presence of other employees when walking through the workplace.

Dr. Jeffries, who was responsible for emergency services of a large multi-site health care system, frequently walked through the emergency room area in order to interact with medical staff, clinical staff, clerical staff, and residents. He talked with employees using the opportunity to emphasize one of the new leader roles that that employee needed to improve. It was not unusual to hear a conversation similar to the one we have constructed below to demonstrate the effective use of LeaderWalk.

"Bob, good to see you. It looks like you and your staff have a busy day with trauma cases," said Dr. Jeffries as he shook the hand of the physician leader responsible for the day shift.

"Busy is an understatement," responded Bob, a new recruit to management from a pure clinical role in the emergency room. Bob's greatest management challenge was the use of empowerment, instead of traditional management.

"Days like this make it increasingly important for staff to be able to work at the highest levels of empowerment. How are we doing with increasing the capabilities of your supervisors?" asked Dr. Jeffries who emphasized the need to increase the capabilities of Bob's supervisors and enhance empowerment within the emergency room.

"Last week, Teresa and I completed the conflict resolution course. I think she's well prepared to take on greater challenges. I'm in a better position to understand and support her as she deals with conflicts. In terms of Don's development, as you know, he has greater skill levels than Teresa. I'm handing over to him the responsibilities for the trauma program director position. I need to talk through that transition with you to give you comfort that we've progressed to where we need to be."

Dr. Jeffries patted Bob on the shoulder. "I'm impressed and very pleased with the progress you've made in such a short period of time. You've jumped into a snake pit down here and worked feverishly to build your management staff to the point where you can increase their effectiveness. You should be pleased with such quick success."

"It's been an uphill climb for me and the others. But now that we've gotten to this point, I look back and see it wasn't as difficult as I thought."

"Where do you go from here, Bob?" asked Dr. Jeffries as he looked for vision and use of the personal development plans.

"For Teresa, we're ahead of schedule and should be to the critical stage in her development plan. I need to immerse her in some tough issues and see how well she handles the pressure and empowers the staff," Bob answered. "She's going to be wrestling with some folks that have not made a true commitment to the changes. As far as Don, I need to back away and give him more space. He's at the point in his personal development plan where he needs to intensely use all of the skills and tools we've been working on. In light of the trauma program and its infancy, he'll get the opportunity of a lifetime to use his new skills. This will be the first time for him to grasp an entire program and shape it. Needless to say, I'm a bit nervous because this means I'm waiting to see if I did a very good job getting him this far. And if he stumbles, I'm going to have to show some restraint. I can't jump in like I used to and take over the situation."

Dr. Jeffries carefully listened as Bob pointed out the key steps. "Let me just make sure I am understanding what you are saying. Teresa is ready for her full set of skills to be tested by a group with concentration on the use of her recently acquired conflict management skills. Don is well along with his development plan. He needs to be fully empowered. And, I need to support you in your nervous moments," chuckled Dr. Jeffries as he reassured Bob.

Dr. Jeffries added, "It's time to see how well we've prepared folks for greater empowerment. As I've said many times before, you sell yourself short, Bob. You're a good leader; however, you need some tangible results to give you personal confidence. It's coming. You're well on your way to attaining your personal development goals. You've completed all of your skills training with the completion of the conflict resolution course. We need to go out for lunch soon and celebrate your achievements." Following a quick handshake and another pat on Bob's back, Dr. Jeffries continued his walk through the emergency department to engage employees.

How to LeaderWalk is summarized in the table below.

LeaderTalk

Employees must be empowered in order to maximize productivity and improve customer satisfaction. How can leaders provide an empowering environment for their employees if empowerment is not supported and

LeaderWalk

The Walk	Explanation
Plan your LeaderWalk time	It is recommended for leaders to LeaderWalk at least 30 percent of work time.
Plan your apparel	If you normally wear a tie and coat, consider walking around without a coat and a loosened tie. If you normally wear a dress/skirt, identify ways to look less formal. Set the tone for less formality.
Plan your walk	List those employees you intend to interact with. Identify those items to emphasize that relate to the new roles and, possibly, their personal development plan.
Walk the talk	LeaderTalk as you interact with employees. Educate and provide positive reinforcement. Emphasize those points that were identified in the step "plan your walk."
Summarize the conversation	At the end of your conversation, summarize the conversation, emphasizing the points that were key to walking the talk.
Keep a record	Record the conversations you had to keep a diary on the personal development of each employee. Periodically (at least quarterly), a leader should review how each subordinate is progressing on their personal development plan.

modeled throughout the organization? If it's good enough for the first line leaders, it should be consistently practiced at all levels in an organization. Many leaders fall into a "prescriptive trap" in an effort to achieve desired results. They prescribe how a certain situation or task should be handled instead of helping an employee to think through a problem. One of the key challenges of helping others grow is to offer help without taking responsibility.

LeaderTalk is the effective use of communication by a leader to help others work through problems and issues without a leader taking responsibility for the problem or issue. LeaderTalk is more than motivation or desirable reinforcement. It is largely using questions to help employees logically focus on and approach difficult problems or issues.

We observed LeaderTalk in action when we flew aboard a small commuter plane to a workshop. We sat in the front row just inches from the flight deck. The pilot of the commuter plane was very much in command as she prepared the plane for takeoff and effectively flew the plane around some weather. However, she was obviously trying to use this flight as an opportunity for her young copilot to increase his skills and confidence level.

At one point during the flight, she told the copilot that she was going to turn over the flight responsibilities to him. We heard her say, "In order for you to increase your skills and confidence, I'm going to sit quietly and observe. When we complete the flight, I'll offer suggestions for you to improve. If you have any questions while you are in control, please feel free to ask any questions. OK?"

The copilot raised the nose of the plane and reached a higher altitude. At one point, he asked the pilot about a technical readjustment in the flight pattern because they were encountering some inclement weather to one side of the plane.

"Ok," the pilot responded, "What's your intended direction? What's the most effective approach for concentrated weather? Does this apply here?"

The copilot listened carefully. He quickly talked through the questions she raised and immediately identified the alternative readjustment that was appropriate for the weather he was encountering.

Instead of providing the answer, the pilot asked several questions to help her copilot discover the answer and keep responsibility for the problem. She also praised him for being able to work through the issue and arrive at the decision point. LeaderTalk in action. She offered the questions to help the copilot work toward the desired point. She ended up using positive reinforcement following the copilot's decisions.

If everyone is not singing from the same hymn book, they may not be singing the same song! The second part of LeaderTalk is consistency. A leader needs to be singing from the same hymn book as others in the organization and using LeaderTalk as the compass for others to be consistent in their words, as well as actions.

A good exercise to illustrate this point is to ask an individual to hold their hands in an open position in front of them within a couple inches of touching a leader's hands. The individual is asked to mimic or follow the movement of the leader's hands. Then, the individual is asked to move his or her hands in the opposite direction from that of the leader. When asked what is more difficult to do, an individual usually responds it's more difficult to move in an opposite direction. It's easier, more natural, to follow a leader's hands than to do the opposite. This is also true in the workplace. It's easier, more natural, to follow LeaderTalk and LeaderWalk than the opposite.

In other words, a leader must carefully conduct all development discussions, such as performance appraisal and counseling. The way a leader conducts these discussions will likely affect the way their subordinates approach their employees. A leader must consistently walk the walk and talk the talk that is desired.

How to LeaderTalk is outlined in the table below.

SO, WHAT'S THE POINT?
There's another old saying—what you do speaks so loud that I can't hear what you say. This is certainly true in many parts of our lives. However, it underscores the importance of words and actions being in alignment. LeaderTalk and LeaderWalk are critical. Individuals watch what we do and hear what we say. Both must be consistent and blend harmoniously.

LeaderTalk

The Talk	Explanation
Outline conversation	Outline the key points of the conversation you want to have with each subordinate employee.
Review points	Review the outline to make sure you will emphasize new roles and personal development plan areas.
Create informal environment	Create an informal environment for the conversation. This will enhance the conversation and openness.
Questioning	Use questions; don't lead; don't criticize.
Reinforce	Where appropriate, provide desirable reinforcement.
Summarize	At the end of the conversation, summarize the major points.

PIERCE THE VEIL: LEADERLISTEN

"Pierce the veil" is a phrase borrowed from business law that means looking beyond the surface and understanding what's really being stated or accomplished. When applying the phrase to management, it means that a leader needs to look beyond what is stated by employees and understand the reality. **LeaderListen** is gaining feedback from others while understanding what is being communicated and why. This is critical to the survival of organizations because a leader is probably one of the most lied-to people in an organization.

Employees do not lie in order to deceive a leader. Employees lie in order to please a leader. No one wants to risk anger and negative reactions from telling a leader, who has a higher formal rank in the organization, that things are not going well or are not as positive as they seem. This is especially true where a leader who is receiving the communication has been the architect of a new service or product that is being criticized. Rather than taking a risk, many employees will allow incorrect perceptions of leaders to remain intact. They will avoid the issue or even lie.

Does a leader want to know there is a problem? Too often, a leader loses sight of the fact that her job exists in order to deal with problems. Human nature being what it is, a leader does not like to hear anything other than perfection or success. However, a leader will not reach a vision without knowing the reality with all of its warts and human failures. A leader cannot understand where an organization is at in its journey unless employees are comfortable sharing their perception of reality.

How Do You Pierce the Veil?

First, leaders need to be good listeners. Most people have had very little, if any, training in skilled listening, while they have had a significant amount of training in the areas of reading, writing, and speaking. (It is not the purpose of this book to teach a course in listening but the listening skill set was reviewed in the previous role on communication.) Good listening skills are a prerequisite, though. It is also a prerequisite for encouraging employees and first-line leaders to be open and honest. In order to be good listeners, a leader must be willing to hear good and bad news. A leader should not "kill the messenger." Where bad news is communicated, a leader should be thankful that the information was shared and the organization avoided possible further harm.

Employees must see that a leader is willing to receive bad news. This requires a leader to use two general types of learning: positive learning and negative learning. Positive learning is where an individual obtains information that is consistent with one's experiences, thoughts, and beliefs. Negative learning is where an individual obtains information that is contrary to one's experiences, thoughts, and beliefs. If a leader doesn't value negative learning, it is impossible to grow others because a leader will not understand or appreciate what is going on. If a leader cannot effectively adopt a Lead-Coach-Manage paradigm, leaders cannot effectively supervise employees.

The second way to pierce the veil is that a leader must visibly reward those who take reasonable risks and communicate their perceptions of reality. A leader must find situations to provide praise for employees that take risks and offer their perceptions of reality.

The third way to pierce the veil is a leader needs to be in touch with employees at all levels of the organization. A leader needs to gain information that is not always filtered through levels of hierarchy within an organization. A leader must regularly tour work areas in order for employees to feel comfortable to share information that may be negative. Employees may feel more comfortable sharing negative information with someone other than their leader because they do not have to work with other leaders and face possible daily recriminations.

Negative feelings do not go away if unsurfaced. Instead, these feelings surface in uglier ways. It is important and positive when people are communicating with a leader. So long as employees are talking with a leader, there is greater opportunity for a leader to gain their perceptions and concerns. When employees stop talking to a leader, they are probably talking to others in the organization and spreading their growing animosity.

How to LeaderListen is outlined in the table below.

LeaderListen

Listening	Explanation
Establish communication channels	Early in the conversation, show your interest in constructive feedback through words and body language. Also show an interest in what employees think and feel by being attentive.
Engage leaders and employees	Listen by being nonjudgmental. Minimize the number of interruptions. Don't preach and don't advise. Show you are listening by summarizing important points made by the employee.
Clarify points	Once an employee has finished his/her thoughts, clarify any points that were unclear. From the behavior shown, understand what is being said and why.
Reflect the conversation	Summarize the major points made by an employee and ask if the summary is accurate.
Provide feedback	Later, provide feedback to the employee who offered the comments. Feedback may consist of a brief note thanking the person for the comments, action to correct a problem cited and communication of the corrective action, or a request for further information for addressing the issue.

Brenda was the senior vice president responsible for all medical management services provided by her employer, a workers' compensation insurance company. Brenda and her staff provided case management to employees injured on the job by periodically calling employees to make sure appointments with physicians were kept, interacting with physicians and others providing care to an employee to coordinate care and minimize work time lost, and reporting the case status to employers.

In the past, the company had a very low employee turnover rate. However, turnover rates were rising. Rob, president of the company and Brenda's immediate supervisor, was pleased with Brenda's performance but concerned about the negative trend in employee turnover. He increased his communication with leaders and employees to better understand the problem.

Rob used informal opportunities to discuss the growing problem with Brenda by stopping at her office when he knew she might be available. He was careful to make sure he met within her territory where the meeting may be seen as less threatening. Conversation never started out with the issue at hand. Rob made sure he talked about personal issues that were important to Brenda. Since he knew she was a gardening enthusiast, Rob always started out the conversation by discussing her plans for the growing season. Once sufficient time was given to open up conversation, Rob would inquire how matters were progressing in the areas ripe for improvement. The conversation would follow similar to the format used below.

"I'm trying to apply my green thumb to my work, Rob. I'm investing in more training time for staff. I think that the turnover problem in our area may be related to staff feelings that systems have changed but training has not kept pace," said Brenda as she reached for a report on her desk.

"You have caught my interest, Brenda. Please, tell me more," asked Rob.

"I got to thinking about what changes have taken place internally and externally. At first, I couldn't identify any from the past year. Then, it occurred to me. Our major competitor had made a major investment in training. In the past, they had been behind us in training," Brenda related as she turned to the middle of the report. "The real key came to light when I browsed through the systems upgrade report. Do you realize that we made seven upgrades to our information systems last year instead of the typical three or four?"

"I see," said Rob nodding his head.

"Despite all of the changes, we didn't even provide the same level of training as in the past. And when I compared the employee satisfaction rates, I noted a lower score in employee satisfaction with training. What had been a strong suit for us in the past was becoming our weakest point. I tested this with staff by asking them if they felt as well informed on system capability as they have in the past. Everyone felt that was a major gap for us."

"What I understand you to say, Brenda, is that training is creating the problem," asked Rob.

"Training appears to be a major cause of helplessness and aggravation on the job. Sure, the pace is picking up. But, we have failed to keep up with the pace of knowledge while our competition has kept up. I would like to say that I picked up the slack by increasing the amount of training within our department, but I didn't," she answered.

"Let me summarize what you've just said. Our pace of business has increased but our revisions to information systems have far outstripped our training commitment this past year. This has led to increased stress on the job and increased turnover," said Rob as he carefully restated the problem. Rob quickly assessed whether the issue was clearly stated or whether Brenda may have been less open regarding the issue. Since she had only positive experiences with information systems in the past and stated in her conversation that she failed to increase training in her own area, Rob felt confident that he had pierced the veil and understood what Brenda was really saying.

"That's right. The increased grumbling and dissatisfaction is related to a great extent to our training commitment," observed Brenda.

"As usual, our conversation has been very helpful. Did you think of this when you were planting your delicious sweet corn?" asked Rob.

Later in the week, Rob forwarded a copy of an e-mail he had received from the vice president of organization development. Organization development agreed that increased training time for staff and team sessions to work on internal systems was needed because survey feedback substantiated the growing barriers for employees. In an attached note, Rob thanked Brenda for her shared insight. Six months later, employee turnover started to drop.

SO, WHAT'S THE POINT?
A leader is lied to because he or she wants to be, and employees know it. It is human nature to want to hear about success stories, not failures. More effective listening skills (LeaderListen), risk taking rewards, and accessibility to employees should encourage increased openness and honesty in communications.

WHAT SHOULD A LEADER DO . . . ?

This lesson began with the recognition that leaders are not born, they are made or developed. If a leader doesn't grow, those employees reporting to a leader will probably not grow.

Therefore, it is important that leaders at all levels continue to grow. A number of issues that should be continually evaluated by a leader in order to grow are outlined below.

One issue deals with perception versus reality. A leader needs to continually assess how he/she is doing. The biggest enemy of a leader is that he/she is at a higher level in the organization. Because of this, it becomes more difficult for other employees to provide feedback on how well a leader is doing his/her job. It is very difficult, if not impossible, for leaders to see themselves as others do. It is a continual struggle but one that needs to be pursued using the skills outlined above.

In order to gain feedback, a leader can pursue the following: Ask people during development discussions how you are doing; utilize written anonymous surveys with your employees; periodically ask other employees as to how you are doing as a Leader-Coach-Manager; and ask for input from internal and external consultants.

A second issue is the expectation of a leader versus employees who report to a leader. Many times, a leader expects he/she won't be as involved in the new roles because new leader roles really pertain to the first line leaders. In reality, a leader should have a greater expectation to use the new leader roles than employees who report to them. Without this support, employees will not have sufficient role modeling.

WHAT SHOULD AN EMPLOYEE DO IF A LEADER ISN'T USING THE NEW LEADER ROLES?

Where a leader is not using the new leader roles, an employee has four basic alternatives. One alternative is the employee can resign or transfer, because there is a low likelihood that empowerment will succeed under these conditions.

A second alternative is for the employee to try to subtly encourage use of the new leader roles. Frankly, we have real concern whether this can be effective. It generally does not work. If employees try this, they may want to involve the leader in employee development efforts. The leader may transfer what she sees to her situation and recognize the need to work together in order to make empowerment an effective approach in the organization.

However, we noted above that without strong support from the leader, there is low likelihood of success. Whether an employee should attempt this second alternative depends on such factors as culture, relationships, and politics. There are obvious risks associated with the second alternative, especially where empowerment is at an early development stage.

A third alternative is for some type of third party intervention to help the leader. Top management could play a more active intervention role. This could include additional training for the leader.

A fourth alternative is for an employee to muster courage and use the Solution(s) Model and an empowering style to engage the leader. This usually requires mastery of these tools and skills to be successful.

SO, WHAT'S THE POINT?
Leaders are developed, not born. Leaders at all levels need personal development. Without it, empowerment and teams will not be effective.

Lesson 3

Lesson 3

How to
Select a Leader

WE GREW UP in an era where stories were songs—where folk singers sang about taxi cab drivers, sunken ore boats in the Great Lakes, and Bad, Bad Leroy Brown. These were the '70s stories about memorable people with character. Many of these storytellers have since passed on, but they've left behind a legacy. They taught us to value people with character and a strong sense of purpose. These songs also taught us that values and character move people and organizations.

Somewhere along the way, the lessons from the '70s were forgotten. There was a point where leaders became convinced that they must mirror business tradition. Command and control leaders were sought for their ability to command the masses and control every meaningful aspect within an organization. The management selection process favored candidates who were outspoken, domineering, and opinionated.

Leaders must challenge these paradigms and make selections outside of their traditional comfort zones. New leader roles demand a new leader selection process. For most leaders, this means that we must put an end to HALism.

In the movie, "2001: A Space Odyssey," a supercomputer named HAL attempted to kill his human overseers on the spacecraft Discovery. HAL perceived that they were ready to pull the plug on him and replace him with a better computer. Some leaders suffer from a similar malady though more subconsciously. Leaders tend to suffer from "killing the best candidate." This leadership malady is sure to raise its ugly head as leaders are encouraged to hire candidates that are more effective with people than the command and control crowd.

Why select the best candidate and risk potential competition within the management ranks? Instead, pull the plug on those candidates. Stop! Pulling the plug on the best and brightest candidates may in fact create greater misery and likelihood of failure for existing leaders. Instead, diversity among the leader ranks is required to balance people and technical skills.

"How to Select a Leader" is focused on the principles and the process to target the right candidates for the new leader roles. This lesson is built on the principle that new leader roles require a new selection process and principles. However, this message does not mean that existing leaders should be demoted or terminated because they are suspect by their association with a bygone era. This lesson is intended to help leaders select individuals who will help organizations make the transition from a command-and-control to a Leader-Coach-Manager culture. And in so doing, they will also help traditional leaders make an easier transition to new leader roles.

ELEVEN PRINCIPLES THEY NEVER TAUGHT YOU IN SCHOOL

New leader roles require a different set of principles for selection of leaders. There are eleven principles that leaders must master to create a new selection environment.

1. The past is past. The traditional selection process was focused on technical skills and achievement of short-term success. Leaders underinvested in people and long term value creation. Because of this, organizations reaped what they sowed. They attained short-term successes and employees with waning loyalty. New leader roles run counter to the past. New leader roles require a long-term focus based on helping others grow. Therefore, management selection requires leaving the past behind and creating new paradigms when searching for the right candidates.

2. Focus on Leader-Coach-Manager. In the past, organizations looked to find leaders that were both good strategists and technical experts. The new leader roles require a balanced focus on the three functions—Leader-Coach-Manager. People skills must be given an equal emphasis with technical skills when selecting future leaders.

3. Fire in the belly. A leader must have fire in the belly. New leaders must have a basic, gut feeling or passion for management. Leaders should have a maniacal passion to lead, coach, and manage. There are too many cadaver leaders walking the floors of organizations today. They do not create energy for those who look to them for direction. Instead, they instill boredom, malaise, and sarcasm. Passion sustains energy for change agents.

4. Diversity is a key. Have you ever worked in an environment where all leaders were expected to wear the same clothes, espouse the same thoughts, and show the same interests at work or in play? Where everyone is expected to talk, walk, and breathe the same, there is little or no diversity. In these environments, new thoughts are contrary to corporate life. Sameness creates the same. New leader roles require diversity in the management ranks because many views of life and work are needed to improve an organization's strategies, quality, and customer relations. Therefore, the selection process should strongly support diversity through the selection process.

5. Synergistic fit is fine. Teams are important because of the synergy that is created. The old saying—two heads are better than one—underscores the importance of two minds working together to create more value than two heads working separately. It is also important that synergy occur naturally as opposed to a forced fit. There are countless examples on the football and baseball fields in America where teams clicked but then fell apart because they really didn't fit together in the first place. Business leaders and teams are affected in a similar fashion. Leaders must strive for natural synergy. This is where team members are comfortable working together and are not thrown together without consideration of their culture preference and work habits. The leader selection process must include consideration of the potential fit with the existing culture and the potential for synergy.

6. Know the Skills and Roles. It is important to clearly understand the new leader roles that were outlined in part 1. It is just as important to understand the job competencies or skills that fit with these new leader roles. Without the right skills, the new leader roles are meaningless. The skills make it possible for leaders to effectively perform the new roles. Without clearly defined skills that fit the new roles, most leaders will revert to using their old skills because of their comfort level. The leader selection process requires early definition of leader roles and the skills to complement these.

7. Selection Team Needs To Use Job Skills. In the past, it was fashionable for leaders to make management selections in a vacuum. The other departments that worked with an area would not have an opportunity to participate in the selection process. The command and control management world looked upon management like farming. Departments and areas were neatly stacked in clearly defined silos. In sharp contrast to the silo effect, the new leader roles are based on a recognition that leaders must be able to work across divisional or departmental boundaries. Only leaders that work across boundaries should be selected as part of the management team. In addition, everyone who participates on the selection team must use the same job competencies or skills criteria. Otherwise, candidates will not be judged based on consistent expectations.

8. Focus the Resumé. In most organizations, it is common for resumés of the top two or three candidates to be shared among selection team members. Usually these resumés are designed by candidates and are not focused on a specific job opportunity. Where such a resumé is reviewed, it will be difficult for selection team members to determine relevant material that applies to the job search. Some organizations ask final candidates to revise their resumés to fit specific criteria for the job being considered. Other organizations restate the information based on specific job criteria. Focused resumés help to pinpoint the fit or lack of fit and keeps the selection team focused on relevant material.

9. **Past is Important.** What is the best indicator of the future behavior of a leader in a new job? Research shows that past behavior is a good indicator of future behavior, in the absence of intervention. Otherwise, leaders would have to be assessed based on their expected reactions. Oftentimes, candidates don't accurately predict what behavior would be used in a certain situation because they fail to consider all aspects and may want to please the interviewer by providing the expected answer. For lack of better indicators, the past is the best way to predict the future.

10. **Mission, vision, and values are core.** The mission helps to set the purpose of an organization while the vision outlines what the organization will be in the future. The values outline what is important to the organization and the type of behavior that is encouraged. It is important to use mission, vision, and values during the selection process because these components are basic to the long-term success of an organization. If a candidate does not fit the mission, vision, or values, they should not be considered despite their technical expertise. All the expertise in the world cannot overcome an unaligned organization.

11. **Balance internal and external.** Some organizations pride themselves on the fact that all leaders have come up through the ranks of their organization. This approach usually creates a strong level of loyalty to the organization. Other organizations pride themselves on diversity of management because it provides a broad experience base. During times of change, organizations must have a broad experience base to provide expertise to adapt. Where leaders are only experienced in one organization, their base of experience will be shorter and may decrease their ability to create innovative solutions. Because change should continue to be a major factor for all organizations, the selection process should be balanced between internal and external candidates.

NEW ROLES DESERVE A NEW SELECTION MODEL

In the early days of automobiles, it was commonplace to start an automobile by winding up the engine from the front. In the latter half of the century, the process no longer required the driver to dismount and wind up the engine by standing directly in front of the car. Like the automobile, the leader selection process must be adapted to fit the new reality. Therefore, leaders must consider a new process to use. The structure of the automobile changed during the twentieth century with the removal of the crank in front of the automobile and the addition of an electric starter. Like the automobile, a leader selection structure has changed to reflect the greater preponderance of teams and a stronger emphasis upon aligned organizations.

The first place to begin with a new leader selection model is structure. There are three critical dimensions that must be directly and visibly tied to the selection process. The new roles, job competencies, and mission, vision, and values must be well defined from the start. If these are not in place, leaders must develop these dimensions before pursuing the selection process. Two other dimensions should also be included for purposes of structure. Succession planning expectations or plans must be defined and ready for implementation, and diversity must be included in the selection process.

As shown below in the Leader Selection Model, there are two components to the selection model: structure and process. Structure tells us what the job is and how it fits with the rest of the organization. Process tells us how the selection should be pursued to be consistent with the structure. It consists of seven considerations including job opening, raise hand, resumé and focused resumé, multidisciplinary selection team, interview preparation, focused interview, and decision. Structure and process should be consistent. For example, matrix leadership positions should involve many leaders in the selection process.

Leader Selection Model

Structure/Dimensions	⬅━━━━━━➡	Process
Mission/Vision/Values/Strategy		Job Opening
Job Competencies		Raise Hand (Encourage/Candidate List)
New Roles		Resumé/Focused Resumé
Succession Planning		Multidisciplinary Selection Team
Diversity (Synergistic Fit)		Interview Preparation
		Focused Interview
		Decision (Selection Rating Form)

Job Opening

This part of the process will depend upon the policy used by an organization. Some organizations will post all job openings while some organizations will post certain job openings but not all job openings. Some organizations will post the job internally only when the job is advertised for external candidates. No one way is preferred over another because it will depend upon the circumstances of a situation and the culture. Generally, though, some form of job posting is preferred in an empowering organization.

Raise Your Hand

The second step in the process is directly related to the human resources philosophy that management supports. Some organizations create an expectation that leaders will be considered for a new position by invitation only. Other organizations encourage candidates to pursue such opportunities where they have the appropriate background and skills. The latter situation is preferred because it clearly tells employees they must be proactive and pursue growth opportunities in order to be considered.

Resumé

The resumé is a helpful tool that must be used in the proper manner to maximize the outcome. A general resumé helps to underscore the basic qualifications of a candidate and potential experience fit. However, until a resumé is written to specifically address leader roles and competencies required for the job, it is difficult for interviewers to clearly understand how the experiences of a candidate fit the roles and competencies required to succeed in a job.

Multidisciplinary Selection Team

The selection team should consist of individuals from divisions, areas, and/or departments that will interface with the position, as well as individuals from the specific area being developed. This will require careful consideration of who is best prepared to provide feedback relative to the roles, job competencies, and mission, vision, and values. In addition, employees and leaders that will interface most with the position should be given the opportunity to participate in the selection process. It is quite common for the initial interviews to include small teams of interviewers while later interviews will be narrowed to a more select group of leaders and employees. This approach leads other employees to buy into candidates that are selected more easily, enhances empowerment, and increases employee responsibility for tasks.

Interview Preparation

It is amazing how few leaders spend time on preparation for interviews. Instead, they wait until the hour of the interview before quickly jotting down potential questions. Worse yet, some leaders do not prepare any questions because they will react to information provided or statements made. Because leader selection is a critical and expensive endeavor, it is important for leaders to spend at least twice the amount of time in preparation as used for the actual interview. Consider what types of questions are important for the position being considered.

Focused Interview

The interview itself should be scripted beforehand to make sure that the most important points will be focused on. Some leaders like to use a checklist and mark off each key area to be covered as they work through the interview. In order to stay focused, it may be necessary for the interviewer to steer the conversation back to the points that are crucial to the selection decision. Sometimes, interviewees will follow tangents and will meander from the important issues unless the conversation is strongly focused. An interviewer can gently remind the candidate that the question raised needs to be the focus of their answer. If a candidate continues to avoid a question or meander, this may be a sure sign that the candidate will not be productive and efficient.

Decision

If the previous steps in the selection process are carefully planned and preparatory time spent, the decision step will be easy to administer. A selection rating form should be developed and used for interviewers to score each of the candidates. The ranking should be clearly linked to the roles associated with the position, job competencies, and mission, vision, and values. Too often, political decisions or compromise are used and may result in the selection of a second rate leader.

QUESTIONS, NO DOUBT

Because leader selection is more an art than a science, questions are inevitable. There are several key issues that seem to reappear for every organization.

Can a selection process be developed where the new roles are not defined? Would you feel safe flying on a commercial airline where they select pilots without a clear definition of their roles? Imagine the conversation that could take place in such a case.

"Gosh, Bob, I guess I wouldn't have taken this job if I had known they expected me to be able to make an emergency landing without a runway."

"That is too bad. Especially for the one hundred fifty passengers we have on board. Well, just give it the old college try."

We certainly wouldn't want to be on that plane. We are continually amazed how many organizations essentially take a blind flight because they have yet to define the new leader roles. The new roles clarify the selection criteria and process. First, define the new roles. Second, outline the related job competencies. Third, design the selection process.

How much education is required when organizations change their selection process to fit the new roles? Where new roles are implemented, the selection process and skills will change. Because of this, education is a must. Some organizations will educate all leaders en masse regarding the new selection process. Other organizations will provide just-in-time education. If the new leader roles are clearly understood by leaders, the amount of time required for the selection process should be minimal.

Should the selection process be piloted in the senior leader level before using it in other parts of the organization? The selection process is usually best piloted in the senior management ranks. This provides an opportunity for senior leaders to role model the new approach, gain an intimate understanding of the new selection process, and develop greater support for a new process. Where a new selection process is piloted in the middle or lower levels of management, it is easier for the traditionalists in organizations to place roadblocks in the way.

SO, WHAT'S THE POINT?

The new selection process for leaders must reflect well-defined new roles and competencies of leaders. A selection team should be used in assessing candidates and making the final decision.

Lesson 4

How to Develop a Leader

A FRIEND'S SON broke his collarbone playing basketball against a rival high school. There were two things vividly remembered. First, the home team lost the game. Second, but more importantly, the friend's son's injuries caused problems for months. His left hand replaced his right for all daily tasks including eating, writing, and dressing. His class work suffered as well.

Changing roles is very much like the basketball player's experience. For example, place your writing hand behind your back and attempt specific functions without it. Aside from a lack of agility, leaders feel awkward or out of sorts because they have changed the way they function. Developing new leader roles and becoming a Leader-Coach-Manager is similar to this change. Leaders are asked to change from a traditional leader where they felt comfortable. The new leader roles initially make leaders feel uncomfortable and experience great difficulty.

In this lesson concentration will be on the ever-important process required to make an effective transition and become an effective Leader-Coach-Manager. Each step will be outlined in the process. In addition, the blind spots that leaders must overcome to excel will be explored. New leader roles and Leader-Coach-Manager are interchangeable terms and will be used as such in this lesson. These terms refer to the new way of leading in an ever-changing world.

A ROLE CHANGE IS MORE THAN SKIN DEEP

Why are role changes so difficult? To answer this question, you must understand how the mind works. Scientists have estimated that each human has as many cells in the brain as there have been seconds in time since our galaxy took form—over one quadrillion cells. And, one thousand cells are destroyed each day. Despite the continual loss, the basic patterns and memory remain intact.

The mind is basically a very sophisticated warehouse, storing numerous experiences in the subconscious. A leader experiences natural conflict where new ideas are introduced in the workplace, such as new processes, theories, and practices.

Experiences are like brush strokes. Every individual has knowledge and experiences acquired over the years. These are referred to as historical brushstrokes. For example, we all have historical brushstrokes that two plus two is four. Similarly, leaders have historical brushstrokes regarding the proper ways to supervise employees. Most of these brushstrokes relate to the command and control style of management. For example, "I am boss and employees will do as I say. After all, I get paid the big bucks to make the decisions."

Where leaders are asked to be a Leader-Coach-Managers instead of bosses, they have new brushstrokes that are contrary to the still-existing, historical brushstrokes. This creates conflict. This conflict or stress drives leaders out of their comfort zones, because of the difference between what happens and what leaders expect to happen. As a result, leaders resist change. Where new experiences go against old brushstrokes, leaders will feel awkward just as the star basketball player who switched from using his disabled right hand to his left hand.

Will leaders ever change their comfort zones? It takes repetitive actions or experiences seven to twenty-one times for habits or historical brushstrokes to be established. In unusual situations, one significant emotional event may create a habit. New habits become historical brushstrokes if, and only if, leaders make a long-term commitment to change. Therefore, repetition is important where a new comfort zone needs to be created.

Ellen was appointed as chief nursing officer for a large flagship hospital in a healthcare system. In her previous work, she had shown strong allegiance to the hospital and an ability to accomplish projects despite great odds. She used command and control with an iron fist to manage the clinical staff. This was very acceptable during the boss era but it was totally unacceptable to the new CEO. He appreciated her adept ability to complete projects but he did not accept her micromanagement style.

The CEO first narrowed Ellen's span of responsibility. Next, he regularly met with Ellen to review project status reports and used the opportunity to coach her in the use of new leader roles. In addition, he sent Ellen to executive courses to increase her experience base about new management styles. Despite these learning experiences, Ellen fought the CEO openly. She expressed discomfort to her colleagues because she was distancing herself so far from the decision making taking place on the nursing units. For Ellen, she was feeling very uncomfortable because she had always micromanaged staff.

Some of Ellen's colleagues in senior leadership were rather vocal about their concerns regarding Ellen's ability to change from a boss to a Leader-Coach-Manager. In the face of growing sentiment, the CEO continued along the course he had created at the outset. After eighteen months had gone by, he began to give more responsibilities to Ellen. The naysayers were now in shock. They couldn't believe that any sane CEO would give additional responsibilities to someone who showed little or no promise to turn around.

As if a wand had been tapped on her head, Ellen began to quicken her pace and loosen her hold on employees. Her doubters continued to predict that disaster was just around the corner; however, it never came. At the end of thirty months, Ellen was a clear choice for most improved player. She was comfortable in her role and was less tense when involved in conflict resolution with her colleagues. Ellen even talked jokingly about her micromanagement disease and how she was trying to kick the habit. Her employees recognized that she was still a hard taskmaster, but she had learned to master the new leader roles.

What changed Ellen's course? The CEO had to get her attention. He knew she was a team player deep down and that her old leadership style was ingrained. Given the right information, she would change.

How did the CEO know when the time was right to start adding to her responsibilities? When she became more relaxed and at ease, the CEO knew she had reached another plateau in her development as a leader.

SO, WHAT'S THE POINT?
Leaders must be open and willing to accept new brushstrokes. Expansion of a leader's comfort zone is critical in transitioning from a traditional leader to a Leader-Coach-Manager.

HOW DO YOU DEVELOP A LEADER-COACH-MANAGER?

New leader roles have developed because of the demise of Taylorism (i.e., narrowly defined jobs because of poorly educated people). Today, technical skills of leaders are not as important as they used to be. Leaders must be able to empower others to perform various functions and make certain decisions on their own. Leaders are expected to develop employees and teams. In other words, leaders must be effective at the new leader roles. Therefore, how should Leader-Coach-Managers be developed?

Organizations have a number of options. It depends on the type of business, culture, available resources, commitment of senior management, and capabilities and skills possessed by leaders. Some options are stronger than others but all require a clear vision for the organization before approaching new leader roles.

Leader-Coach-Manager development options can be generally classified into one of the following eight categories. Some organizations may provide a mixture of a couple of the options outlined below.

1. Go be a Leader-Coach-Manager. No preparation or real support is provided by an organization
2. Go be a Leader-Coach-Manager and other leaders will help. Once again, this is an informal approach with informal support provided
3. Read some books and practice on your own. Let other leaders within the organization know if there are any questions
4. An organization provides some formal preparation without any formal support from others within the organization
5. An organization provides some formal preparation with formal support
6. An organization provides extensive, formal preparation with no formal support
7. An organization provides extensive, formal preparation with formal support
8. An organization provides extensive, formal preparation with formal support and a certification system

All options have advantages and disadvantages. Some options may prove more effective for an organization than others. For each of the options, limitations exist and are presented in the following Leader-Coach-Manager Options table.

What option is best for you? That's a decision that is best made by your organization. In terms of the strongest approaches, option 8 provides the most effective model for consideration by an organization. Because of this, the remainder of this lesson outlines option 8 in greater detail, as shown in the Leader-Coach-Manager Development Process diagram.

Understand Leader-Coach-Manager Focus And Beliefs

The first step in the development process is to understand the focus and beliefs. Senior leaders need to have a basic foundation of understanding with respect to Leader-Coach-Manager and its effect on empowerment, work redesign, and quality. Why senior leaders? Internal and external consultants can be helpful in order to understand these issues. However, an organization will not embrace and understand new leader roles, empowerment, and quality unless it is discussed and supported by senior

Leader-Coach-Manager Options

Option	Relative Cost	Limitation(s)
Go be a Leader-Coach-Manager	No cost	Because Leader-Coach-Manager is in its infancy, organizations need to provide formal support and resources for progress to be made. Where no support or resources are provided, the subtle message to both leaders and employees is Leader-Coach-Manager is not that important.
Go be a Leader-Coach-Manager and other leaders will help	Low	This is too informal. A training and support network for new skills/roles is needed to produce long-term habits.
Read some books and practice on your own	Low	If an organization has 150 leaders, this approach is likely to result in 150 different definitions and approaches. Integration throughout an organization is almost impossible.
Some formal preparation without support	Low	New leader roles is about changing brush-strokes, changing habits. Without support, use of training will most likely fail.
Some formal preparation and support	Medium	Because new leader roles are a major change in skills, habits, and culture, "some" formal preparation is not likely to change leaders and culture as quickly as the market may demand.
Extensive formal preparation without support	High	Training without support will not sufficiently reinforce development to produce new habits.
Extensive formal preparation and support	High	This approach is high cost but may have a greater return and likelihood to change quickly to the desired environment.
Extensive formal preparation and support and certification program	High	Same as above except higher cost and longer learning curve.

management. A review of the first three roles of this book is recommended to develop this level of understanding.

Assess Alignment With Organization Mission/Vision/ Values

The new leader roles are one of several methods that can be used to achieve an organization's mission/vision. In this step of the process, senior management needs to assess whether Leader-Coach-Manager is consistent with achieving an organization's mission and vision and is supportive of its values. If employees within an organization would be shocked or surprised by the pursuit of Leader-Coach-Manager, chances are good it's not consistent with an organization's current practices.

A division of a large manufacturing organization implemented new leader roles. Management made a commitment because it was believed to

Leader-Coach-Manager Development Process

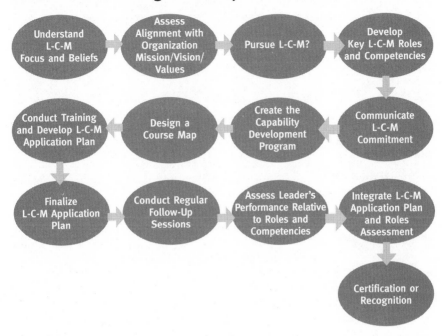

be the "in thing to do" and fear of being left behind by the rest of the organization where new leader roles were strongly embraced and supported. Formal preparation was provided to first line leaders and a shortened course was taught to middle and senior leaders of the division. Following the training, support was provided by the organization development section of the company and middle and senior leaders. This was similar to the training and support provided in other parts of the organization where they experienced improved performance.

Unfortunately, this division did not have a clear vision of its empowerment commitment and relationship to quality management. They were pursuing the new leader roles for all of the wrong reasons. As a result, it showed in the way middle and senior leaders supported the new program. Leaders said the right words but employees could tell that there was minimal appreciation of the new roles. Because of this, the level of support for the program was not invigorating. In addition, some decisions made by senior management were inconsistent with the new leader roles. Despite their verbal commitment to empowerment, management still used the old inspection system that was part of the mainstream command and control system.

As a result, the front line employees were supportive of the new roles but leaders were frustrated and confused. Front line leaders used most meetings to ask why the new roles were being pursued. Middle and senior leaders inter-preted these questions as lack of support and pushed harder for a program that was not well integrated into the division. This environment continued for well over eighteen months. Finally, division leadership was changed. One of the first actions taken was a management retreat to discuss the mission and vision of the company and division and the Leader-Coach-Manager fit. Each leader created a plan of action to better integrate the new leader roles into the division. Leader-Coach-Manager was clearly integrated into the mission and vision of the division by including the concept in the statements and placing related goals and objectives in the strategic plan for the division.

Because the new leader roles were more clearly linked to the division's operations, leaders were able to understand the concept and how it improved productivity and work life. This showed in their vigorous support of the new roles both in words and actions.

It was like someone had turned on a light bulb in a dark closet. Everyone had a common sense of mission and vision that clearly integrated Leader-Coach-Manager into the day-to-day tasks and projects. The new roles came off the shelf and came to life. The bottom line improved by over twenty percent and employee turnover decreased by 8 percent.

If Leader-Coach-Manager does not align with an organization's mission and vision, it should not be pursued. In this case, an organization will need to assess whether is has the right mission and/or vision for its' long term business strategy.

Pursue Leader-Coach-Manager?
(Make a Decision Regarding the New Roles)

If the new leader roles do align with an organization's mission and vision, they should be pursued. At this point, it is critical to involve all leaders in the learning and development process. All leaders need to appreciate and understand the new focus and beliefs and its fit with an organization's mission and vision. Senior management should communicate this message to all leaders and solicit their input into the development of the roles. If new leader roles are not pursued at this time, they should be reassessed on a periodic basis, along with other relevant issues such as work redesign, quality management, and empowerment.

Develop Key Leader-Coach-Manager Roles and Competencies

Senior management and other leaders should work together to develop key leader roles and competencies for their organization. This collabora-tion provides greater likelihood of buy-in by leaders throughout an organization. In addition, this would provide a deeper understanding of and appreciation for the new roles. This book provides major roles that should be considered.

One issue that may arise is whether all new leader roles should be identified and implemented at once or whether several roles should be implemented during the first year. A reason for implementing only some of the new roles is to allow leaders the opportunity to master these. A problem with this approach is that leaders will not appreciate the synergy to be gained from all of the new roles. Also, a partial implementation of the new leader roles would not underscore the complete expectations. We tend to encourage organizations to implement all the new roles at one time. This is a long journey, not a destination. Leaders should not expect to master all of the new roles at the beginning.

Competencies are the knowledge, skills, and values needed to carry out the roles. Developing competencies is essential in order to design an effective course map.

Communicate the Leader-Coach-Manager Commitment

Communicate, communicate, communicate! Leaders cannot possibly over-communicate where new leader roles are or have been implemented. Without communication, employees will make up their own stories about the reason and purpose of the new leader roles. Normally, these stories are distorted and negative. An atmosphere of "they're about to do it to us again" will prevail. A first step in helping employees understand the new roles is to cover the major points outlined in the Expectations of Employees role. These, in part, include: learn, learn, learn; willing to be coached; pursue empowerment; help a leader grow; and understand what the new leader roles are and are not.

Create the Capability Development Program

Capability development is an important concept to understand because of the difference between this type of development and training. Capability development is the planned use and creation of skills and knowledge developed during the training phase and on the job. Training alone is insufficient. The actual use of skills and knowledge gained from training is critical.

Capability development includes training, application of training, feedback from employees and a leader's leader, and integration of capability into an organization's system of human resource development. Training, then, is the acquisition of knowledge and skills primarily within the classroom setting.

Leaders need to be involved in training and application of training. Leaders need to be directly involved in the five phases of training: design, development, delivery, on-the-job application, and assessment. This will increase leaders' knowledge, support, and comfort. Where leaders are involved in all phases of capability development, their new roles will be reinforced and they will be able to role model empowerment principles.

With the above advice, an organization is ready to create the general outline of the capability development program. The remaining blocks in the

Leader-Coach-Manager Development Process diagram outline the major components of this program.

Design A Course Map

A development process requires the creation and implementation of specially designed training modules. Training should consist of courses, books, videos, practice sessions, tours to better understand supplier-customer relationships, and attendance at team meetings to learn from other leaders. These should cover philosophy and principles, system used by the organization, tools, employee and/or team development, empowerment, conflict resolution, goal setting, decision making based on principles, FOCUS, work redesign, continuous quality improvement, leadership, and interpersonal skills. All of these topics are interrelated. The absence of any of these topics will result in an incomplete understanding and application of the new leader roles. Course map design work is very intense and requires a significant amount of input from leaders and fine-tuning by senior management to fit an organization's environment.

There are few people in the United States who have extensive experience in the design of coaching training. Therefore, don't expect to find someone with "the answers." Also, don't expect that you will create a perfect course map the first time. Leaders need to create the course map, pilot it, improve it, pilot it, improve it. . . .

A division agreed upon a series of training measures to be used for that area. The division leader had extended debate on the proper location for display of the measures. An enormous amount of time and effort was taken trying to make a decision. In the meantime, a new division vice president was appointed for that area. His first action was to place a white, hand-drawn, cardboard sign on his door that displayed the key divisional measures. Leaders immediately responded with criticism. Over time, however, leaders within the division began to suggest and implement improvements on measures and displays. The leaders had finally gotten out of the huddle and taken action. The moral of the story is leaders shouldn't stay in a huddle too long or they will never get to play. Create a course map designed around roles and competencies, implement it, and continue to improve it.

Conduct Training And Develop The Leader-Coach-Manager Application Plan

Once a course map is designed and developed, training sessions should be offered to leaders. Several issues should be considered at this point:

• Should leaders be asked to spend full time or part of their time in training;
• Who should provide the training;

- What resources are available for conducting the training sessions;
- What is the role of the leader's leader in training and/or support of training;
- What preparation is needed for employees;
- Should there be some pay considerations, such as leaders from third shift attending the first shift training sessions;
- Who should attend the training sessions from management;
- Will soon-to-be retirees in the leader ranks be involved in training; and
- Will temporary relief be provided for leaders that attend training on a full time basis for a long period of time?

One organization we are familiar with has a sixteen-week development program for first level leaders. These leaders are expected to spend all of their work time concentrating on training. In their absence, some areas are provided other management resources from various sources. In some situations, second level leaders provide general relief while other areas expect their teams to be self-supporting during the absence of first level leaders.

Second level leaders and above in the organization also attend an abbreviated development program which is designed for their specific needs. This program is more general in scope than the first level leader training. Many of the first level leaders have expressed opinions that all other leaders need full training as much, if not more, than first level. The issue is further compounded by the fact that most second level leaders and above have been technically trained with college experience.

As we discussed earlier in this book, most technically trained leaders have not received extensive training in people skills in college. In this particular organization, the first assignment for technically trained individuals in manufacturing is as a leader responsible for seventy-five to one hundred team members. It is recommended that new leader roles training should be conducted for all levels of the organization, not just first level leaders.

As each leader progresses through a course map, each leader should develop an application plan for each learning experience associated with a new leader role. For example, a leader completes a course in conflict resolution that is related to the communication role. An Application Plan for the Communication Role would be filled out as shown in the Generic Application Plan table.

Leaders record the learning experience, identify the major points learned, and identify how this will be applied on the job. Application plans are necessary because leaders too often will receive training but not use a skill or tool on the job. If a new tool or skill is not used within a short period of time following a training session, it is unlikely that leaders will retain the knowledge or skill level.

Generic Application Plan

Role	Competency	Plan	Status
Communication	Understand You	Use the cycle at least twice a day for two weeks. Note the experiences and evaluate their effectiveness. Gain feedback from your employees.	

Finalize The Leader-Coach-Manager Application Plan

After a leader has been trained and has developed application plans, a number of possibilities for implementation will be identified, selected, and prioritized by a leader and his/her supervisor. They will agree upon those plans that are most important and timely to be pursued. The reason for a leader and his/her supervisor to meet is to properly align a plan with an organization's mission, vision, and key organization documents. This creates an expectation that formal support will be provided.

Conduct Regular Follow Up Sessions

A leader and his/her supervisor should meet on a regular basis to review progress made on the application plan. During these meetings, they should identify and discuss what they are doing relative to the plan and issues that require further discussion.

An application plan is based on what is known. As conditions change, the application plan may be changed. Application plans are living documents. Regularly scheduled meetings provide a good point to reassess whether a plan is in need of revision. First, they need to focus on principles to be used during these sessions.

- Discuss perceptions of performance. Perceptions, not reality, are what they offer during these discussions.
- Individually take responsibility for performance (action and inaction). The critical part of taking responsibility is to have an open and honest discussion about successes and failures. A leader's supervisor must set the tone to facilitate this type of discussion. This involves maintaining the self-esteem of a leader. Critique behavior, not the leader.
- The sessions are intended to help them grow. If they grow, employees grow. If employees grow, the opportunity for business success is greatly enhanced.
- A basic premise of quality management is continual improvement. Continual improvement applies to coaching just as much as it does to other areas in the business world. Each and every leader can and needs to improve in a competitive world.

- Giving and receiving constructive feedback is essential for continual improvement. In order to do this, both must be good listeners as well as good speakers. Remember: communicate.
- The reason for having regular sessions is to improve skills. The reason for improving new skills is a means, not an end, to improving business success and quality of work life.

With these principles in mind, a draft agenda is outlined below that can be used for the meeting of a leader with his/her supervisor.

1. Review the action plan prior to the session or jointly review it during the first part of the session
2. The leader's leader should begin by offering opportunities for his or her own improvement. This should be a good role model for encouraging a leader to offer suggestions later in the meeting relative to his or her performance
3. The leader's leader should ask for feedback. How well did he/she perform relative to the application plan? Once again, this is good role modeling to further develop a leader
4. A leader should provide feedback to his/her leader on successes and opportunities for improvement. Sometimes leaders may think they should not provide positive comments. However, desirable reinforcement is a two-way street regardless of one's level in an organization
5. The leader's leader should ask to discuss performance on the application plan implementation
6. The leader should provide feedback to his/her leader similar to that outlined in "B" above
7. The leader should ask his/her leader for feedback. How well did the leader implement the application plan?
8. They should finalize any revisions to an application plan and any actions for the next review session

Assess Leader's Performance Relative to Roles and Competencies

Development of roles and competencies was the primary focus early in the process. The development of an application plan and the need to conduct regular follow-up sessions for implementation of the application plan were also discussed. Following these steps, leaders need to obtain feedback from employees on how successfully they have implemented their roles and competencies.

Feedback can be gained formally or informally. It can come from individuals or from groups. One of the most effective tools to date is use of an employee survey. A survey is provided to employees to rate the performance of a leader. A leader can be rated on roles and competencies using a Likert five point scale where "one" indicates the leader never used this role, and a "five" means a role is continuously used. A simple illustration of this is provided in the Key Role Assessment table using several roles covered in this book. Employees should be asked to anonymously complete surveys in order to help a leader grow.

Key Role Assessment

Role	Assessment				
	Never				Always
Does your leader continuously learn and challenge his/her own beliefs?	1	2	3	4	5
Does your leader believe in the nine basic beliefs of Leader-Coach-Manager?	1	2	3	4	5
Does your leader use the new roles of a leader on a daily basis?	1	2	3	4	5
Does your leader coach you and other employees on a routine basis?	1	2	3	4	5
Does your leader use the Empowering Style where appropriate?	1	2	3	4	5
Does your leader work with the employees to help them understand the need for change in your organization?	1	2	3	4	5
How effectively does your leader intervene?	1	2	3	4	5

Surveys are excellent tools if used properly. However, if employees use survey instruments to "get even" with a leader, management must look behind the numbers. Harsh scores may indicate that a leader is dealing head on with necessary change that is being resisted by some employees.

In other situations, some leaders may garner excellent scores. On paper, they appear to be excellent leaders who have mastered the new roles when, in fact, they have discovered how to go easy on employees and gain their adulation. Once again, leaders must consider what the numbers are telling them.

Although the surveys are excellent tools, there are also limitations. The survey data is an indicator of an environment. The challenge for management is to understand that environment. On the day of a survey, an employee may be upset with a leader or the organization and reflect that on the survey. Otherwise, a leader may be perceived as an excellent Leader-Coach-Manager.

One last word of caution—employee surveys must be used as learning tools, not hammers or sticks. If surveys are used as weapons, leaders will no longer use them as one of several growth barometers. Where surveys have been used as hammers, oftentimes leaders "game the system" to defend themselves. Leaders may figure out how to gain excellent scores through manipulation of who takes the survey, timely use of employee perks, or other methods.

Integrate the Leader-Coach-Manager Application Plan and Roles Assessment

The application plan and key roles assessment are used to discover where a leader has developed and where additional efforts are required. Where these tools are integrated, the application plan becomes more of a barometer for a journey, instead of an end point. Leaders begin to see the plan as a living document that helps them grow while roles assessment tools, such as employee surveys, are viewed as signposts along the road.

The application plan and key roles assessment should also be critical inputs into an organization's employee development system. The first assessment data from employee surveys can create a baseline. This baseline can be used to gauge how much progress is made in the future as application plans are implemented. This data can also provide important feedback for management to concentrate organization development resources. If leaders show minimal improvement in conflict resolution skills over time, additional or different training may be indicated to help leaders overcome these barriers. Some organizations use this data as one way to identify the cost/benefit of training in their organization.

Certification and/or Recognition

The last step in the development process is certification and/or recognition. Certification and/or recognition are provided where leaders demonstrate effective use of the new leader roles. Certification could be accomplished through written and/or performance testing. Emphasis should be placed upon written and performance testing because the new roles require an ability to "walk the talk." Many leaders score well on paper but are dismal performers. Satisfactory completion of the certification process is indicated with the presentation of a Leader-Coach-Manager certificate.

Recognition can be provided in many ways. For example, advancement in an organization's career ladder, plaques, and publication in a newsletter can be effective ways to provide recognition. Some leaders respond more to certain types of recognition than other types. A leader must consider what others value the most and use that method to provide recognition.

SO, WHAT'S THE POINT?
A development process is a significant journey. It is not a matter of taking a couple of courses and telling someone to be a Leader-Coach-Manager. It is a partnership that involves all leaders. It isn't a quick fix. It is an art, skill, and profession.

WHERE DOES A CEO FIND A MENTOR?

Every leader and employee in an organization has a leader to help them grow and develop, save one person. CEOs don't have someone to help them grow. A board of directors isn't prepared, in most cases, to coach a CEO except through feedback provided by a board's management committee where they critique a CEO's performance on an annual basis. Board members rarely have the experience, motivation, or time to provide such painstaking, one-on-one relationships. How many CEOs would feel comfortable in sharing concerns and weaknesses with such a group of people who first and foremost have the interests of shareholders or members in mind? Few CEOs reading this book will run to a telephone and volunteer as the next guinea pig on such a mission.

Leaders within an organization may help CEOs grow, but it is unusual to find because it is difficult to coach upward. The gap between a CEO and other leaders in an organization is quite wide due to the difference in experiences and breadth of issues. Besides the gap, leaders must overcome substantial pressure if they are going to provide open and straightforward comments on a continuous basis to a CEO. Leaders would be providing criticism to a senior officer that has input in regard to their own performance review. The fear is always potential recrimination. At the same time, it takes a rather unique relationship for a CEO to feel comfortable and allow a subordinate to provide criticism, though constructive, on a continuing basis. Such a relationship definitely goes against the grain of traditional management. Basic human behavior also teaches us that we need to be very cautious about showing any weaknesses to those who are subordinates within an organization.

Where does a CEO find such help? This book was published because there were no books that helped leaders make a transition to the new leader roles. CEOs and other leaders didn't have anyone within their organization to help them grow, and this book could help to fill some of that void. However, there's a need for additional interaction to stretch paradigms and test perceptions.

So, where can we find a CEO's coach? In addition to this book and other learning tools such as videos and self-evaluation, there are three sources. CEOs can use information and feedback from professional organizations, other CEOs, and consultants.

Professional organizations, such as American Management Association and American College of Healthcare Executives, may be beneficial sources of feedback. These organizations are likely, however, to be limited in their knowledge and resources related to new leader roles because this is a new frontier. If resources do exist, they are likely to be offered for mass consumption. They would lack a one-on-one relationship that is the essence of Leader-Coach-Manager.

Other CEOs can be a good source of support where such talent exists. Other CEOs understand a CEO's world. They share similar concerns regarding confidentiality. Because of the lack of experience in new leader roles, knowledgeable CEOs with a strong Leader-Coach-Manager track record are difficult to find. Most CEOs are swimming in the same shark infested waters looking for long-term solutions to management shortfalls.

The most likely source of help for CEOs is consultants. They don't have the inherent conflict of interest as other leaders within an organization. They definitely have a capability to provide one-on-one service. Some may even have previous experience as CEOs sharing an understanding of that unique environment. Once again, though, consultants suffer some of the same shortcomings as professional organizations and other CEOs. Experienced consultants in new leader roles are few and far between because of the infancy of this area and paucity of hands on experience in this area. CEOs may find this out, but only after they have paid substantial dollars and received little in return.

Here's a recap. CEOs must initially look inward. This will require excellent CEO skills in scanning the horizon—a CEO must be able to observe and clearly interpret their level of understanding and effectiveness. This requires extraordinary listening, conflict resolution, team building, decision making based on principles, goal setting, and FOCUS skills as a foundation. Assuming the skills are present, CEOs must religiously commit a block of time each week learning, implementing, and assessing their new leader roles abilities. If a CEO is devoted (not just committed) to the new roles, talents should blossom.

One of the first legitimate Leader-Coach-Managers in corporate America learned how to overcome the mentor void. He was a senior leader in a large organization managing well over ten thousand employees in the company's largest division. His company was driven by professionals but was carried by the toil and sweat of common laborers. Bill became an informal leader of the new roles because of an overriding interest in people and productivity. He had a thirst to break through old barriers and carve out a new vista for all employees.

Like other leaders, Bill didn't have someone to show him the path. Instead, he created a path not unlike the modern-day roller coasters. Experimentation was most important in those early days. Bill developed his capabilities through an inward vision, consultants, other CEOs, and other leaders.

Early in the experiment, Bill learned that the transition required continual questioning of oneself and numerous paradigms. He was brave enough to question his own actions as well as others, but in a constructive way. The company really began to grow when it searched the globe for experiments in new leader roles. The many management books and videos only confirmed that little was understood and appreciated. To fill that void, consultants were pursued.

Inward vision was not enough to light the way for Bill. A number of consultants were used to find the best of breed. As each role became more self-evident, Bill urged his organization development staff to search and find answers from consultants that were the best of the best for each role. When the communication role became clearer in definition, Bill encouraged his staff to find the leading models and thoughts on listening skills and conflict resolution. The pioneers were building the Leader-Coach-Manager paradigm brick by brick.

Other CEOs were somewhat helpful because they could debate the needs and direction of management for the millennium. However, most CEOs were still caught up in their thirst for immediate success and the latest management fads. As time passed, it became clearer that the new leader roles would have to come from within an organization to be defined and developed. There were too few success stories to help Bill's division grow.

This inevitably led Bill to work closely with a number of leaders within the organization who were dedicated to finding a better way to work and increase productivity. Interestingly enough, the human resources department did not provide the answer. They were too committed to the systems and structure of command and control management. Instead, the new leader roles were defined by a group of middle-level leaders bumping around the organization, experimenting with innovative ways to build a successful organization. This unique group was created within Bill's division for the sole purpose of channeling energy and efforts toward a better way of working.

Despite their subservient role to Bill, this unique group of leaders felt comfortable to challenge paradigms that even Bill may have cherished. They knew that Bill believed in self-esteem and would protect it to the end. That's not to say that Bill always agreed with every concept that the group created. But, he did understand employees and how they responded to genuine relationships.

The unique group was challenged to create pathways for Leader-Coach-Managers. Once the early model was designed by trial and error with some support from several consultants, it was given a trial run. After each trial, the program was improved based on the learnings from each session. The group of leaders made a number of mistakes along the way. They learned that the new leader roles required a strong top down commitment. In the beginning, they failed to appreciate this splitting of the organization between the believers and the uninformed.

With each step, Bill grew in his determination and support. His inner vision began to take hold, reinforced by the group of leaders. The new leader roles really became a natural part of his division when front-line employees sang the praises of this new program. No longer was Bill the lone cheerleader fighting doubters within the organization. He had many disciples.

Despite the early questions and doubts, the new leader roles were finally accepted as one of the most effective strategic weapons of his company. It was sold one employee by one employee. It required the personal involvement of senior leaders in the process before it gained strong support. Most likely, success would not have materialized without risk-taking leaders who spoke the message, walked the talk, and were brave enough to fight even senior leaders.

Bill learned a lesson from his journey. Innovations in management can only come from within, borrowed from the best of breed, reinforced by senior leaders, and role modeled by a few cheerleaders just as willing to receive as to give constructive feedback. First and foremost, leaders must feel it burning in their gut.

Some CEOs may see this challenge as too daunting and dangerous. However, many more CEOs will see the inherent strength in the new leader roles and rise to the challenge. These pioneers will pave the way as their successes become more recognized. Success will feed on success, removing any earlier doubts about the new leader roles.

SO, WHAT'S THE POINT?
Leader-Coach-Manager is a solitary undertaking for CEOs. Some support mechanisms exist but they are limited. Management, like medicine and law, will become an art because it is not solely based on technological skills. The practice of management will be strongly founded on the new leader roles.

Lesson 5

How to Maintain
the Competitive Advantage

THE RIGHT CHOICES create great things. Tim Cordes expects to receive his medical degree and a Ph.D. from the University of Wisconsin by the year 2006. His accomplishments to date are impressive—valedictorian at the University of Notre Dame, black belt in jujitsu, canoeist, water skier, biochemistry researcher, and music composer.

These accomplishments are even more impressive considering that Tim Cordes was born legally blind and has been totally sightless since sixteen years old. While other teenagers were getting their driver's license, Tim received his guide dog.

Despite the challenges of blindness, Tim succeeded because he chose to believe in his ability to grow. He was able to overcome his sight deficiency by using his hands and brain to visualize. When asked in a survey to rate the impact of blindness upon his life, Tim replied that the problem was a minor inconvenience. Tim mastered a mindset, at a very early age, and recognized that he and other people had a limitless ability to grow. Tim is a profile in Leader-Coach-Manager.

Tim is not alone in his journey. Camilla Jaquette awoke one day to a world that was totally foreign to her. When she slipped into her deep sleep possibly brought on by a stroke, she left behind all memory of her previous life. In the middle of her life, Camilla began life from scratch. She had to become acquainted with the husband she didn't know and the children who were complete strangers to her. Just like Tim, Camilla chose to believe that she could overcome her challenge because she could grow. Unmoved by the depth and breadth of her challenge, Camilla persevered and learned all over again.

Most leaders don't face substantial personal challenges like Tim or Camilla face. However, many leaders have chosen to pursue new leader roles and accomplish great things. Their stories of transition to new leader roles underscore the personal and professional rewards that abound.

Despite his senior leadership position, Jeff personally fought the new leader role transition required throughout the company and his manufacturing division. Unbeknownst to him, Jeff felt threatened by the new leader roles and the loss of his identity as the divisional decision maker. He also felt complete in his knowledge of and ability to thrive as a leader. Because of his company's strong commitment to new leader roles, Jeff finally chose to learn and utilize the new leader roles. Much to his surprise, he realized that he had been ill prepared to deal with employees' needs. As if overnight, his job became rewarding and his interactions with employees became more meaningful. At home, his newly found roles and skills were also helpful. Over the past several years, a gulf between he and his daughter had grown. Jeff found himself spending more time at work because he didn't want to face the problems at home.

Capitalizing on the new roles and skills, Jeff was able to deal with conflict in a constructive fashion versus the destructive manner in the past. He began to listen more and understand his daughter. The worsening family condition was reversed. When it came time to reassess the importance of new leader roles, Jeff was a strong proponent of the new roles instead of one of the main detractors.

Jeff was not alone in his journey. Stanley was a hard-driving executive who was a strong believer in technical and strategic skills. In the middle of his career, his emphasis was upon working harder and faster, but he wasn't getting ahead. Despite the use of management fads, Stanley could not increase workforce productivity and he saw his company's bottom line stagnate. To Stanley, the harder he worked the farther he fell behind. He began to realize the work world had changed so dramatically that he needed a different way to work. At first, the new leader roles were frightening to Stanley. He had to place greater dependence on employees during a time when larger companies were stealing market share from smaller companies. Stanley overcame this barrier when he recognized that employees embraced the opportunity to take on greater decision making and responsibilities.

The new leader roles created several advantages for Stanley. Vendors formed a stronger partnership with Stanley because he talked and walked the language of cooperation and collaboration in a meaningful and consistent manner. Stanley's competition, meanwhile, continued to look upon vendors as a necessary evil in the workplace. When he was threatened by increased competition, vendors provided Stanley with long-term contracts at more competitive rates.

Employees were so taken by empowerment and the new leader roles, they were more committed than ever to cutting costs while improving quality. In the past, budgets were a continual nightmare as employees used games to gain as much capital as possible. The new environment changed all of this. Employees were more concerned about external success because they were rewarded for their efforts through an incentive payment program tied to empowerment and new leader roles. The company went from being one of the more costly to being the cost effective leader in the market. Market share increased for Stanley's company while his competition struggled to stop eroding bottom lines and market shares.

In a fast changing world, new leader roles provide a long-term competitive advantage to leaders who choose to make the commitment. New leader roles provide greater flexibility for business success, more effective leaders and employees to improve quality, and continuous growth systems to build on past successes. New leader roles are a never-ending journey providing both short-term and long-term business success and personal rewards. No longer are leaders trying to pull and tug on employees to reach success. Gone are the monthly management fads. Instead, leaders and employees concentrate on the right roles to reach their vision.

CEOs haven't fully tapped the capabilities and commitments of employees and other leaders because they have not transitioned out of the old ways and old roles. For those leaders who have the courage and commitment to leave behind traditional leader roles, they will find personal rewards and long-term business success. With this book in hand, you have the agenda to change your life and your company. For those who choose to accept the challenge, enjoy the rewarding journey!

SO, WHAT'S THE POINT?

As the front cover of this book depicts, new roles for leaders are the keys to transform from a Boss to a Leader-Coach-Manager. It is a choice and a difficult journey to achieve and maintain competitive advantage.

PART 3

Exercises

Role 1

1. Step Out of the Box

This exercise provides an opportunity for leaders to break paradigms and understand that there are other ways to look at management behavior. One form

Step Out of the Box

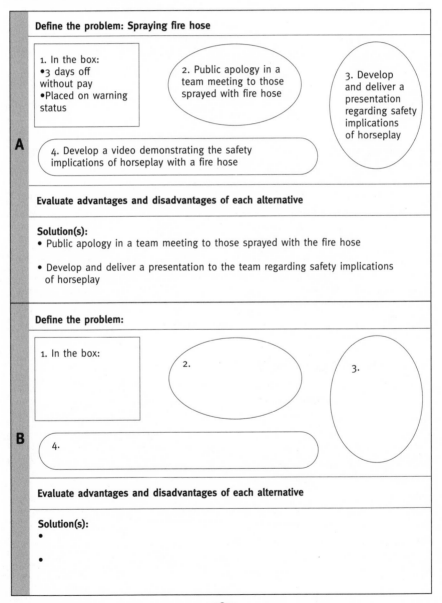

Define the problem: Spraying fire hose

A

1. In the box:
• 3 days off without pay
• Placed on warning status

2. Public apology in a team meeting to those sprayed with fire hose

3. Develop and deliver a presentation regarding safety implications of horseplay

4. Develop a video demonstrating the safety implications of horseplay with a fire hose

Evaluate advantages and disadvantages of each alternative

Solution(s):
• Public apology in a team meeting to those sprayed with the fire hose

• Develop and deliver a presentation to the team regarding safety implications of horseplay

Define the problem:

B

1. In the box:

2.

3.

4.

Evaluate advantages and disadvantages of each alternative

Solution(s):
•

•

of horseplay in a large organization was to take a fire hose and squirt other employees when least expected. In one situation, Harold sprayed several employees from the top of one of the buildings in the plant. A decision was needed regarding proper punishment because horseplay was against company policy. This was a company where team members were encouraged to take on more governance responsibility. The traditional way of handling such a case (thinking in the box) was to provide three days off without pay and place the employee on a warning status. This status meant that Harold could be terminated if another breach of company policy took place. The team was asked for its opinion about the best way to handle this matter.

This situation is outlined above in the Step Out of the Box diagram. The traditional way of thinking is noted in the box. The team was asked to provide a minimum of three alternative ways to deal with Harold's situation. These are listed outside of the box. As listed at the bottom of the diagram, think of the advantages and disadvantages for the alternatives provided. The solution selected by the team was to pursue a combination of punishments, which are listed as solutions. Was this the proper solution? There is no one best solution. The key point of this exercise is that the team "thought out of the box" and did not blindly follow rigid, prescribed rules.

In part B of the diagram, you are asked to think of a management situation where you are currently experiencing difficulty. List, in the box provided, the traditional way of dealing with the matter. Then, create at least three alternative ways of dealing with the problem. Finally, record the advantages and disadvantages at the bottom. After considering the advantages and disadvantages, you may find that the traditional solution is appropriate or inappropriate. The point of the exercise is that it is important that you consider different ways of looking at and dealing with situations in the workplace. Because people and the environment are rapidly changing, past ways of thinking may be inappropriate.

2. Feedback Assessment

There are a number of sophisticated instruments available to assess feedback effectiveness. One simple way to measure yours is reflected in the Feedback Assessment—Exercise. First of all, consider the horizontal axis along the top of the diagram. When given the opportunity, do you solicit feedback from others? Consider the range from 0 percent to 100 percent. Place a dot on the horizontal axis in the diagram corresponding to your answer. The vertical axis reflects a similar rating but focuses on how often you give feedback when given the opportunity. Once again, place a dot on the vertical axis in the diagram corresponding to your answer. Where the two dots intersect from the vertical and horizontal axes, a boundary is created. This boundary represents your self-assessed utilization of feedback. Most leaders have a self-assessment of 50 percent by 50 percent—the larger the box, the better. Consider several specific projects and rate each on the diagram. Next,

Feedback Assessment

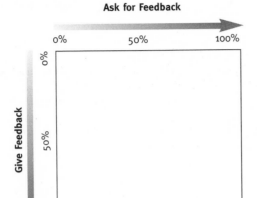

Plot the percentage time you ask for or give feedback when given the opportunity to do so.

analyze opportunities for increasing feedback and possible mechanisms to be used in each of the projects. Feedback is maximized when you and your employees actively solicit constructive feedback and actively give constructive feedback. This is no time for egos to get in the way! Is increased feedback an opportunity for you?

3. What Do You Believe?

Beliefs are the cornerstone of effective leaders in an organization's journey, and it is important to understand your current reality with respect to beliefs required of a leader. On the left side of a piece of paper, list the nine beliefs, which were described for Role 1. Next, create five columns to the right of the beliefs and number the columns 1 through 5, consecutively. For each belief, place a value on how well you have practiced that belief. This exercise requires straightforward answers. "1" is the lowest value and "5" is the highest value. For those beliefs with a value of "3" or lower, identify ways to improve upon that belief in day-to-day activities and include these ideas in your personal development plan. This exercise can also be used with employees or colleagues to gain their perception of your beliefs as a leader. For employees, a written survey can be used which incorporates the beliefs. Compare the scoring you have given for each of the beliefs with that of employees or colleagues. Too often, leaders see themselves in a much different light than others around them. However, management effectiveness is affected by perceptions.

Levels of Belief

Definitions:

A. Value—What is important or inherently worthy.

B. Belief—What is held to be true about something.

C. Principle—What is done to put values and beliefs into action.

D. Vision—Mental picture of a desired future state.

Examples (Safety):

Value — Human life is of high importance. Safety is more important than financial success.

Belief — All injuries can be prevented.

Principle — Our plant will be operated in such a manner that people will not be injured.

Vision — We have a safe work environment; everyone works toward achieving an injury-free operation.

Application (Highway Safety):

1. _____ Have an effective highway safety communications campaign that reaches all age groups in a way that positively impacts driving habits.

2. _____ The well-being and safety of people using our state highway system is an important issue for all.

3. _____ Excessive speed on highways is responsible for unnecessary suffering and death.

4. _____ The public will be aware of the impact of excessive speed. People drive safely within speed limits.

4. Levels of Belief

Values, beliefs, principles, and vision have been underscored as important building blocks of a leader in a learning organization journey. This exercise allows you to understand the differences among vision, values, beliefs, and principles and to apply this knowledge. In the Levels of Belief—Exercise, basic definitions and examples are provided for each of the four terms. Following this, match one of the four concepts with your statements regarding safety. (Answer key: 1. C, 2. A, 3. B, 4. D)

5. Levels of Ownership

In the Levels of Ownership—Exercise identify five important programs/initiatives that are being pursued by your organization. Next, think how you feel about and act towards these programs (level of ownership). To the right of each noted program, classify your level of ownership; is it at the level of politics, knowledge, or commitment? Finally, identify what personal actions are required by you to reach the commitment level. Include these changes in your personal development plan.

Levels of Ownership

Programs/Initiatives	Levels of Ownership	Personal Actions
1.	P K C	1.
2.	P K C	2.
3.	P K C	3.
4.	P K C	4.
5.	P K C	5.

KEY
P=Politics
K=Knowledge
C=Commitment

Role 2

1. Coaching Diary

Coaching is not a natural function for most leaders. Instead, leaders spend the majority of their time on leading and managing. The first point in the coaching journey is to find out how much effort is being spent on coaching. Take out a clean piece of paper. Across the top of the page, create three columns: leader, coach, and manager. On the left hand side of the paper, list the days of the business week for a two week period. The purpose of this exercise is to find out how much time is being spent on coaching versus leading and managing. At the end of each day, estimate the time that was spent on each of the three functions. At the end of the first week, add up the number of hours in each column. If you find that the coaching efforts totaled far less than one-third of your time, examine how you can focus more time on coaching. Examine each employee's needs and estimate how much coaching time is spent with the person. What other efforts are required? Be proactive and plan coaching opportunities for the second week.

During the second week, fill out the coaching diary as you did during the first week. Tally the hours spent in leading, coaching, and managing for each business day and the week. Have you made any progress? You should see an increase in coaching time because of the focus and planned efforts in this area. This exercise should clearly underscore the need to plan your coaching efforts. Otherwise, coaching will continue to be secondary to leading and managing.

2. Readiness To Be Coached

Coaching requires finesse at understanding the key moments where coaching will be most effective. It is more of an art than it is a science.

For each employee who reports to you, identify his or her major responsibilities or key areas in need of further improvement. Use the Readiness diagram to identify where the employee is located on the diagram. This will allow you to identify what coaching emphasis is required to help an employee progress to the upper left-hand quadrant (capability and ownership). Next, outline what formal coaching action steps you will take to help each employee grow. Every week or twice a month, review this plan. What progress has been made to help an employee grow to the desired quadrant? What additional efforts are required? Have you provided sufficient authority for him/her to succeed? Is this employee in need of transfer or termination? The above information is vital where you help create a personal development plan for an employee.

Role 3

1. Style Times Five

This exercise is intended to increase your awareness and understanding of the different leader styles. Reference the Leader Styles diagram. The five leader styles are listed in the left column. In the middle column, describe three different real-life situations which are appropriate for that leader style. In the right column, describe three real-life situations that are inappropriate to use in each style. Several reflection questions are listed at the bottom of the exercise for self-assessment considerations.

2. What's Your Style?

Leaders can change their styles only by changing their beliefs and application of new behaviors in the business setting. In this exercise, you are asked to keep a diary for one week (see Leader Styles Diary on p. 288). Identify one

Leader Styles

Leader Styles	Appropriate Situations	Inappropriate Situations
Sidestepping		
Telling		
Yo-yoing		
Liking		
Empowering		

Reflections:
1. Which style(s) was (were) most difficult to describe an appropriate situation? Why?
2. Should the Empowering Style be used in every situation? Why or why not?
3. What is your estimate to the percent of time you use the Empowering Style?
4. What would others (direct reports, peers, supervisor) estimate the percent of time you use the Empowering Style?

major decision-making interaction from each day of the workweek in the left column. Next, identify whether the situation was urgent or nonurgent. In the next column, identify whether the situation involved potential business loss or potential people loss. Classify the style you used for each situation. Finally, identify what style was preferred for each situation. The diagram includes urgency level on one axis and business/people loss potential on the other axis. In each quadrant of the two-by-two diagram, the preferred styles are listed. This can be of help as you consider what preferred style is appropriate for each major interaction. Finally, weekly reflections are listed: What happened? What have you learned? What should be your top focus area next week?

An accomplished leader should avoid using side-stepping and liking styles on a consistent basis. However, side-stepping and liking styles may be

Leader Styles Diary

Date _____ through _____

Major Interaction	Urgent or Nonurgent	Business or People Loss	Leader Style Used	Preferred Leader Style
Monday				
Tuesday				
Wednesday				
Thursday				
Friday				
Saturday				
Sunday				

Urgency (High / Low)

Empowering / Yo-yoing	Empowering / Telling	
Empowering / Yo-yoing	Empowering / Telling	

Low — High

Liking / Sidestepping

Business/People Loss

Weekly Reflections:
- What happened?

- What have I learned?

- What should be my top focus area this week?

appropriate in some interpersonal issues in order to promote long-term work relationships. The empowering style should be the most prevalent while the telling style should only be used when the situation creates high urgency and high potential loss. The yo-yoing style should be used where risk of harm to people or business success is low. If you deviated from the preferred leader styles, a plan of action should be designed to identify how more appropriate styles will be used in the future. This plan should be added to your personal development plan for future monitoring and growth. Appreciate the fact that this exercise and the models used rely on subjectivity to a great extent, and the exercise is intended to help you appreciate possible areas for improvement.

Role 4

1. ChangeVision in Your Own Land

Using the ChangeVision—Exercise chart, look around your part of the organization and ask yourself and your employees where employees have learned helplessness. Identify the top three to five areas of learned helplessness. Prioritize them based upon which ones are the most significant barriers to change. Using the ChangeVision process, create a plan of action to help the employee(s) overcome learned helplessness. Following implementation of this plan, monitor the success of your ChangeVision plan and take whatever additional steps that are needed.

2. Get Out Your Brush and Go To Work

Review the five leader styles defined in Role 3 prior to completing this case study, focusing specifically on telling and empowering styles. Sue was vice president of human resources for a ball bearing manufacturer. She was a

ChangeVision

Source of Learned Helplessness	Areas of Learned Helplessness		Most Significant Barriers to Change
_____	_____	**=**	_____
_____	_____		_____
_____	_____		_____
_____	_____		_____

Change Vision Action Plan

Map the journey _____

Begin the journey _____

Share the ride _____

Complete the journey _____

Brushstroking

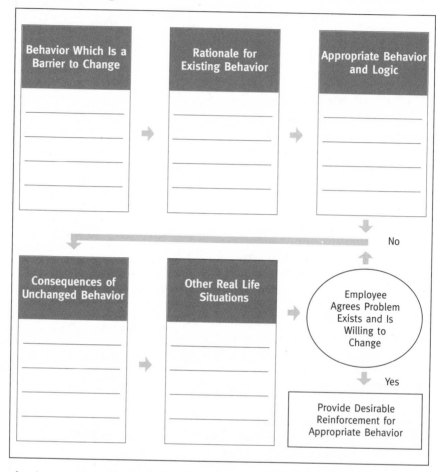

classic user of the Telling style. She took pride in being the person with "the answer," because she had thirty years of experience. Sue had so much knowledge and experience, she thought that employees should follow her problem-solving suggestions.

Typically, Sue took pride in telling employees what needed to be done and specifically how it should be done. For two years, Sue had been involved in significant empowerment training because it was very popular in management circles. Sue did not really understand or agree with empowerment offering only verbal support when she needed to be responsive to management. Despite her lack of true support for empowerment, Sue had convinced herself that she used an empowering style. Sue was not able to recognize that she was not able to change while others around her were able to change. Sue had been unable to see herself as others saw her. She definitely had a blind

Purposeful Growth

Employee Name: _____

Major Job Emphasis Area: _____ _____ _____

_____ _____ _____

Key Development
Opportunities: _____ _____ _____

Change Journey:

Shared Vision	Current Reality	Current Performance
_____	_____	_____
_____	_____	_____
_____	_____	_____
_____	_____	_____
_____	_____	_____

Resources Needed	Boundaries to Manage	Feedback
_____	_____	_____
_____	_____	_____
_____	_____	_____
_____	_____	_____
_____	_____	_____

spot. Sue found it increasingly more difficult to continue to provide detailed instructions because her area of responsibility had almost doubled in size over the last eighteen months.

Using the Brushstroking—Exercise diagram, develop a plan of action to deal with Sue's situation which describes how to approach Sue and gain the needed change in behavior.

3. Purposeful Growth

Think of each employee that reports directly to you. Determine the major responsibilities (what they should be doing) for each of their jobs. Is the employee primarily valuable because of technical expertise? Does the job require expertise in empowerment? Are quality management and redesign valuable factors for an employee in this job? Is the employee primarily valuable because of team meeting leadership skills? Is process improvement a key factor for this job? Identify the major emphasis areas that are most important for the employee's development. You should apply to each employee the Change Journey (see diagram on p. 291) and create a plan of action. As an added part of the exercise, provide each employee with a copy of the Change Journey and ask each of them to create a plan of action for themselves. Once completed, you and individual employees will meet and jointly review the two plans. Finally, implement the plan of action after the joint review. Monitor the employee's progress at least on a quarterly basis, providing desirable reinforcement for accomplishments to date.

Role 5

1. Clarifying Expectations

In the Clarifying Expectations—Exercise, the expectations of employees can be reviewed either in a group setting or individually. The preference is

Clarifying Expectations

A	B	C	
List Expectations You Have of Employees	Employee Understanding of Expectations (1-Low; 3-Avg.; 5-High)	Employee Commitment to Expectations (1-Low; 3-Avg.; 5-High)	Total (B+C)
_____	_____	_____	_____
_____	_____	_____	_____
_____	_____	_____	_____
_____	_____	_____	_____
_____	_____	_____	_____
_____	_____	_____	_____
_____	_____	_____	_____
_____	_____	_____	_____

Action Plans:

_____

_____

_____

for employee expectations that are created through the interaction of leaders and employees. Under column "A," list the expectations the leader has of employees. For each expectation, the employee's level of understanding and commitment are rated on a scale. A score of one is used for low, while average and high levels are rated three and five, respectively. After understanding and commitment are rated, the two columns (B and C) are added together. For those expectations that are rated a three or lower, an action plan should be created to identify how this area will be improved. The action plans should reflect the components listed in the Leader Influence Model that was reviewed in Role 5. For example, if employees are rated "one" related to the expectation of learn, learn, learn, the following action plan may be appropriate for an organization: have discussions with employees. Link the learning expectation to the business and quality plans providing specific examples related to their area. Ask employees if they understand this is an expectation, what does this expectation mean, and how can improvements be made in this area. The overall objective of the meeting is to strive for agreement that the learning expectation is important and should be followed. Monitor future outcomes related to this expectation and provide feedback to employees.

Plan an Intervention

Intervention Steps	Planned Comments
Greeting	
Appropriate Behavior	
Inappropriate Behavior	
Reasons	
Discussion	
Agreement	
Practice	
Feedback	

Role 6

1. Plan an Intervention

This exercise is intended to increase your planning skills related to interventions. In most cases, leaders will "think through" the intervention prior to approaching an employee, instead of writing down the intervention steps and approach to be used. For purposes of fine-tuning your skills, this exercise involves a written plan of action.

Following your review of the situation, refer to the Plan an Intervention diagram on page 293 and develop your planned communication.

Jennifer was the vice president for sales of a large real estate development firm. One of her leaders, Don, was responsible for twelve employees who created marketing brochures and other materials used in the sales process. Recently, Jennifer has been hearing rumors that Don's employees are upset with him and some are looking to leave his department. One employee from Don's area asked to meet with Jennifer. Since this person was very objective and a past strong supporter of Don, Jennifer thought this should provide an opportunity to examine whether intervention may be needed in Don's area.

Dear Diary

Intervention Types	Monday	Tuesday	Wednesday	Thursday	Friday	Total
Appropriate Behaviors						
Inappropriate Behaviors						
Focus Areas						
Safety						
Self-esteem						
Cost						
Legal						
Customer/Supplier Relationships						
Other						

Considerations:
1. How well did you use the Intervention model as a guide?
2. Did you use the Intervention model with a proper blend of questions (rather than statements)?
3. Did you maintain or enhance the self-esteem of individuals involved?
4. Was feedback kept in the Healthy Zone?
5. Did you demonstrate good listening skills in order to understand the individual's point of view?
6. What is your follow-up and reinforcement plan?

Don't Put Failure in Your Future

Problem	Rate the Problem				
	Low				High
Lack of early involvement by all management	1	2	3	4	5
Lack of programmed education	1	2	3	4	5
Span of responsibility too broad	1	2	3	4	5
Too much change	1	2	3	4	5
Absence of daily coaching pressure	1	2	3	4	5
Technical leaders	1	2	3	4	5
Leader roles not defined or understood	1	2	3	4	5
Leader rotation	1	2	3	4	5
Lack of good communication skills	1	2	3	4	5
Assuming all leaders can coach	1	2	3	4	5
Leader dependency culture	1	2	3	4	5
Some leaders do not walk the talk	1	2	3	4	5
Lack of interdependent management culture	1	2	3	4	5
Fear	1	2	3	4	5
Action Plan					
Problem Defined	Action		Progress		

The employee related that most of the employees in the area were unhappy with their work relationship and some were now considering leaving the company. The employee offered examples of issues related to Don's increased absences from the department, tardiness, last minute cancelled meetings, and diminished communications with all employees.

Following this discussion, Jennifer was approached by some of her colleagues who had witnessed some of the behavior issues outlined by the employee. Two employees who were leaving the department to take promotions within the company provided the traditional exit interviews and shared similar problems with Don and situations where the inappropriate behaviors occurred. From all information Jennifer was provided, she felt it was necessary to intervene in the situation. Despite Don's past record as a dedicated and thoughtful leader, it appeared that there were some problems that required her attention.

2. Dear Diary

Effective use of intervention requires continual use of tools and skills. This exercise is focused on the use of intervention skills by recording intervention trends and auditing your behaviors. In the Dear Diary—Exercise, collect data

Integration Audit

Intervention Steps	Training Experiences	How Communicated	Knowledge & Use	Score
Mission				
Vision				
Values				
Quality				
Safety				
Strategy				
People				

Development Plan:

_____

_____

_____

_____

on your intervention types. At the end of the week, review the information and perform a self-analysis to improve your skills.

Role 7

1. Don't Put Failure in Your Future

New leader roles require a vast amount of energy and time to succeed. For this reason, organizations must scan the environment to see if there are problems on the horizon that could lead to failure. This exercise is designed to help leaders do just that. A checklist is provided on page 295 that can be used to identify the potential threats to implement new leader roles. The checklist can be used prior to or after implementing new leader roles. As with any tool, the checklist is only as effective as the leader's objectivity in using the tool. Be honest with yourself and your organization. If your organization has problems, recognize them, create an action plan, and solve the problems. This checklist should be used periodically during your journey. It's not unusual to find that some areas have deteriorated over time.

Role 8

1. Integration Audit

A good place to start when considering integration in any organization is to perform an audit of present documents, systems, skills, and projects. A chart is provided above to assist you in this exercise.

First, list the key organization documents in your organization. The chart has several documents listed for consideration.

Second, list training experiences for understanding and skill building relative to principles in your organization.

Third, review how the documents are communicated in your organization.

Finally, identify the knowledge and use of the key documents in your organization for decision making.

After the chart has been completed, use Low (L), Medium (M), or High (H) to score your organization and assess development opportunities.

2. FOCUS on Your Organization

This exercise is intended for you to use FOCUS in your own organization. Identify the stakeholders, mission, vision, values, and strategies of your

FOCUS on Your Organization

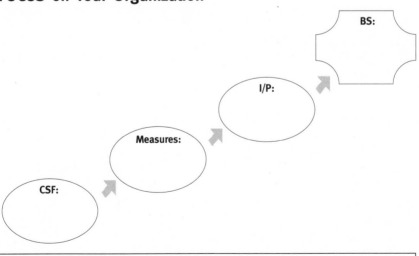

| BS: |
| I/P: |
| Measures: |
| CSF: |

| M/V/V/S: |
| Stakeholders: |

organization. Also, consider what factors are crucial to your organization's success in your industry. Develop a list of potential critical success factors (CSFs) and select one to focus on for purposes of this exercise.

The next step is to consider what major processes affect this CSF. Based on the processes related to each CSF, identify a measure that would show if your organization is being successful in that CSF. The measure should be quantifiable if possible.

To improve the CSF, think of an improvement project (I/P) that your organization could concentrate on. If you are a president of a company or leader of a division, select a project that has the most impact on your organization. If you are a leader of a department, select a project that involves several of your employees. The key to this project is involvement. If employees are not trained in the necessary tools, training may be required prior to implementing the project. The purpose of the project and how it relates to employees should be clearly communicated.

Prior to implementing a project, identify the baseline or where your measure is at present. Implement the plan using the tools covered in this role. When the project is completed, use the measure to identify what improvements have been made. Finally, identify what results or business successes (BS) were achieved. Find out what employees thought about the exercise. How would they approach it differently?

Following completion of the first project, select another CSF, and follow the process outlined above.

Role 9

1. Understand It Diary

Use your knowledge of the Solution(s) Model in your next meeting when you're trying to resolve a problem. Without using the model, observe how an employee handles it. You can map it out on paper by outlining the major stages of the discussion. Use the Solution(s) Model to check off what elements from the model were used and which elements were not used. Think about what could have been said during the conversation to provide a more effective and efficient solution. How might this have been handled? When you complete this exercise you should be able to see how the use of the model could have streamlined discussions because employees and leaders would have been focused on the right issues. Write down these observations to reflect on at a later date as you work on improving this skill.

2. Do It Diary

There is no better way to perfect a skill than to use it, use it, use it. Perfect practice makes perfect. With this in mind, set goals to use the Solution(s) Model within the next two weeks during a meeting with an employee or group of employees. Before you go into a meeting or become involved in the discussion,

It Can Happen Here

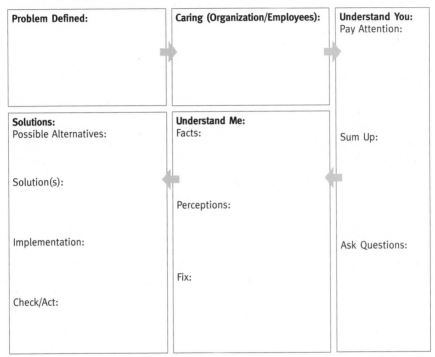

Problem Defined:	Caring (Organization/Employees):	Understand You: Pay Attention:
Solutions: Possible Alternatives: Solution(s): Implementation: Check/Act:	**Understand Me:** Facts: Perceptions: Fix:	Sum Up: Ask Questions:

choreograph your use of the model in your own mind. Athletes continually report that they think through how to hit the home run, run the hurdles in record time, or set up an excellent break-away play. Think about the potential responses to your use of the Solution(s) Model. Take it step by step. After you have become comfortable, try it out in the meeting or discussion you have been thinking about. As the meeting or discussion evolves, make some mental notes about points that you can use in the future to improve your use of the model.

Once you've mastered the model, teach it to your employees. There is no better way to thoroughly understand a topic than to teach others. First, plan your outline for the educational event. Then, make sure you include a number of poignant stories to use during the session. These stories hook employees. Later on, you will find that employees remember the model because of these stories. Use pictures to help tell the story. Keep notes on how your experience went. Reflect on these notes prior to your use of the model in the future.

Role 10

1. It Can Happen Here

Think of a major problem that you recently encountered with a barrier. Use the above diagram as a checklist to identify what method was used to remove the boundary. Consider whether the steps in the Solution(s) Model were effectively used. Identify an existing boundary problem and plot out a strategy to use the Solution(s) Model.

Role 11

1. Self-assessment

There are three areas to assess your level of preparedness:

1. Time and effort spent on learning to increase job capabilities
2. Understanding of and applying new leader roles
3. Meaning and pleasure derived from work

Each of these areas should be assessed and plotted on a scale from zero to one hundred. If a leader has no level of accomplishment in this area, it should be rated as a zero. If a leader has reached the highest level of accomplishment that is possible, it should be rated as a one hundred.

Once each area is rated, the three scores should be plotted on the radar screen. Once the areas in need of attention are determined, it is time to create a plan for developing the needed skills. Part 2 of this book provides processes, skills, and tips on how to use a plan to grow as a leader.

Self-assessment

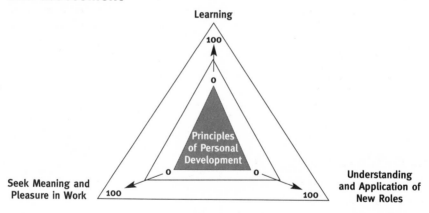

2. One Plus One is Three

If you feel comfortable, ask employees that report to you or your colleagues in management to rate you according to the three principle statements outlined in this role. They should use the scale of zero to one hundred. Average all of the scores for each statement. Prepare a personal development plan.

One Plus One Is Three

Areas of Development	Self (0–100)	Others (0–100)	Gap
Learning to increase capability			
Understanding and application of new roles			
Meaning and pleasure derived from work			
Personal Development Plan:			
_____			
_____			
_____			

Lesson 2

What's Your LeaderWalk?

LeaderWalk is a skill that leaders must continually develop. The best way to develop skills is to continually practice. This is referred to as "running wind-sprints." As in sports, repetition increases comfort and skill levels. In this exercise, you are asked to keep a journal of the *LeaderWalk* experiences. The journal format is outlined below. This exercise helps you to understand how often you are using these skills and how effectively these are tied to the development of leaders.

Select a normal week to keep the journal. At the end of each workday, enter your comments in the journal. Identify the different situations where *LeaderWalk* was used. Was this situation used to implement the personal development plan for that leader? How much time overall are you spending on *LeaderWalk*? After you've kept the journal for a week, create a plan of action to improve on your *LeaderWalk* skill. Later, select another week and keep a journal of *LeaderWalk* activities. Compare your progress from the first journal week to the second week outlined in the journal. Consider how you can improve your time spent and activities associated with *LeaderWalk*.

Lesson 3

Play It Again Sam

Consider a management job opening in one of your areas of responsibility. Create the structure or dimensions for this position. This will include the new roles and job competencies. Outline the mission, vision, and values to apply to the position. Once these dimensions are complete, outline the process to be

LeaderWalk Journal

Day	Situation	Relates to Leader's Development Plan	Time
Monday		Yes or No	
Tuesday		Yes or No	
Wednesday		Yes or No	
Thursday		Yes or No	
Friday		Yes or No	
Development Plan:			

followed using the process steps outlined below. A grid has been provided for use in this exercise.

Lesson 4

Application Plan Can

If you're going to develop as a Leader-Coach-Manager you will need to create a map. The map is basically an application plan. Look at the new leader roles and decide which of these roles fit within your organization. Then, consider what you need to learn to grow in this new role. How are you going to learn? Will you use a book, video, seminar, or some other learning opportunity? Next, identify what key learning you expect to gain from that exercise. Finally, identify how the new knowledge and experience will be specifically used immediately following this experience (Application).

You can use this plan on a monthly basis to judge whether you are improving in your talents and skills to fill the voids. If not, you may need to revisit your application plan and revise some areas. An application plan should be looked upon as a living document that is intended to help you grow.

Play it Again, Sam

Job Opening: _____	Process		
Mission:	Identified who is interested?	Yes	No
	Reviewed resumé?	Yes	No
Vision:	Reviewed focused resumé?	Yes	No
	Identified and appointed multidisciplinary selection team?	Yes	No
Values:	Preparation for interview completed?	Yes	No
	Focused interview session conducted?	Yes	No
Strategy:	Selection rating form completed?	Yes	No
	Decision:		
Job Competencies:			
New Roles:			
Succession Planning:			
Diversity:			

Application Plan Can

Role	Learning Needed	Expected Key Learnings	Application

ABOUT THE AUTHORS

TOM HORNSBY designed and implemented one of the first New Roles for Leaders systems in the world. Formerly with Eastman Chemical Company, a Fortune 500 company and recipient of the coveted Malcolm Baldrige National Quality Award, Tom has over thirty years managerial and internal consulting experience including ten years independent/external experience in leadership development, quality management, and organizational development. Tom is presently a principal in VisionWorks, LLC, helping leaders worldwide improve organizational effectiveness.

 LARRY WARKOCZESKI has been a senior executive in the retail wholesale food and health services industries, a business college law professor, and the president of a technology start-up firm. In each of these arenas, he utilized his experience in marketing, planning, leadership development, quality management, and managed care. Larry presently serves as senior vice president for Mountain States Health Alliance, a regional health care system located in the southeastern United States.

VisionWorks can be visited at
www.visionworksllc.net